THE WOLVES
OF ISLE ROYALE

by L. David Mech, PhD.

Fauna of the National Parks
of the United States Fauna Series 7

1966

America's Natural Resources

Created in 1849, the Department of the Interior—America's Department of Natural Resources—is concerned with the management, conservation, and development of the Nation's water, wildlife, mineral, forest, and park and recreational resources. It also has major responsibilities for Indian and territorial affairs.

As the Nation's principal conservation agency, the Department works to assure that nonrenewable resources are developed and used wisely, that park and recreational resources are conserved, and that renewable resources make their full contribution to the progress, prosperity, and security of the United States—now and in the future.

The National Park System, of which Isle Royale National Park is a unit, is dedicated to conserving the scenic, scientific, and historic heritage of the United States for the benefit and inspiration of its people.

United States
Department of the Interior
Stewart L. Udall, *Secretary*

National Park Service
George B. Hartzog, Jr., *Director*

United States Government Printing Office, Washington: 1966
For sale by the Superintendent of Documents, U.S. Government
Printing Office, Washington, D.C., 20402 – Price $1.

Foreword

THOUGHTFUL PEOPLE have advanced many reasons for set-
ting aside samples of our various "wilderness" types to be
preserved in a relatively undisturbed condition. One of the
best is the possibility of using such lands and waters for research. The life communities of primitive times were durable
and productive. We can learn much that applies in our
resource husbandry by studying the mechanisms that worked
so well in the green world of North America before the coming
of the white man.

The principle is good, but a taxing problem today is finding
those primordial communities of living things. Fortunately,
some of the best we have are in the care of the National Park
Service. This study of the wolf by David Mech (pronounced
"meech") could have been made in only one area south of
Canada—Isle Royale National Park.

The fact that this roadless wilderness is an island is fortunate
too, for on islands you stand the best chance of making least-
complicated counts of animals. Isle Royale is a range of
goodly size for wolves and moose. And no one will forget that
it is manned by that particular kind of professional outdoors-
man you find on national park staffs. The logistic support
for such a study was on hand.

These were important considerations when, in 1957, a co-
operative agreement was entered into between Purdue University and the National Park Service for studies of the wolf and
its prey on Isle Royale. It was to be a series of 3-year projects
carried out by graduate students working for their Ph. D.
A National Science Foundation grant was obtained as principal support; the next problem was to find a proper man for
the initial study of wolf ecology.

I met David Mech, then a senior wildlife student at Cornell,
in autumn of 1957, and looked no further. Dave, a native
of Syracuse, was a highly recommended scholar and self-trained
woodsman who spent Christmas vacations tracking fishers in
the Adirondacks. For two summers he had worked on New

York's bear study, including trapping, handling, and marking bruins of every description and temperament. He was hale and eager to learn about wolves.

The fieldwork began in June 1958, and after a fall semester of course work, Dave went to the island for the first 7-week winter period in February and March 1959. By further good fortune, that winter he met Donald E. Murray, of Mountain Iron, Minn., who was engaged as one of the aircraft pilots for the project that year. In the two succeeding winters, the team of Mech and Murray achieved great things in the aerial observation of wolves and their hunting. Don has continued to serve the Isle Royale studies each winter as a mainstay of the program.

David Mech submitted his thesis and received his doctoral degree in 1962. With some modifications, the thesis became this, the seventh in the National Parks Fauna series. It lays the groundwork for the continuing program that is necessary to gather significant information on such long-lived animals as wolves and moose Likewise, it has set a standard that will take some doing to maintain.

Some years ago, people seemed to have all the facts they needed on predator-prey relationships. But the assumptions are breaking down as scientific scrutiny reveals the time-tested adaptations through which wild creatures survive. This account of the great wild dog of North America and its largest antlered prey has something important to add.

Durward L. Allen
Professor of Wildlife Ecology
Purdue University

Contents

Tables

Illustrations

Summary

THE PRIMARY objective of this 3-year investigation was the appraisal of wolf-moose relationships in Isle Royale National Park, a 210-square-mile island in northwestern Lake Superior. The island has supported a moose herd since the early 1900's and a wolf population since about 1948; no other big game or large carnivore is present. The use of a light aircraft for counting moose and following wolves during 435 hours in February and March 1959–61 facilitated gathering the most significant information; field work during three springs and summers provided supplementary data. Sixty-five weeks were spent in the field.

The primary wolf pack, composed of 15 to 16 animals, was the same size each winter, as was a pack of 3. An additional pack, of two wolves, probably also was present each year. Copulation was observed in 1959 and 1960 in the large pack, but apparently no young survived to the following winters. Reasons for the lack of increase remain unknown. The large pack traveled over the entire island, but most of its activity occurred on about half the area. The small packs did not frequent this section but traveled extensively in the other half. Strife between the large pack and the other wolves was additional evidence of territoriality.

During 31 days, from February 4 to March 7, 1960, when the entire route of the large pack was known, the animals traveled approximately 277 miles, or 9 miles per day. However, during 22 of those days the wolves fed on kills and did not journey far. Thus in 9 days of traveling, the animals averaged 31 miles per day. The normal pace was about 5 m.p.h. During the entire study, the longest distance known to have been traveled in 24 hours was approximately 45 miles. On the basis of 25 observations, the maximum distance traveled between kills was 67 miles; the minimum, 0; and the average, 26.5.

The moose herd numbers about 600 in late winter. Probably most moose are host to the winter tick (*Dermacentor albipictus*), and a substantial number of older animals are infected with hydatid cysts (*Echinococcus granulosus*) and actinomycosis, all of which undoubtedly are important in predisposing moose to wolf predation. The tapeworm *Taenia hydatigena* and the lungworm *Dictyocaulus* sp. also are present in the herd, but the incidence of infection and the effect of these parasites are not known.

The primary moose-mortality factor is wolf predation, since the large pack alone killed an average of one moose per 3 days during the winter study periods. Average daily consumption per wolf, based on estimated weights of kills, ranged from 9.7 pounds in 1960 to 13.9 pounds in 1961. Individuals apparently ate as much as 20 pounds at a meal but sometimes went 5 days without food.

Special effort was made to observe hunts by the large pack, and in 68 hours 66 hunts involving 132 moose were witnessed. The pack actually tested 77 moose (held them at bay or chased them long distances) and killed only 6 of these, a "predation efficiency" of 7.8 percent. Running is the first defense of the moose, but if the wolves are not discovered soon enough, many moose stand and defy the pack. Of the 36 that stood at bay until the wolves gave up, none were killed, but 5 of the 41 that ran were dispatched. Defense of the calf is strong and stereotyped. The cow protects the rear of the calf, which seems to be the favorite point of attack. If any wolf closes in, the cow charges and sends it scurrying.

Nine hunts were observed in which moose were killed or wounded. To kill a moose, the wolves attack its rump and flanks. They cling to the animal and slow it down. Meanwhile, one wolf grabs the nose of the moose and occupies the animal's attention until the others inflict significant damage to the rump. Usually moose are killed within 10 minutes, but some wounded animals manage to hold off the wolves for several hours.

When possible, wolf kills were examined on the ground. Fifty-seven kills were found and 51 examined; 18 were calves, but most of the others were 8 to 15 years old. None was 1 to 6 years old. Only bones of most kills could be examined, but 39 percent of the adults showed symptoms of debilitating conditions. One of the two intact, wolf-killed adults examined harbored 57 golf-ball-sized hydatid cysts in its lungs, and the other 35.

On the basis of the winter kill rate, annual adult moose mortality approximates 83 animals. About 17 percent of the moose herd is composed of yearlings in late winter, so the annual increment just before calving season should be 85 yearlings. Thus the herd is believed to be relatively stable. The total annual kill is calculated to be 142 calves and 83 adults. On the basis of consumption figures, it is estimated that approximately 5,823,300 pounds of browse are required annually to support the moose herd that produces the 89,425 pounds of moose consumed by about 1,512 pounds of wolves.

The wolves appear to have kept the moose herd within its food supply, culled out undesirable individuals, and stimulated reproduction. Wolves and moose probably will remain in dynamic equilibrium, although the moose herd may decline in the next decade because a large proportion of the browse is growing out of reach of the moose.

Figure 1—Wolves holding a moose at bay. Note that the only close individuals are behind the moose. The pack harassed the animal for 5 minutes, then left (see Hunting Account 16). (c) National Geographic Society, courtesy National Geographic Magazine.

Introduction

L ESS than a century ago, the timber wolf (*Canis lupus*) occurred
throughout North America, but today
it is absent as a resident from 45 of
the 48 contiguous States. Probably
less than 500 individuals inhabit the
remaining three—Minnesota, Wisconsin, and Michigan. Undoubtedly
the most important factor leading to
the decline in wolf numbers throughout most of the country was habitat
destruction. Just as a drained pond
cannot support fish, a destroyed wilderness cannot support wolves.

However, persecution is also responsible for the present low wolf
population. Wolves have been persecuted ever since the first settlers established colonies over three centuries
ago. On every part of the frontier,
wolves competed with man for prey
that man wished to reserve for himself—his livestock—and therefore
they had to be eliminated. Trapping,
hunting, poisoning, and den-digging,
much of this by Government preda-
tor-control agents, took their toll.
Wolves were not allowed to remain
even in remote wildernesses in the
West because it was feared that the
surplus from these reservoirs would
flow into the cattle and sheep country.
Persistent harassment of the species
thus has resulted in its extirpation
from the West, with the possible ex-

ception of a small remnant population in the Sierra Nevada of California (Ingles, 1963). Even today,
occasional stragglers from Canada are
quickly eliminated. Young and Goldman (1944) and Young (1946) have
traced the history of the species in
North America in detail.

The size and habits of the timber
wolf probably help make it more of
a target for crusading citizens than are
other carnivores. It is one of the
largest predators, adult weights ranging from 65 to 175 pounds, depending
on the subspecies. There are 23
North American subspecies of *Canis
lupus,* the more northern generally including the heaviest individuals.
The largest wolf on record seems to be
the 175-pound Alaskan wolf reported
by Young and Goldman (1944).
Total lengths of wolves range from 59
to 69 inches, and shoulder heights
from 26 to 38 inches.

The wolf's habits of howling and
of hunting in packs no doubt have
been important factors in the pub-
lic's acceptance of the animal as evil-
incarnate. Most wolf packs contain
less than 10 members, but there are a
few authentic records of packs num-
bering up to 50. Although a group
of 50 wolves would be a spectacular
sight indeed, some popular writers
have not been content to deal even

with this large number; they had to create absurdly enormous packs. Thus we get such a fantastic tale as that by Alexandre Dumas in his book *Voyage en Russie*, supposedly dealing with his trip to Russia in 1859. A translation of certain sections, concerning a wolf hunt, published in *Sports Afield* (1960), contains the following passage:

Their number increased so rapidly that they seemed to be literally rising out of the earth. There was something uncanny about the way they appeared out of nowhere. It was hard to account for the presence of 2,000 or 3,000 wolves in the middle of a treeless desert where no more than two or three isolated animals could be seen in the daytime.

The anti-wolf prejudice of most of us was instilled when we were naive and innocent tots. One of the first songs many of us learned was "Who's Afraid of the Big, Bad Wolf?", and a few years later we learned the stirring story of "Peter and the Wolf." The plight of "Little Red Riding Hood" and of the "Three Little Pigs" reinforced our view of the wolf as a most undesirable creature. With such priming, how could we have helped believing the perennial tales that used to emanate (and sometimes still do) from Alaska and Canada about the poor soul who had been torn limb-from-limb and devoured mercilessly by some bloodthirsty wolf pack? Such stories often give the full name, address, age, and other detailed information about the victim, but when traced down, these tales prove to be masterpieces of fabrication. Lee Smits (1963) soberly reviewed the subject of wolf-man relationships and concluded that ". . . no wolf, except a wolf with rabies, has ever been known to make a deliberate attack on a human being in North America."

But the wolf *is* a killer. Nature endowed the species with a type of digestive system that requires meat. Unlike humans, however, wolves cannot push the job of butchering onto a few individuals while the rest of the population righteously looks the other way; they must all do the job. In their present dwindling range, they feed on wild prey almost exclusively. Yet many people feel that the wolf competes with man every time it kills a game animal. On the other hand, most biologists insist that wolves merely take surplus game that man would never get anyway (e.g., Stenlund, 1955). Nevertheless, ruthless persecution continues today. It is generally agreed that the remnant wolf populations of northern Wisconsin and Michigan (except for Isle Royale) probably totaling less than 50, are on their way to extinction. These wolves may not even be breeding successfully. Although Michigan removed its wolf bounty in 1958, it maintains an open season on the species. Wisconsin has not only removed its bounty on wolves but it has even given the species the protection of a closed season. Many people feel it is too late, however, to save the Wisconsin wolves.

There are probably only 300 to 400 wolves remaining in Minnesota, but that State still has a bounty. About the only time a bounty might help decrease a predator population is when the species has a low reproductive rate, when the population itself is low and the bounty payment high, and when there are very efficient methods of capture. Such is now the case in Minnesota. The use of aircraft and snowmobiles have greatly expedited wolf capture. Thus there is genuine concern that unless the bounty is removed, the voice of the timber wolf will soon be silenced in the State that now so rightly boasts of its great wilderness.

With prospects so poor for the timber wolf over most of its present range, it is important that the species be studied while it is still possible to do so. Ecological research on this big-game predator so far has yielded somewhat conflicting theories. Do wolves kill indiscriminately, or are they limited to sick and weak individuals? Do they affect prey populations only incidentally, or do they control or deplete them? What controls a wolf population? What is the function of the wolf in a wilderness area? The answers to these and other questions were sought during the present study of wolf ecology.

Isle Royale National Park in north-western Lake Superior is an ideal location for such a study. Fifteen miles from the nearest mainland, this outdoor laboratory has supported a discrete population of moose (*Alces alces*) for about 60 years and of wolves for about 15. No other big-game animal or large carnivore is present, and all wildlife is protected from hunting. Preliminary work by Cole (1957) and others indicated that intensive wolf and moose research on the island would be highly rewarding.

Long before wolves populated Isle Royale, biologists speculated about how they might affect the moose herd, which had greatly exceeded the carrying capacity. After the wolf population became established, the possibilities for research were apparent to many.

In June 1958, Purdue University initiated the present 3-year study, the first of a series. Essentially, the objective was to explore the dynamics of wolf-moose relationships. Use of an aircraft in winter facilitated gathering the most significant information, but ground observations in spring and summer provided additional data.

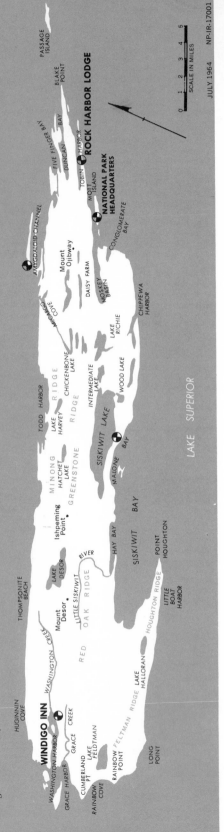

Figure 2—Isle Royale.

PASSAGE ISLAND

BLAKE POINT

ROCK HARBOR LODGE

FIVE FINGER BAY

DUNCAN BAY

TOBIN HARBOR

MOTT ISLAND

NATIONAL PARK HEADQUARTERS

AMYGDALOID CHANNEL

Mount Ojibway

CONGLOMERATE BAY

DAISY FARM

MOSKEY BASIN

McCARGO COVE

LAKE RICHIE

CHIPPEWA HARBOR

TODD HARBOR

M I N O N G   R I D G E

LAKE HARVEY

HATCHET LAKE

CHICKENBONE LAKE

G R E E N S T O N E   R I D G E

INTERMEDIATE LAKE

SISKIWIT LAKE

WOOD LAKE

MALONE BAY

THOMPSONITE BEACH

LAKE DESOR

Mount Desor

LITTLE SISKIWIT RIVER

Ishpeming Point

HAY BAY

R E D   O A K   R I D G E

SISKIWIT BAY

POINT HOUGHTON

HUGININ COVE

WASHINGTON CREEK

WASHINGTON HARBOR

WINDIGO INN

GRACE HARBOR

GRACE CREEK

CUMBERLAND PT

LAKE FELDTMAN

RAINBOW COVE

RAINBOW POINT

FELTMAN RIDGE

LAKE HALLORAN

HOUGHTON RIDGE

LITTLE BOAT HARBOR

LONG POINT

LAKE SUPERIOR

SCALE IN MILES
0 1 2 3 4 5

JULY 1964   NP-IR-17001

Figure 3—Main foot trails of Isle Royale.

M I N O N G   R I D G E

GREENSTONE RIDGE

RED OAK RIDGE

FELTMAN RIDGE

HOUGHTON RIDGE

0 1 2 3 4 5

Study Area

MICHIGAN'S Isle Royale, in Lake Superior, is 50 miles northwest of the Keweenaw Peninsula and about 20 miles southwest of the Canadian shore (89° west longitude, 48° north latitude). Forty-five miles long and 2 to 9 miles wide, the 210-square-mile island parallels the northwest shore of the lake (figure 2). The nearest mainland is Prince Location, Ontario, 15 miles northwest of the southwest end of the island.

In 1940, Isle Royale became a National Park, insuring the preservation of its wilderness character. Copper mining (prehistoric and modern) pulpwood cutting, hunting, fishing, and trapping had been carried on to some extent before 1940. Since then, however, Isle Royale has been protected from such disturbing influences except fishing (commercial and sport).

Although there are no roads in the park, approximately 100 miles of little-used foot trails provide access to most of the interior (figure 3). Bays and harbors enable boaters to explore some of the periphery, but much of the shoreline is rugged and unsuitable for mooring boats. Rock Harbor Lodge at the northeast end of the island and Windigo Lodge at the southwest end are the centers of tourist activity. (Summer head-quarters of the National Park Service are on Mott Island.) Between these areas are two ranger stations, three forest-fire lookouts, and a few isolated abodes of commercial fishermen. The tourist season extends from Memorial Day to Labor Day. Park Service staff and resident commercial fishermen live on the mainland from December to April.

Physiography

The topography of Isle Royale is characterized by series of parallel ridges and valleys, narrow points and bays, numerous nearby islands, and slender lowlands and lakes. The island originated when a bed of pre-Cambrian lava and sedimentary layers faulted, tilted upward from southeast to northwest, and protruded from the sea. Erosion, submersion, and deposition of Cambrian sediment followed, and the process was repeated. "Similar processes continued until the marked elevation of the land, which took place at the close of the Tertiary, and which initiated the repeated glaciations of the Ice Age" (Adams, 1909:32).

The last (Wisconsin) ice sheet completely covered Isle Royale by several thousand feet. After it receded, Lakes Duluth and then

Figure 4—Aerial view of northeast end of Isle Royale.

Algonquin covered the island. Eventually, new outlets developed and the lake level dropped by steps, as evidenced by the ancient beach lines seen today on Isle Royale and the north shore of Lake Superior (Adams, 1909). The present lake level is 602 feet.

Because of the direction of the original tilting, the southeast sides of most ridges slope, whereas the northwest sides form escarpments. One main central divide, the Greenstone Ridge, extends the length of the island. Its summit, Mount Desor (elevation 1,394 feet), is the highest point on Isle Royale. Minong Ridge and Red Oak Ridge parallel this on the northwest and southeast,

respectively. These and numerous lesser crests produce a "washboard effect." At the northeast end of the island, ridges project for miles into the lake, forming points, peninsulas, and over 200 surrounding islands (figure 4).

The soil is shallow, sandy or stony loam; there is little glacial till. Postglacial disintegration of rock, plus deposition of organic remains, has produced most of the soil, but lacustrine clay and sand are present in isolated locations (Adams, 1909). Erosion has left many ridgetops bare or covered with thin, azonal soil, whereas deposition has built up many poorly drained valleys. Where accumulation has occurred in upland areas, there has been light podzolization (Linn, 1957).

Between the ridges there are hundreds of ponds, swamps, and bogs, and approximately 30 lakes. Siskiwit Lake, the largest, is 7 miles long and 1½ miles wide. Most watersheds are small, so many streams are intermittent; the few permanent ones are slow-moving. Numerous narrow bays, harbors, and channels interrupt the shoreline, particularly along the northeast half of the island. In winter, these frozen waterways provide landing fields for the research aircraft and travel routes for wolves. The 200-mile shoreline is also a favorite wolf travelway.

Climate

The climate of Isle Royale is similar to that of the rest of the upper-Great-Lakes region. Some snow may be expected any time from September to May, but it accumulates only from mid-November to April. Temperatures are moderated by Lake Superior, especially on Isle Royale, where daily lows in winter may be 6° warmer than those of the mainland. In summer Isle Royale is much cooler than the mainland. Trees are not fully leaved until about June, and traces of autumn color appear in late August.

Weather records for Isle Royale are incomplete, for in most years no one is there from December to May. Table 1 gives the data recorded at Mott Island, near the northeast end of the park, from 1940 to 1952. Since snowfall records are unavailable for Isle Royale, data are presented from the nearest other U.S. Weather Bureau station, Grand Marais, Minn., approximately 36 miles west of the southwest end of the island (table 2).

Figure 5 — Northward view of the south-central section of Isle Royale, well used by wolves every winter.

TABLE 1.—WEATHER RECORDS FROM MOTT ISLAND, ISLE ROYALE, 1940–52

[U.S. Department of Commerce, 1956a]

	Jan.	Feb.	Mar.	Apr.	May	June	July	Aug.	Sep.	Oct.	Nov.	Dec.[a]
Mean total precipitation (in.)	2.21 [b](3)	1.86 (3)	2.12 (3)	2.27 (4)	2.19 (10)	3.58 (12)	2.81 (12)	3.34 (12)	3.99 (11)	2.35 (10)	2.68 (9)	1.52 (4)
Mean snowfall (in.)	...	...	...	...	.8		0	0	.4	.9	12.2	...
Mean temperature	...	...	...	...	45.2	52.2	58.3	60.5	52.9	44.6	30.9	...
Mean maximum temperature	...	...	...	...	54.4	61.1	67.5	68.1	?	51.4	35.8	...
Mean minimum temperature	...	...	...	...	35.8	43.0	49.0	52.8	46.1	37.8	26.0	...
Maximum temperature	...	...	...	...	79	86	87	86	81	72	62	...
Minimum temperature	...	...	...	...	19	33	37	38	29	12	7	...

[a] Annual precipitation 1941: 30.69; 1942: 35.68 (only years available).
[b] Number of years on which mean is based. All other figures based on 10 years.

TABLE 2.—WEATHER RECORDS FROM GRAND MARAIS, MINN., 1931–52

[U.S. Department of Commerce, 1956b]

	Jan.	Feb.	Mar.	Apr.	May	June	July	Aug.	Sep.	Oct.	Nov.	Dec.	Annual
Mean total [a] precipitation (in.)	1.53	1.01	1.40	1.90	2.53	3.48	2.72	3.07	3.06	2.25	2.02	1.36	26.33
Mean [b] snowfall (in.)	14.3	12.8	9.4	5.4	.1	Tr.	0	0	.1	.9	7.9	12.9	63.8
Mean [c] temperature	15.2	16.1	25.0	36.3	45.5	51.7	58.5	61.1	54.2	44.1	30.7	20.4	38.2
Mean maximum [c] temperature	24.4	25.4	33.2	44.5	55.0	61.9	69.8	69.8	62.2	52.0	37.7	28.6	47.0
Mean minimum [c] temperature	6.0	6.8	16.9	28.2	35.9	41.7	47.9	52.7	46.2	36.2	23.7	12.1	29.5
Maximum [d] temperature	48	51	63	70	85	88	94	94	86	72	62	55	94
Minimum [b] temperature	−34	−34	−24	5	17	25	28	33	23	6	−13	−27	−34

[a] Based on 21 or 22 years. [b] Based on 19 years. [c] Based on 20 years. [d] Based on 18 years.

Microclimates in the interior of Isle Royale differ significantly from those along the shore. Robert M. Linn (1957:96–97) in a study of the island's climax forests and their microclimatological differences found that ". . . in areas near to Lake Superior, temperatures are lower and have less range, and atmospheric moisture is greater than at the higher elevations in the center of Isle Royale. Here temperatures are highest and atmospheric moisture is lowest. These two extreme habitats possess climatic patterns which differ enough to be expressed by different climax vegetation types."

During the present study, the February–March snow depth on the level in wind-protected areas was 16 to 24 inches in 1959, 12 to 16 inches in 1960, and 20 to 26 inches in 1961. Drifts on the northwest sides of ridges were 3 to 6 feet deep, but exposed

Figure 6 — Greenstone Ridge (in background) which runs the length of the center of the island, as seen from the north.

southeast slopes and thick swamps often had less than a foot of snow. Hakala (1953) reported snow depths of 18 to 36 inches for a similar period in 1953.

By January, extensive sheets of floating ice surround Isle Royale on calm days; during windstorms these break and wash up on shore. This action keeps the lake open south of the island, but a shelf forms along the shoreline and across the smaller bays. In 1959 and 1961 all the harbors and bays (including Siskiwit Bay) were frozen their entire lengths by February. Similar conditions were not encountered in 1960 until March.

During 1959 and 1960 ice often appeared to connect Isle Royale with

Figure 7—Lush, second-growth hardwoods in the 1936 burn.

Canada, but after each high wind the ice span disappeared. However, in 1961, the "bridge" remained intact from February 15 until at least March 21, despite several windstorms.

Flora

Isle Royale is in the Canadian biotic province (Dice 1943: Map I), just south of the arbitrary boundary of the Hudsonian province. Thus, it is actually in the transition zone between the two, and characteristics of both are evident.

In the cooler, damper regions close to the lake, and in the narrow northeast section of the island, balsam fir (*Abies balsamea*) and white spruce (*Picea glauca*) comprise the climax forest; white birch (*Betula papyri-*

fera) forms small pockets in this type. According to Krefting (1951) the spruce-fir forest composes 29 percent of the island's cover. This climax is characteristic of the Hudsonian biotic province.

Typical of the Canadian province is the climax consisting of sugar maple (*Acer saccharum*) and yellow birch (*Betula lutea*), which predominates on the warmer, more mesic sites in the southwest third of the park. About 10 percent of the island's forest consists of this type (Krefting, 1951). Small local stands of northern red oak (*Quercus rubra*), white pine (*Pinus strobus*), red pine (*P. resinosa*), or jack pine (*P. banksiana*) occupy the most xeric ridges.

Swamps and lowlands support black spruce (*Picea mariana*), white cedar (*Thuja occidentalis*), and balsam fir.

Figure 8—The 1936 burn in winter.

Figure 9—Heavily browsed birch and aspen.

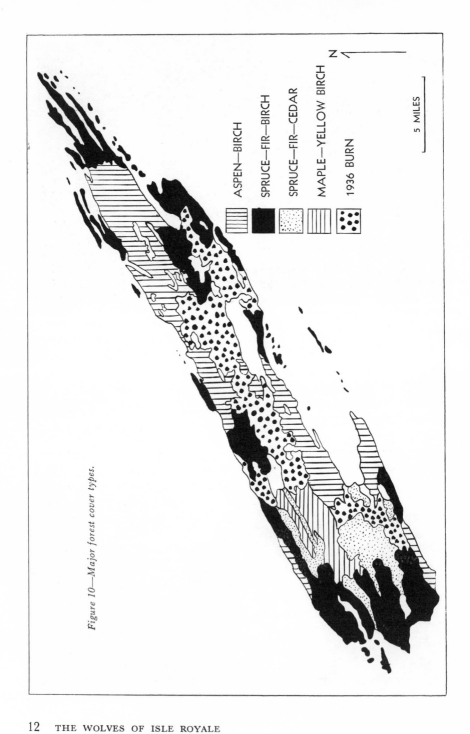

ASPEN—BIRCH

SPRUCE—FIR—BIRCH

SPRUCE—FIR—CEDAR

MAPLE—YELLOW BIRCH

1936 BURN

N

5 MILES

Figure 10—Major forest cover types.

About 56 percent of the forest cover is subclimax aspen (*Populus tremuloides*) and white birch, interspersed with conifer reproduction (Krefting, 1951). This type results from fires, and since most of Isle Royale has been burned over (Brown, n.d.), these subclimax stands are widespread. According to Hickie (n.d.), extensive fires occurred between 1870 and 1900. In 1936, fire swept approximately one-fourth of the island (Aldous and Krefting, 1946), and this area now supports predominantly white birch and some aspen. Willow (*Salix* spp.), fire cherry (*Prunus pennsylvania*), and choke-cherry (*P. virginiana*) also are scattered throughout the burn (figures 7 and 8).

Figure 10 shows the location and extent of the major cover types.

Shrubs and lesser trees are represented primarily by speckled alder

Figure 11—American yew, a favorite moose food, on Passage Island, one of the islands surrounding Isle Royale. Since there are no moose on this island, yew grow profusely, but on Isle Royale this species is now very scarce.

(*Alnus incana*) along streams and in old beaver meadows; mountain alder (*A. crispa*) around lakes, bays, and rock openings; beaked hazelnut (*Corylus cornuta*) in rock openings and old burns; mountain maple (*Acer spicatum*) in mixed woods and on rocky cliffs; mountain ash (*Pyrus americana*) on islands and in rock openings; black ash (*Fraxinus nigra*) in damp upland areas; serviceberry (*Amelanchier* spp.), blueberry (*Vaccinium* spp.), bearberry (*Arctostaphylos uva-ursi*) and wood rose (*Rosa acicularis*) on open ridges; red osier (*Cornus stolonifera*) along shores, bogs, and swamps; red rasp-

Figure 12—Lush stand of young aspen making a return in the Washington Harbor area.

Figure 13—Moose browse in winter.

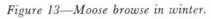

berry (*Rubus idaeus*) in forest clearings, rock openings, and old beaver meadows; bush honeysuckle (*Diervilla lonicera*) and thimbleberry (*Rubus parviflorus*) in rock openings, mixed woods, and old burns. The latter probably is the most abundant and widespread shrub on Isle Royale.

One of the most common herbs is large-leaved aster (*Aster macrophyllus*), which grows in old burns, mixed woods, and rock openings in all parts of the park. Cow parsnip (*Heracleum maximum*) is widespread, in clearings and lightly shaded areas. Bunchberry (*Cornus canadensis*), twinflower (*Linnaea borealis*), yellow clintonia (*Clintonia borealis*), and wild sarsaparilla (*Aralia nudicaulis*) are also conspicuous in the understory. Open ridges support wood lily (*Lilium philadelphicum*), fireweed (*Epilobium angustifolium*), columbine (*Aquilegia canadensis*), bluebell (*Campanula rotundifolia*), self-heal (*Prunella vulgaris*), pearly everlasting (*Anaphalis margaritacea*), strawberry (*Fragaria virginiana*), goldenrod (*Solidago* spp.), and others.

Skunk cabbage (*Symplocarpus foetidus*), marsh marigold (*Caltha palustris*), sedges (*Carex* spp.), and rushes (*Juncus* spp.) are typical herbs of Isle Royale swamps. The common aquatics are *Nuphar, Nymphaea, Brasenia, Potamogeton,* and *Utricularia*.

The most abundant and widespread fern appears to be bracken (*Pteridium aquilinum*), which grows in old burns, along trails, on ridges, and in birch-aspen stands. Interrupted fern (*Osmunda claytoniana*) and several species of *Dryopteris* occupy the more shaded sites, and polypody (*Polypodium virginianum*) is widely distributed in shaded rocky areas.

C. A. Brown (n.d.) listed 671 ferns and flowering plants present on Isle Royale.

History of Isle Royale Mammals

SINCE the study area is isolated, relatively few mammalian species are present. Furthermore, when a species disappears, it may not return for decades, if at all. Thus, significant shifts in species composition have been noted since Adams (1909) published the first list of mammals for Isle Royale. Man's role in these events is not fully known. However, he probably is responsible for exterminating the lynx and marten. The caribou and coyote apparently disappeared for other reasons. No attempt was made during the present study to complete a mammal survey, but incidental observations of mammals were made, and long-time summer residents of the island were interviewed regarding the past status of various species. (One cooperator first camped on Isle Royale in 1902!) Table 3 summarizes the information on shifts in the Isle Royale mammal community.

The lynx must have been plentiful on Isle Royale, for Adams (1909: 413) reported: "Victor Anderson and son, John, secured 48 skins during the winter of 1903 and 1904. Most of these were from about three miles southeast [sic] of the head of Rock Harbor, in the vicinity of Lake Richie." Tracks or specimens were reported from most sections of the island.

Milford Johnson of Amygdaloid Island relates that lynx were being trapped by Bill Lively of the Michigan Conservation Department about 1925. Glen Merritt (Tobin Harbor) believes the species was present until about 1930, and Zerbey (1960: 4) wrote that "In the early 1930's the Michigan Conservation Office trapped over 25 lynx." This is the last record of the species on Isle Royale.

Martens undoubtedly were common on the island at one time; Adams (1909: 414) wrote: "During the past season [1905] Chas. Preulx took eleven Martens along the Desor trail . . ." Apparently, soon after this, the valuable and easily trapped furbearer disappeared. None of the interviewed early residents remembered the animal, and no other reports or mentions of it were found.

Adams also recorded that residents observed 2 woodland caribou near Blake's Point in the winter of 1904, and 9 on the ice near the Rock Harbor lighthouse in 1905; an ice fisherman about 5 miles out from Pigeon Point, Minn., spied 11 caribou on the ice toward Isle Royale. Julian G. Cross, whose father lived for many

TABLE 3.—HISTORY OF ISLE ROYALE MAMMALS
[X=present; O=not observed]

Species	Present in 1905	Interim	Present status
Woodland caribou *Rangifer caribou*.............	X	To about 1925.	O
Canada lynx *Lynx canadensis*.............	X	To early 1930's.	O
Marten *Martes americana*............	X	O	O
Coyote *Canis latrans*...............	O	X	O
Beaver *Caster canadensis*...........,....	O	X	Common
Moose *Alces alces*.................	?	X	Common
Red fox *Vulpes fulva*................	O	From about 1925.	X
Timber wolf *Canis lupus*................	O	From about 1948.	X
Snowshoe hare *Lepus americanus*............	X	X	Common
Red squirrel *Tamiasciurus hudsonicus*........	X	X	Abundant
Mink *Mustela vison*..............	X	X	X
Long-tailed weasel *Mustela frenata*............	X	?	X (*Mustela* sp.)
Short-tailed weasel *Mustela erminea*............	X	?	X (*Mustela* sp.)
Muskrat *Ondatra zibethica*............	X	X	Scarce
Deer mouse *Peromyscus maniculatus*.........	X	X	Common
Red-backed vole *Clethrionomys gapperi*..........	X	O	O [a]
Little brown bat *Myotis lucifugus*.............	X	X[b]	X
Keen's myotis *Myotis keenii*...............	X	X[b]	X [c]
Big brown bat *Eptesicus fuscus*.............	X	X[b]	O
Silver-haired bat *Lasionycteris noctivagans*........	O	X[b]	O
Hoary bat *Lasiurus cinereus*............	O	X[b]	O
White-tailed deer *Odocoileus virginianus*..	(12 introduced in 1906 eventually disappeared; Cole, 1956.)		
Otter *Lutra canadensis*.............	O	O	O[d]

[a] A fragment of skull believed to be from *Clethrionomys* was found in a fox scat.
[b] Listed by Burt (1957) for Isle Royale.
[c] Reported by Johnsson and Shelton (1960).
[d] See page 20.

Figure 14—Red squirrel.

years at Silver Islet (near the tip of Sibley Peninsula, Ontario), wrote (personal correspondence, 1961) concerning the movement of caribou: "Previous to 1900, when caribou were abundant, they were often observed on the ice outside of Silver Islet singly, or in small herds. . . . These animals often could be observed traveling back and forth, apparently to Isle Royale, or following the shoreline in both directions."

Pete and Laura Edisen observed a band of 14 to 16 on the ice near the Daisy Farm in 1922. Pete also noticed a single animal a few summers later in Conglomerate Bay. Milford and Myrtle Johnson saw caribou as late as 1925. This appears to be the last definite observation of the species on Isle Royale. Cole (1956: 53), without giving details, reported that "small numbers of caribou or single animals were seen in 1904, 1915, 1920, 1921, and 1926." It is not known whether the caribou population was resident on Isle Royale or whether small bands merely migrated there from the mainland in winter.

The reason for the caribou's disappearance has not been ascertained. However, the history of the species on Isle Royale correlates well with that on the mainland. Before 1900 the caribou was common in northeastern Minnesota (Swanson *et al.*, 1945) and in Ontario (de Vos and Peterson, 1951; Peterson, 1955), but it began to decline in numbers about the turn of the century (Hickie, n.d.). At present, it is rare along the north shore of Lake Superior. Perhaps the forest fires and invasion by man which occurred in the early 1900's altered the environment too drastically. If the Isle Royale herd was migratory, it also might have succumbed to these factors.

The most abundant mammal on Isle Royale in 1905 (possibly except for the deer mouse) was the snowshoe hare, according to Adams (1909). Commercial fisherman Sam Rude reported that hares were also plentiful in 1911 and 1922, but that since he settled in the southwest section of the island in 1927 he has seen none. Pete Edisen at the northeast end stated that in 1916, when he arrived, hares were abundant and remained so until the 1930's, but since 1936 he has seen very few. Murie (1934) reported hares very scarce in 1930. According to residents of Mott Island, the hare population there was high about 1950, but it decreased markedly by 1955. Cole (1956:53) observed that "the population level in the winter of 1955–56 was considerably below that of the winter of 1952–53."

The earliest record of the red fox on Isle Royale was furnished by Pete Edisen. He remembers seeing wild foxes outside the cages of black foxes raised by Bill Lively about 1925. Murie (1934), working in 1929 and 1930, also observed foxes. Later reports indicate that the population, although persisting, never was high.

Although Adams failed to mention the coyote, Glen Merritt of Tobin Harbor recalls that in 1902 "brush wolves" were plentiful. Mrs. William Lichte, also of Tobin Harbor, heard her grandfather, C. F. W. Dassler, speak of "wolves" on Isle Royale in the early 1900's, but her father, J. C. Dassler, informed her that these were coyotes. Pete Edisen said coyotes were present in 1916 when he arrived; Sam Rude remembers them in 1922; and Milford Johnson reported that they were common in 1925. Zerbey (1960) noted that coyotes were persecuted by residents from 1915 to 1935.

Murie (1934) found coyotes present in 1930, and Hickie (n.d.) stated that about 50 were taken in 1934–35. The occurrence of the species in 1945 was recorded by Aldous (1945), in 1946 by Gensch (1946b), and in 1949 by Krefting (1949b). Cole (1956: 53) summarized more information:

Brush wolves trapped in the 1920's are believed to have been coyotes. A number were trapped in the winter of 1928–29 and from fifty to one hundred more the winter of 1934–35. During six months on Isle Royale, two observers saw 18 coyotes in the winter of 1941–42. They were reported plentiful in 1944 and scarce in 1945.

Cole, a National Park Service biologist, did much field work on Isle Royale from 1952 to 1957. During 3 weeks in the park in February 1957, he (1957:37) saw no coyotes and only one track, and concluded: "Apparently the Isle Royale coyote population has declined substantially the last five years." This is also the opinion of most island residents.

Beavers inhabited Isle Royale in the 1800's but apparently disappeared and then reappeared since. According to Adams (1909), the William Ives survey in 1848 indicated the presence of old beaver sign, and island residents in 1878 saw beaver dams and cuttings. Glen Merritt asserts that beavers were present in 1902. However, Adams obtained no recent evidence in 1905 and believed that trappers had exterminated the species. Pete Edisen saw no beavers from 1916 until the early 1920's, when they again were evident. In the southwest section of Isle Royale, Sam Rude noticed them first in 1927. Aerial photos taken in 1930 showed evidence of a small population (Gilbert, 1946).

According to Gilbert, beavers were trapped before the island became a National Park in 1940, and not until 1943 was an increase in the population noticed. "At that time the gradual spread of colonization could be easily discerned. Outlets to inland lakes began to show signs of beaver damming, a few isolated swamps showed beaver work, and dams began to appear in series along the streams." By 1945, beavers had colonized almost every stream, lake, swamp, and bay. Several worked-out colonies were found, and aspen had been depleted severely along many waterways; white birch was being resorted to.

Gensch (1946a) studied 57 beaver colonies and their food supplies in 1946, and Krefting (1963) studied 28 colonies in 1948. Many had been abandoned, and new ones had been established in almost every available location. The latter authors concluded that the food reserve in the center section and especially the southwest section was low; the northeast section had the best reserve. In 1951, Krefting again reported a dwindling aspen supply. Pete Edisen (Rock Harbor) and Sam Rude (Siskiwit Bay) noticed a decline in beaver numbers about 1950, and Cole (1954) found a significant decrease in the population in the Siskiwit Bay region from 1952 to 1954. All island residents interviewed agreed that the beaver population decreased sharply in the 1950's.

Although there is no definite record of the presence of otters on Isle Royale, it seems odd that such an aquatic mammal would not have found its way to the island. Indeed, certain circumstantial evidence was obtained during the present study indicating that otters are present. Milford Johnson reported that in the autumn of 1959 he found several 3-to-4-pound whitefish bitten into while in nets in the mouth of McCargo Cove and around Round Island. This damage sounded like something

for which only an otter could be responsible. On August 23, 1960, I found mustelid-like tracks 2 inches long by 2⅜ inches wide along the outlet of Hatchet Lake, and suspected they were otter tracks. Again, on June 14, 1961, I noted similar tracks on the beach at the head of Conglomerate Bay. These, too, looked like otter tracks I have seen on the mainland. A final piece of evidence came from Lt. Comdr. C. G. Porter, skipper of the U.S. Coast Guard's *Woodrush,* who observed what he believed to be an otter in Washington Harbor on June 17, 1960, for 10 minutes at a distance of 75 feet. Porter is familiar with both beavers and mink and was certain the animal was neither of these. Nevertheless, it remains for future studies to gather indisputable evidence.

Moose Irruption

Authors writing about the history of moose and caribou in the Lake Superior area (Hickie, n.d.; Swanson et al., 1945; de Vos and Peterson, 1951; Peterson, 1955) agreed that as the caribou population decreased from 1890 to 1910, moose, which had been scarce, became more common. By 1912 moose were "very common" in Lake County, Minn. (Johnson, 1922). Fires and logging probably benefited the moose at the caribou's expense.

Adams (1909) did not list moose as present on Isle Royale in 1905. He did mention an observation of some maples which had been broken down and stripped of leaves and bark

and whose small branches had been eaten. He attributed this to caribou, but Murie (1934:10) wrote that it was probably ". . . the work of moose, for this type of feeding agrees exactly with the feeding habits of the moose and is not characteristic of the caribou." Hickie (n.d.) also believed that moose reached Isle Royale about 1905.

The popular theory is that the animals immigrated during the winter of 1912–13 when ice bridged the island with Canada. However, in 1915 the population size was estimated at 200 (Hickie, n.d.). Since moose are not herding animals, whenever they did reach the island, they probably did so in groups of one, two, or three. It seems unreasonable that there arrived enough separate groups to increase to any number near 200 in 2 years. Moreover, moose hesitate to cross even small stretches of

Figure 15—Cow and calf swimming between islands in mid-July.

ice, for it is difficult for them to maintain their footing there. Since moose are excellent swimmers and have been seen swimming in Lake Superior several miles from shore (Hickie, n.d.), it appears more likely that they reached Isle Royale by swimming from Canada. Indeed, P. M. Baudino of Calumet, Mich., told me that in the early 1930's in late June he observed a bull moose about half-way between Amygdaloid Island (part of Isle Royale) and Sibley Peninsula, swimming toward Canada.

If the first moose which arrived on Isle Royale swam from Canada, they probably arrived in the early 1900's when the moose population increased substantially along the north shore of Lake Superior. By 1915, moose were well established on the island. Conditions apparently were ideal, for the herd increased to an extremely high density, as is shown in table 4. Most of the estimates presented are subjective and show only trends, but it is interesting that the figures (until 1930 when the peak was reached) fit the theoretical sigmoid curve expected when any species invades new favorable habitat.

Adolph Murie spent the summer of 1929 and spring of 1930 studying moose on Isle Royale. He (1934) found that all the winter browse species and several of the summer foods were overbrowsed and predicted that disease and starvation soon would cause an extensive die-off. According to Hickie (1936) this began in 1933. In the spring of 1934, approximately 40 dead moose were found on about 10 percent of the island; the few carcasses autopsied were emaciated. Hickie spent the winter of 1934–35 investigating the situation, and established that the browse was all but gone. Don R. Coburn, game pathologist, examined 24 carcasses, finding "little but malnutrition as the cause of death." In 1936, the population was estimated to be down to 400–500 animals. From 1934 to 1937, the Michigan Conservation Department livetrapped 71 moose and released them on the Michigan mainland. The starving animals were easy to lure into the traps (Hickie, n.d.).

Besides the harm to several species caused by overbrowsing, great damage to the balsam had been inflicted by the spruce budworm since 1929.

TABLE 4.—ESTIMATES OF ISLE ROYALE MOOSE

Year	Estimate	Source
1915	200	*vide* Hickie, 1936
1915–16	250–300	*vide* Hickie, undated: 10[a]
1917–18	300	*vide* Hickie, undated: 10[a]
1919–20	300	*vide* Hickie, undated: 10[a]
1921–22	1,000	*vide* Hickie, undated: 10[a]
1925–26	2,000	*vide* Hickie, undated: 10[a]
1928	1,000–5,000	*vide* Hickie, 1936
1930	1,000–3,000	Murie, 1934
1936	400–500	Hickie, 1936
1943	[b] 171	*vide* Cole, 1957: 8
1945	[b] 510	Aldous and Krefting, 1946
1947	[b] 600	Krefting, 1951
1948	800	Krefting, 1951
1950	500	Krefting, 1951
1957	[c] 300	Cole, 1957

[a] Based on biennial reports of Michigan Game, Fish and Forest Fire Department and from Department of Conservation.
[b] Derived from aerial sampling.
[c] Attempt at complete aerial census.

In 1936 fire destroyed browse on more than a quarter of the island. Aldous and Krefting (1946) believed that the lowest moose population existed between 1935 and 1937.

A few years after the fire, browse was recovering in the burn, and the moose herd began increasing. In 1945 Aldous took an aerial sampling of the population and estimated that 510 moose were present (Aldous and Krefting, 1946). During the same study, an intensive browse survey led the authors to believe that Isle Royale's carrying capacity for moose had been reached.

Another aerial sampling, in 1947, produced an estimate of 600 moose (Krefting, 1951). A browse study in 1948 showed that browse was deteriorating, and another die-off was predicted (Krefting, 1951). Krefting believes that this occurred from 1948 to 1950. Several carcasses were found during these winters. The herd is estimated to have decreased from about 800 in 1948 to 500 in 1950 (Krefting, 1951).

During a month of browse investigation in the park during early 1953, Cole (1953) judged the moose food supply to be adequate. In 1956, he found that some of the browse was escaping, and he, too, believed that a marked moose reduction had started about 1949 (Cole, 1956). In early 1957, Cole attempted a complete aerial count of the moose. He observed 242 animals and estimated from tracks the presence of another 48 (Cole, 1957). (During the present study, this census technique was found to have serious limitations.)

Figure 16 — Washington Harbor. Winter headquarters for personnel involved in wolf study is located at head of harbor.

Advent of the Timber Wolf

The earliest claim we have of the presence of timber wolves on Isle Royale is from J. A. Lawrence. In correspondence of April 20, 1960, to D. L. Allen, Lawrence asserted that, from 1910 to 1920, timber wolves were hunted and trapped on the island and finally were exterminated. However, interviews with other residents of the same area and period indicate that the only wolves present at that time were brush wolves (coyotes).

Milford Johnson spent three winters (1924, 1925, 1931) on Isle Royale and believes he saw tracks of a single timber wolf each winter. During the 1930's or early 1940's Pete Edisen, who also overwintered three times on the island, reported that he saw wolf tracks during each. Ex-superintendent Charles E. Shevlin (1951) wrote:

Several years ago, two rangers on patrol observed what they believed to be a wolf, although, since neither was intimately familiar with the species, they could not be absolutely sure. They are, however, definite in their opinion that the animal was not a coyote. Other reports have been received from local fishermen to the same effect.

Milford Johnson reported hearing J. Cross, who lived all winter on Silver Island at the tip of the Sibley Peninsula, relate (about 1945) that he often watched wolves travel across to Isle Royale on the ice and could almost predict on what day they would return to the peninsula. However, Cross' son, Julian G. Cross, wrote (personal correspondence, 1961) that most of these wolves were of the "smaller or coyote variety." De Vos (1950:171) reported: "Mr. J. Cross saw a wolf pack from the air, several years ago, approximately south of Sibley, halfway between the peninsula and Isle Royale." Both Cross and de Vos noted that wolves crossed to Pie Island and Edward Island, and frequented Black Bay, Thunder Bay, and various other nearby bays and islands.

If a wolf population had been established on Isle Royale during the 1930's or 1940's, it seems there would have been more positive evidence. None of the reports of studies conducted during this period mentions the possibility of timber wolves being present. In contrast, once wolves did become established, their tracks, scats, and howling became evident to anyone spending any period on the island. Thus, it appears that if there were wolves on Isle Royale between 1900 and 1945, they probably were single or visiting individuals.

During the late 1940's several reports of timber wolf sign culminated in the definite establishment of the presence of wolves on Isle Royale. Sam Rude relates that in the summer of 1948 he saw tracks much too big for coyote tracks, on a beaver dam on Little Siskiwit River. Cole (1952a) quoted from a report of N. W. Hosley concerning his trip to the island in September, 1949:

On the trails in the eastern part of the island droppings were found which were estimated to be 1¼ to 1½ inches in di-

Figure 17—Wolf scats.

ameter. Probably half of these contained moose hair. They were so large that the question was raised as to whether timber wolves had not reached the island.

Krefting (1949b) also reported discovering scats "unusually large for a coyote" in September 1949.

In November 1950, Hakala (1954) found tracks measuring 3¾ by 4¼ inches. These are within the usual range of wolf-track dimensions. (The largest measurement of coyote tracks given by Murie [1954] are 2¾ by 2⅜ inches.) In May 1952, Cole (1952a) found wolf tracks and scats abundant.

Meanwhile, before the wolf was known to be present, a plan had gained impetus to establish a sanctuary for it. Murie (1934), Hickie (n.d.), Cahalane (*vide* Aldous and Krefting, 1946:308), Krefting (1951), and Neff (1951) had suggested introducing wolves on Isle Royale.

The original plan was to pay Michigan bounty hunters to secure two pairs of wolf pups, each pair from a different den. These pups were then to be released on Isle Royale with a wild-trapped adult female. However, the bounty hunters were unable to obtain wolves, so arrangements were made for the Detroit zoo to supply the animals. On August 9, 1952, four zoo-bred wolves were imported to Isle Royale. Since the creatures were not in the habit of fending for themselves, the plan was to keep and feed them in pens and allow them to come and go as they please, in hopes they would leave of their own accord and eventually revert to the wild.

Pens were built near the camp of Pete Edisen, Rock Harbor fisherman,

Figure 18—Wolf tracks in sand.

who agreed to feed and care for the wolves while they were in his vicinity. This turned out to be a bit more of a chore than Pete had expected, for the wolves soon escaped their pens and began harassing the Edisens. The creatures tore up one of Pete's nylon fish nets and made off with several handmade rugs that his wife Laura had laid out to air. They began seeking food at various areas of civilization on the northeast end of the island, including Rock Harbor Lodge, the main tourist center of the park. Since the wolves were used to being fed by people, they fearlessly visited local residents and campers, scaring the wits out of most of them. One wolf approached a professor, who was out for a leisurely stroll with nothing but a camera to defend himself, and came so close that the prof ended up in a tree, swinging his cam-

Figure 19—Resort area in Rock Harbor.

era at the persistent animal. He never did get a picture!

No one got eaten up, but many people were certain they had narrowly escaped such a fate. Thus Park Service personnel trapped the wolves and ferried them 30 miles away, but the next day the animals were back harassing tourists. Finally two of them were shot, one was trapped and returned to the mainland, and the fourth escaped. This individual, "Big Jim," had been reared at home by Lee Smits of Detroit and was an excellent retriever. He weighed 90 pounds when 8 months old and was about 15 months old when released. He never returned to the tourist lodge, but a year later, fishermen several times spotted a wolf swimming between islands and supposed it to be Big Jim, the retrieving wolf.

Because of the wide publicity afforded the wolf-importation plan, many people still hold the miscon-

ception that the present Isle Royale wolf population is descended from the zoo-bred wolves. But, as has been stated, wild wolves were known to exist on the island before the tame animals were imported. Since the tame females were disposed of, the present Isle Royale wolf population must be free of any influence from the zoo wolves—with the possible exception of whatever stud service Big Jim may have performed.

On October 2, 1952, Hakala (1954) sighted one large and one small wolf on the Feldtmann Trail. Between February 17 and March 16, 1953, Hakala and Cole observed a pack of 4 wolves on Siskiwit Bay. They believed these to be an adult male, an adult female, and two pups (Hakala, 1953). (However, Stenlund [1955] and Fuller and Novakowski [1955] cautioned that winter size and weight of adults and pups overlap so much that age cannot be distinguished on such a basis.) Hakala and Cole also saw lone-wolf tracks which seemed too small to have been made by Big Jim. Thus, there were at least five wild wolves on Isle Royale in early 1953.

From February 9 to March 8, 1956, Cole (1956) found evidence of a pack of seven wolves (observed northeast of Siskiwit Lake by his pilot), a group of two, a lone wolf, and at least one pack of four. He believes that there were two packs of four and another group estimated to contain four, all inhabiting the southwest end of the island. However, these estimates are based on tracks seen from the ground. The present study shows that wolves travel widely, and that even aerial observations of the animals themselves must be interpreted cautiously. Since Cole's estimated three packs operated in the same general area and each contained the same number of animals, the observed tracks probably could have been made by one pack of four. Nevertheless, it was quite definitely established that during early 1956 there were at least 14 wolves on Isle Royale (Cole, 1956).

From February 12 to March 2, 1957, Cole made an aerial survey of wolves and moose in the park. He observed a pack of seven wolves, a lone wolf, a pack of three, and tracks of a group of four. Although he believed that approximately 25 wolves existed on Isle Royale, he was certain only of the presence of 15 (Cole, 1957).

Figure 20—Cabin in Rock Harbor, where author and family spent summer of 1960 and 1961.

Figure 21—New lean-to, such as at numerous locations along the Isle Royale shoreline.

Figure 22—Type of lean-tos in the interior of the park. This one, on Lake Desor, was well used by the author during the summer fieldwork. Stores of staples and canned and dried food were cached nearby at beginning of each season.

Methods and Extent of Present Research

The results of this study are based upon observations made during 65 weeks in the study area, distributed as shown in table 5.

The base camp during the February-March study period was at Windigo, near the head of Washington Harbor (southwest end of the island). The Park Service stocked this camp with canned and dried food and aviation fuel before the park closed in the autumn. Additional gasoline was cached at Mott Island (northeast end of the park). Since a Park Service employee, the pilot, and I were the only persons on the island, two-way, FM radio contact was maintained with the Isle Royale winter headquarters in Houghton, Mich., 24 hours per day. About every 2 weeks a Cessna 180 from Northeast Airways, Eveleth, Minn., arrived with mail, supplies, and an alternate Park Service employee.

Censuses and observations of wolves and moose were made with the aid of a 90-horsepower, ski-equipped Aeronca Champ aircraft stationed on the island throughout the study period (figure 28). This tandem-seated plane cruises at 80 mph and carries a 2½-hour fuel supply. Two sleeping bags, tiedown ropes, and emergency food were carried in the plane, and two pairs of snowshoes and an ice chisel (to chop anchor holes for emergency tie-down) were lashed to the struts.

Competently piloted by Donald E. Murray of Mountain Iron, Minn., the craft provided rapid access to all parts of the study area and was highly maneuverable, allowing close-up views of the activities of both wolves and moose. Wolves were tracked daily whenever possible, and when located were observed continually until low fuel supply, inclement weather, or darkness interfered. Notes were kept of their hunting,

TABLE 5.—DATES AND EXTENT OF FIELDWORK

Dates	Weeks	Days
June 28 to Aug. 20, 1958..	7	5
Total 1958...........	7	5
Feb. 3 to Mar. 14, 1959..	5	5
May 7 to Aug. 19, 1959..	15	.....
Oct. 27 to Nov. 1, 1959..	.....	6
Total 1959...........	21	4
Feb. 4 to Mar. 21, 1960..	6	4
May 9 to Sep. 1, 1960...	16	5
Total 1960...........	23	2
Jan. 30 to Mar. 21, 1961..	7	2
May 10 to June 15, 1961..	5	2
Total 1961...........	12	4
Grand total...........	65	1

Figure 23—The Purdue "Wolf" — 16-foot boat used each summer.

Figure 24—Army "Weasel" used for transporting gear and drinking water from bay to winter camp.

killing, and feeding habits, and of their social behavior. When we discovered a moose carcass, we landed on the nearest bay or inland lake, and examined the remains. The winter phase of the study involved 435 hours of flying: 115 hours in 1959, 185 in 1960, and 135 in 1961.

The main living quarters during spring and summer were Mott Island dormitory in 1958, a commercial fisherman's cabin on Wright Island in 1959, and another fisherman's cabin (in Rock Harbor) in 1960 and 1961. During extended field trips, I utilized Park Service patrol cabins and lean-tos. A seaworthy 16-foot boat and 35-horsepower outboard motor afforded transportation to all parts of the island's periphery during fair weather Approximately 1,400 miles of hiking supplemented the use of the boat.

Field work from May through August involved many activities. Observations were made of moose, beavers, and snowshoe hare; wolf and fox scats were collected from foot

Figure 25—Wright Island cabin—summer headquarters for author and wife in 1959.

trails for analysis at the university; and all fresh moose carcasses and old moose remains found were examined. Few wolves were observed, but fresh tracks, scats, and scratchings were seen frequently. In spring I attempted to locate wolf dens by broadcasting recorded wolf howls and searching areas from which replies were obtained. Interviews with island residents, and reported observations of wolves and moose by cooperators (commercial fishermen, park employees, and tourists) provided additional information.

During autumn, I was in the field only 6 days. From October 27 to November 1, 1959, a sampling was made of the moose population to measure the calf:total population ratio. For the purpose, a 90-horsepower Piper Cub aircraft with floats was engaged for 11 hours.

Figure 26 — National Park Service patrol cabin on Hatchet Lake in center of island. Author used this cabin often.

Figure 27 — The "clothes grinder" — powered by 1-cylinder gasoline engine.

Figure 28 — Research aircraft and pilot Donald E. Murray.

Figure 29—Aerial view of winter headquarters at Windigo—head of Washington Harbor.

Figure 30—An Isle Royale timber wolf at 15 feet.

Results—The Timber Wolf and Its Ecology

No WOLF or wolf carcass was handled during this investigation, so no vital statistics are available for the Isle Royale animals. However, these wolves undoubtedly are of the same subspecies as those on the nearby mainland—*Canis lupus lycaon*. Stenlund (1955) examined approximately 150 wolves of this subspecies from northern Minnesota and found that the body length of most males was 43 to 48 inches; the majority of females measured 41 to 45 inches. Females averaged about 61 pounds, and males about 78, although some males weighed over 100 pounds. Observations of most Isle Royale wolves from about 50 feet, and of one from 15 feet (figure 30), indicate that these animals are about the same size as those from Minnesota. All of the park's wolves are gray, with so little color variation that individuals are indistinguishable on this basis.

In most of the wolf's range, airplanes are used to hunt the animals. Minnesota wolf-hunters claim that wolves have learned to vacate open areas at the sound of an airplane, and Stenlund (1955) and Cole (1957) provide evidence for this contention. On Isle Royale, Cole found that the wolves reacted unpredictably to his light craft. At times they bolted for the nearest cover, but in other instances they calmly watched the plane pass several times within 100 feet.

The first time we encountered wolves they (six) showed little concern until the plane approached to within about 200 feet; then they arose from their beds (figure 31). Each time we passed within 100 feet, they rushed toward the craft. This continued until we left. When the plane drew near nine other wolves on a ridge a few miles away, they ran onto the ice and tried to chase the craft. A few hours later, the groups were together and responded to us as they had earlier. These wolves were seen again 2 days later; 200 feet below us, they showed little concern. Throughout the rest of the first winter study period they remained oblivious to our presence, except once when continually buzzed at 75 feet. (Unless special conditions warranted, we usually flew at about 300 feet.)

This large pack apparently remained conditioned to the aircraft for a year, since low passes during the first day of the 1960 study period failed to disturb them. Even when we landed within 60 yards of the animals they stood their ground. Several ran back and forth on the ice for 1½ minutes and started toward the plane a few times, but they all

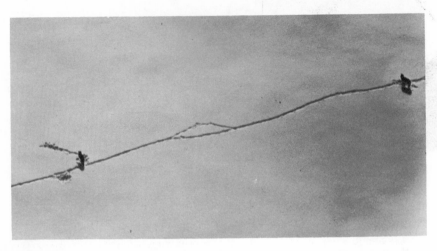

Figure 31—Attitude of wolves upon the initial approach of our aircraft.

finally ran into the woods and howled. When relocated the next day, they were unafraid. Throughout this study period the wolves appeared unconcerned at our presence (figure 32). Even when buzzed 10 times at about 40 feet on the last day, they merely stood around and watched.

Our first approach in 1961 frightened a few of the wolves in this large pack, but most remained unafraid. This disparity in behavior between individuals was noticed throughout February and March 1961, and probably resulted primarily from differences in social arrangement of the pack and the corresponding variations in social status of individuals.

Packs encountered less frequently showed more concern about the airplane. Apparently, wolves become conditioned by the continued pres-

ence of an aircraft that causes them no harm. Burkholder (1959) in Alaska found that wolves which were at first afraid of his craft eventually became accustomed to it.

Several times when the Isle Royale wolves were encountered while resting, they became aroused and began traveling a few minutes after the plane approached. They did not seem to be unduly concerned over the aircraft but may have been bothered by the noise. However, this was not considered enough of a disturbance of natural activity to complicate the results of our observations.

Wolves in most areas are known to be afraid of man, and experiences with Isle Royale wolves demonstrate the extreme to which this is true. On three occasions I chased 15 wolves from a moose carcass upon which they had just begun to feed. Although a few individuals were reluctant to leave until I approached to within, in one case, about 40 feet, all finally retreated and failed to return until several hours after the carcass had been examined. The manner in which the wolves left one carcass was especially interesting. When I approached to within 150 yards, most of the pack ran. Six animals continued tugging at the carcass until I got to within about 60 feet, and then two looked up at me and unceremoniously left. The other four, heads buried in the carcass, apparently received no signals from these individuals. They didn't detect me until I was about 40 feet away. Suddenly all jumped up and ran about 75 yards, stopped, looked back, and then continued to the rest of the pack, about 150 yards away.

On one occasion, after I had disturbed the wolves and examined their kill, part of the pack made a new kill while the others returned and fed on the old. The former animals apparently did not return to the original kill for about 2 days. The behavior of individuals during several other close-up encounters during winter and summer attested to the Isle Royale wolves' fear of man. A pack of three even were afraid of the human scent on a package of crackers tossed from the aircraft; each took one sniff and dashed off. However, the wolves were completely unafraid of docks, cabins, and other manmade structures which had no recent human scent.

Wolf Numbers

The composition of the Isle Royale wolf population makes possible a reasonably precise count but renders difficult an absolutely complete census. The main pack, containing 15 to 16 members, usually was relatively easy to locate. However, groups of three and two, and lone individuals, also were sighted. (These smaller groups

Figure 32—The unconcern shown the aircraft by the large pack throughout most of the study.

Figure 33—Wolf tracks in snow.

shoreline and all major lakes for wolves or tracks (figure 33). Tracks were followed until the wolves were found, if possible. Undoubtedly, no large packs escaped detection, but perhaps one or two lone wolves did.

On February 9, 1959, after a fresh snowfall, the first census was made. A pack of 15 wolves was discovered near McCargo Cove, a lone wolf at Todd Harbor, and another individual in Rock Harbor. A search of the rest of the island produced no other wolf sign. However, on February 23 a pack of 3 was sighted near Five-Finger Point, and a few minutes later the pack of 15 plus a lone wolf were discovered near Davidson Island, demonstrating that at least 19 wolves were present. The extra lone wolf

Figure 34—Tracks of five wolves in sand.

were difficult to find and keep track of.) Thus, censusing involved finding and counting the large pack and then trying to locate all other groups. The wolves' preference for traveling along the Isle Royale shore or on lakes was most important in the success of the censuses.

Censuses were attempted on the first or second day after a fresh snowfall, or under the following combination of circumstances: (1) the known whereabouts of the large pack, and (2) the discovery of a recent kill made by another pack (thus often allowing the prompt locating of this pack), and/or (3) the accidental sighting of other wolves. During censuses, we flew at 300 to 500 feet altitude and surveyed the entire seen February 9 might have been a straying member of the pack of three. No other wolf sign was seen in 1959 which could definitely be attributed to any other animals.

In 1960, four groupings of wolves were noticed: 15 (plus a lone wolf which followed this pack closely), 3, 2, and 1. The two wolves were seen three times, and the pack of three, five times, all on the same half of the island, but both packs never were observed on the same day. Therefore, I thought that perhaps the two wolves were part of the pack of three, and that the single wolf (only noticed once that year) was the third animal. The total estimate remained at 19 or 20.

The census in 1961 was complicated by the fact that the large pack often split up. Nevertheless, this pack still contained 15 animals. Lone wolves and the pack of three again were sighted several times. This year, however, strong circumstantial evidence indicated that an additional pack was present, composed of two animals. Although this never was proved conclusively, general knowledge of the Isle Royale wolves makes me believe that the group of two animals seen in 1960 and 1961 was *not* part of the pack of three.

Therefore, the 1961 estimate of the number of wolves present on Isle Royale is 21 and possibly 22. The difference between estimates in 1960 and 1961 is caused only by the difference in interpretation of the observations. That the pack of two

Figure 35—Wolf tracks in snow.

was not seen in 1959 does not mean it was not present, for during that year even the pack of three was observed only once, whereas in subsequent years it was seen many times. I believe that the Isle Royale wolf population has remained unchanged for the duration of this study. My increasing familiarity with the island's wolves from one study period to the next merely has made the last census most precise.

Figure 36—Wolf tracks in sand.

Packs

A summary of the size of Isle Royale wolf packs observed before and during this study is presented in table 6. Because larger packs sometimes break up into smaller groups, single observations are not always reliable for determining the size of a pack. Nevertheless, it is interesting that sightings recorded before 1959 involved some groupings of the same size as those seen during this study.

Hakala (1954) observed two wolves along the Feldtmann Trail in 1952, and Cole (1956) found evidence of a pair in 1956 near Siskiwit Bay. In 1960 and 1961, a pair (one animal larger than the other) was observed only on the northwest side of the island. Perhaps a pack's territory changes as variations occur in the size or distribution of other packs in a discrete population. If that is so, this pair may be the same as that observed in previous years.

Each winter a pack of three frequented the northeast and northwest parts of the island, where Cole (1957) four times observed a group of three. Probably these are the animals observed by Cole. One of the members is smaller than the others, so it may be a female.

The most significant pack on Isle Royale usually contains 15 to 16 members. This pack probably represents some combination of the seven wolves and the four observed by Cole, and the offspring of either or both groups. It has the largest (and probably best) range, kills the most moose, and dominates in encounters with other wolves. Most of each winter study period was devoted to observing this pack.

Figure 37—Wolf tracks near kill.

During the winters of 1959 and 1960, members of the large pack usually remained closely associated (figure 38). The few times the pack did split up in 1959, it usually separated into groups of 10 and 5 to 6. The smaller group sometimes

Figure 38—A typical formation of the large pack.

continued to rest for about an hour after the other animals started traveling, and it occasionally lagged on long treks. Twice, 5 wolves headed

TABLE 6.—SIZES OF WOLF PACKS OBSERVED ON ISLE ROYALE

Year	Sizes of packs						Source
	1	2	3	4	7	15–16	
1952		X					Hakala (1954)[a]
1953	X		X				Cole (1953)[a]
1956	X	X		X	X		Cole (1956)[a]
1957	X		X	X	X		Cole (1957)[a]
1959	X		X			X	Present study [b]
1960	X	X	X			X	Present study [b]
1961	X	X	X			X	Present study [b]

[a] Some of the wolves reported in these studies were observed just once so may have been straying members of larger packs.
[b] These figures represent basic pack sizes; temporary groupings are not included.

for old kills while the other 10 continued hunting. (In August 1960 and May 1961, tracks of a pack of five were observed along the winter runway usually used by the large pack.) Within the group of five, three animals seemed lighter colored and lankier, and these were thought to be young-of-the-year. If they were, this might explain why the group rested longer and more frequently

In 1960 the large pack still contained 15 to 16 members, but the 3 lanky wolves were not evident among them. The only time we observed any break-up of the pack was during the last 4 days of the study period, March 17 to 20, when three animals were missing.

Figure 39—Moose trail used often by wolves in summer.

However, in 1961 this pack was split about half of the time. On 13 of the 25 days the pack was observed, it was divided, usually into 5 and 10, or 7 and 8. There also were indications that it might have been losing a member, for often when the groups were united, only 14 wolves were present. In Alaska, Burkholder (1959) studied a pack which usually numbered 9 or 10 but sometimes split into 3 and 7.

Within the large pack there appeared to be at least three females, as determined by their behavior during the mating season. One of these, the smallest individual in the pack, was accompanied closely by a large male for a few weeks each winter. This pair, part of the 10 when the pack split in 1959 and in 1961, was the only pair that was consistently evident in the pack.

At least one lone wolf has been seen each year of the present study and of Cole's studies. In 1957 one followed Cole and his pilot for 9 miles across Siskiwit Bay. Cole (1957) believed this may have been Big Jim, the tame wolf released in 1952.

The lone wolf studied during the present investigation followed the pack of 15 from February 23 at least to March 14, 1959. Usually, it remained about 100 yards behind the pack and often was chased. Throughout the 1960 winter study period, a lone wolf (assumed to be the same one) again followed the pack, but it seemed almost to be accepted. It still traveled behind the others and did not mingle much, but

only on February 22, when much mating activity occurred, did I see it run from them. On that occasion, whenever they looked or moved toward the animal, it ran and then followed the group from a distance. The relationship between the pack and this individual in 1960 is difficult to describe, but it seemed more a matter of strong tolerance by the pack than complete acceptance. Therefore, the basic size of this pack is considered 15 animals, although sometimes the "pack of 15 to 16" or the "15 to 16 wolves" will be referred to.

In 1961, two lone animals frequented the large pack's territory, and they could not be distinguished. Neither followed the pack consistently. One was probably the same individual seen in previous years, and the other presumably was the stray-

Figure 40 — View toward Canada (Sibley Peninsula, Ontario, 20 miles in background) from interior of Isle Royale.

ing 15th member of the pack. Neither was exceptionally small, so both probably were males.

Other single wolves were seen each winter, but these may have been just straying members of the packs.

Home Ranges and Territoriality

Evidence that wolves are territorial was presented by Murie (1944) and Cowan (1947), and Stenlund (1955: 37) wrote:

Travel routes [in Minnesota] suggested established home ranges with poorly defined borders overlapped somewhat by ranges of other packs. Home ranges from which the main pack had been removed

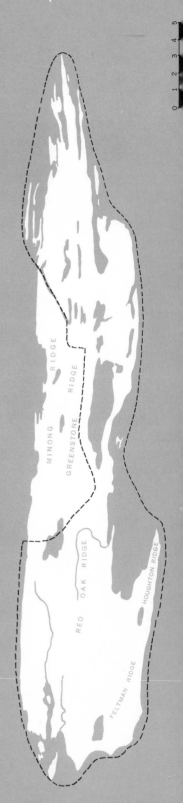

Figure 41—Territory of the large pack—February through March 1959.

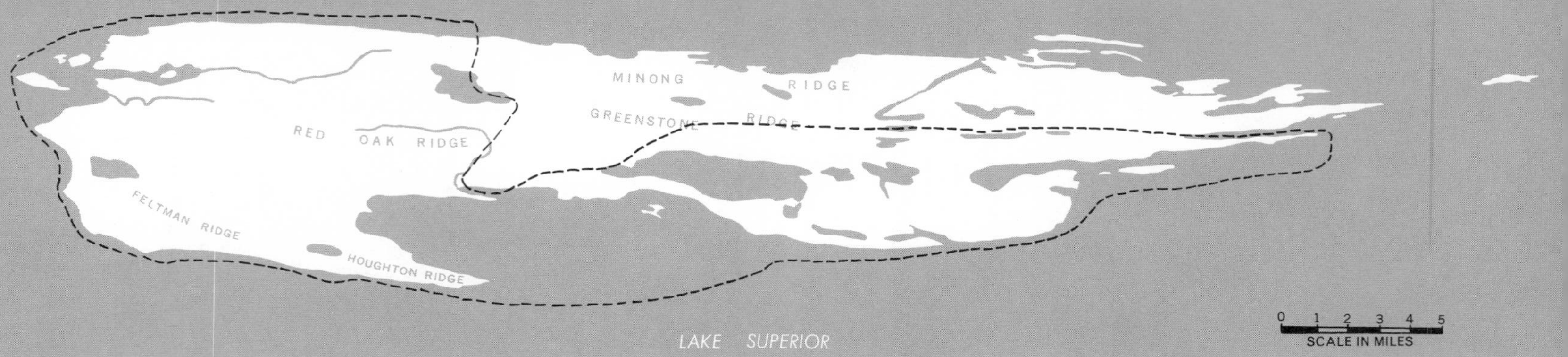

Figure 42—Territory of the large pack—February through March 1960.

MINONG RIDGE

GREENSTONE RIDGE

RED OAK RIDGE

HOUGHTON RIDGE

FELTMAN RIDGE

LAKE SUPERIOR

SCALE IN MILES

0 1 2 3 4 5

MINONG RIDGE

GREENSTONE RIDGE

RED OAK RIDGE

HOUGHTON RIDGE

FELTMAN RIDGE

0 1 2 3 4 5

remained barren of sign for two or three weeks after which other wolves reoccupied the range. Since these vacated home ranges remained free of wolves for a period of time, it is probable that wolves and wolf packs on the periphery respected the established territory of the home pack.

Schenkel (1948) believes that urine sprayed on scent posts serves to mark territories. This may explain Young and Goldman's (1944) report that urine from a strange wolf causes great excitement in other wolves and that scratching and kicking up of dirt, and often excessive deposits of excreta, are noted when such urine is found on scent posts.

Isle Royale's packs also seem to be territorial, at least in winter. Although the large pack used all parts of the park, it frequented certain sections much less than others. During 5 weeks in 1959, this pack only once visited the northwest shore from Duncan Bay to Thompsonite Beach, and spent but 4 days there. For the remainder of the period, the animals used the southeast side of the island (figure 41). In 7 weeks of 1960 the pack spent a few days on part of the northwest side, but continued to use the southeast half extensively (figure 42). However, in 1961 the range of the large pack seemed to have shifted somewhat. The southwest end of the northwest shore was used more, and the northeast end of the southeast shore, less. Even so, most activity of this pack occurred on the southwest end of the southeast side, as it had in 1959 and 1960 (figure 43). The shifts in range during the

three study periods may have been apparent only, because throughout most of the year the wolves may have used many other regions than indicated in the figures.

The only summer observation of wolves which probably were members of this pack was reported by K. Knoble of Gays Mills, Wis. On July 17, 1958, he saw six wolves on the Huginnin Cove Trail. Tracks of a pack of five were seen in August 1960 and May 1961 along the southeast and southwest shore of Isle Royale, and a large group was heard howling north of Siskiwit Lake in June 1960. All these locations are within the winter range of the pack of 15. A large pack also was heard several times near Daisy Farm in Rock Harbor, a less-used section of the winter range.

Thus the winter range of the large pack could be considered to be about half of Isle Royale, or 105 square miles. The approximate density of wolves in this territory, then, would be one animal per 6.5 square miles. It probably is significant that this area contains the best moose range and about two-thirds of the winter moose population. Of course, it might be more appropriate to consider the whole island as the range of this pack, since the entire area is available to the wolves, and indeed they do occasionally visit all of it.

The pack of three and the pack of two frequent the northwest side of Isle Royale, apparently with complete coincidence of territories (figure 44). Four summer observations

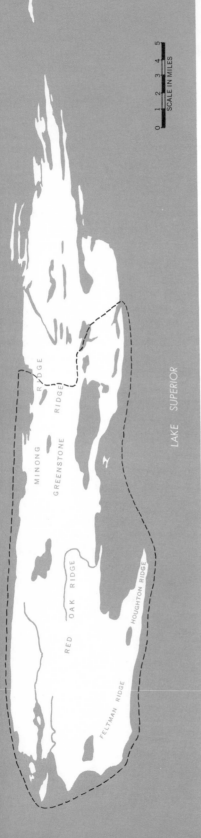

Figure 43—Territory of the large pack—February through March 1961.

LAKE SUPERIOR

MINONG RIDGE

GREENSTONE RIDGE

RED OAK RIDGE

HOUGHTON RIDGE

FELTMAN RIDGE

SCALE IN MILES
0 1 2 3 4 5

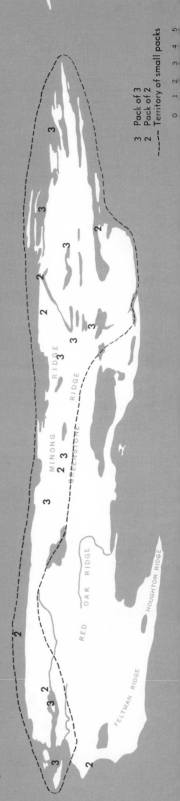

Figure 44—Territory and observations of the small packs—February through March 1959–1961.

MINONG RIDGE

GREENSTONE RIDGE

RED OAK RIDGE

HOUGHTON RIDGE

FELTMAN RIDGE

3 Pack of 3
2 Pack of 2
――― Territory of small packs

0 1 2 3 4 5

of three wolves were all made in regions within the winter territory of the pack of three. Campers saw three wolves at the head of Tobin Harbor about August 20, 1958, and Milford Johnsson observed three in October 1958, near Amygdaloid Channel. On July 28, 1960, Park Service Naturalists Robert A. Janke and Robert G. Johnson spotted three wolves just northwest of Mount Ojibway, and on August 20, 1960, Prof. and Mrs. W. Warth of Oberlin, Ohio, frightened three animals from a kill along the Huginnin Cove Trail.

Since the two smaller packs range over about half of Isle Royale, the approximate density of wolves in their territory is one animal per 21 square miles, about one-third the density on the other half of the island. The average approximate density

for the entire island is one wolf per 10 square miles, but this figure should be viewed cautiously because of the disparity in densities between the two sections of the island. Wide differences exist among figures reported from other areas, but Isle Royale has one of the highest densities recorded. Stenlund (1955) estimated that northern Minnesota supports one wolf per 17 square miles. For three study periods in Saskatchewan, Banfield (1951) estimated densities of 39.5 square miles, 58 square miles, and 83 square miles per wolf. Cowan (1947) believes that in Jasper National Park there was one wolf per 87 to 111 square miles in summer, but one per 10 square miles in winter. Reported home-range sizes of individual packs are listed in table 7.

TABLE 7.—REPORTED HOME-RANGE SIZES OF INDIVIDUAL WOLF PACKS

Location	Size of pack	Sq. mi. of home range	Sq. mi. per wolf	Source
Wisconsin.................	3 or 4	150	40 or 50	Thompson (1952)
Michigan.................	4	260	65	Stebler (1944)
Alberta...................	8	540	68	Rowan (1950)
Northwest Territories.......	7	90	13	Banfield (1954)
British Columbia...........	4 or 5	50	10 or 12	Cowan (1947)
Alaska....................	10	500	50	Burkholder (1959)
Minnesota................	7	126	18	Stenlund (1955)
Minnesota................	2	36	18	Stenlund (1955)
Minnesota................	5	50	10	Stenlund (1955)
Minnesota................	3 or 4	85	21 or 28	Stenlund (1955)
Isle Royale..............	2+3	105	21	Present study
Isle Royale..............	15—16	[a] 105	[b] 6.5	Present study
Isle Royale (total).........	21	210	10	Present study

[a] If the entire island were considered to be the range, this figure would be 210.
[b] If the entire island were considered to be the range, this figure would be 13.

The winter range of the smaller Isle Royale packs overlaps with that of the large pack in the Rock Harbor and Washington Harbor areas. It is interesting to speculate whether the smaller packs chose to inhabit the portion of the island with proportionately fewer moose or whether they were forced there by the large pack. Murie (1944:44) wrote that ". . . it is advantageous for minor packs to find territories where they are unmolested." This may be especially important on Isle Royale because of the great numerical difference between the large pack and the smaller ones. Schenkel (1948:90), during a study of wolf behavior, concluded that ". . . as soon as the society controls a certain number of individuals, the manifestation of all individuals toward individuals from outside becomes more secure. . . ." Thus, it appears that the smaller packs probably have been forced to inhabit the part of the island in which they are least molested.

Two instances were observed of direct encounters by the large pack with other wolves. On February 7, 1960, the 16 wolves chased a single animal at least halfway across Moskey Basin (about one-half a mile) to the north shore of the bay. All ran extremely fast, but the pursued wolf outran the others. Upon reaching shore, it continued at top speed into the woods and then northeastward at least a quarter of a mile without stopping. The pack gave up when it reached shore, and the animals lay down and rested.

The second instance was observed on March 4, 1961, near Cumberland Point. The large pack was traveling along the shore from Rainbow Cove to Cumberland Point when two wolves, which had been feeding on an old kill, ran out of the woods about 125 yards ahead. The pack gave chase, and the larger of the two wolves headed into the woods and was not pursued. The smaller individual continued with utmost haste for a few hundred yards along the shore, stopped momentarily, looked back at the oncoming animals, and assumed the attitude of complete submission described by Schenkel (1948), i.e., front legs stretched forward and head and shoulders lowered. After a few seconds, it turned and headed along the shore, with the pack in continued pursuit. All ran swiftly, but the pack did not gain on the lone wolf. The pursuers stopped after covering about one-half a mile; the single wolf continued at the same speed for at least another mile before entering the woods.

There also were indirect indications of enmity by the large pack toward outside wolves. On March 6, 1960, the pack of three ran "anxiously" from Grace Island to Washington Island while the 16 wolves were heading across Grace Harbor, a quarter of a mile away. Grace Island prevented each pack from seeing the other, but the 16 animals kept looking toward the 3, which were running and watching their back-trail. The large pack did not pursue. On February 22, 1960, the large pack was traveling overland south of Ishpeming Point when suddenly half of the wolves struck out on a fresh wolf track. They followed it excitedly for about a quarter of a mile before returning to the others. The actions of the pack of 15 to 16 toward other wolves gives the impression that if the dominant animals ever caught the outsiders, a mortal fight would ensue. Indeed, Cowan (1947) reported an instance related to him in which a large wolf was found mangled by others, and another instance in which four wolves attacked a fifth and wounded it badly. He also wrote of a situation in which a wolf wounded a dog and then rushed it again as its master leaned over it. Cowan believes the wolf's action was a manifestation of territoriality. Murie (1944:43) also described an observation of a wolf pack wounding an alien wolf. On Isle Royale, Cole (1956) found tracks indicating that a pack had attacked a strange wolf. Bloody snow and a 2-inch piece of lip showed that a serious fight had ensued.

Movements

"The desire to travel appears to be an inherent trait in wolves" (Stenlund, 1955:30). This statement seems to apply well to wolves on Isle Royale, for they often travel long distances, bypassing areas with high moose concentrations, and sometimes doubling back on their own tracks before making a kill. Kelsall (1957) analyzed 71 wolf observations involving 2,552 minutes, and found that 34 percent of the wolves' time was spent in traveling. Although no such figure was sought during the present study, indications are that Isle Royale wolves probably spend a comparable amount of time traveling.

Much travel seems to be necessary to the island's wolves for locating susceptible prey. Once they con-

Figure 45—Part of large pack traveling along shore of Washington Harbor.

sume a carcass, any moose they detect is subject to attack, but before encountering a vulnerable animal, the wolves may travel 60 miles or more (table 8). Burkholder (1959) in Alaska found that distances between kills made by the pack he studied varied from 6 to more than 45 miles, and averaged 24.

It is well established that wolves travel where going is easiest. In winter they follow frozen rivers, lakes, and streams; open ridges; and hard-packed drifts. Isle Royale wolves use such features also, but they follow the shoreline most extensively. There the snow is wind-packed, and the footing is good. Travel habits similar to those of the island's wolves were noted by de Vos (1950:174) in wolves on nearby Sibley Peninsula, Ontario:

. . . in late winter and early spring wolves travel extensively on the ice along the shores of lakes. They may either follow the shoreline into bays or cross those in a straight line. Often they run from land point to land point or from one small island to another in the bays around the peninsula.

He concluded that travel routes are determined by topography, distribu-tion of prey, and seasonal changes. Stenlund (1955) stressed the importance of topography, and this factor seems most significant on Isle Royale also.

Isle Royale wolves usually travel single file in winter, especially during overland forays. This appears to be a common habit of wolves, for it has been reported often. Not only is this mode of travel more efficient, but the packed trails that result become convenient overland travelways for the future. Regular use of such a runway keeps it easy to travel despite a heavy accumulation of snow.

Although the wolves commonly use the same trails whenever they pass through an area, they do not have a predictable travel routine. This agrees with work by de Vos (1950) and Stenlund (1955). The island wolves usually do not even follow a circuitous route, although circuits of runways do exist. Most authors agree that wolves follow their circuits in both directions. The Isle Royale animals are no exception, for they often double back on their own tracks.

Established wolf trails are used year after year on Isle Royale, just

TABLE 8.—DISTANCES (MILES) TRAVELED BY LARGE PACK
BETWEEN KILLS

Year	Minimum	Maximum	Average	Number of observations
1959...............	0	60	30	9
1960...............	10	67	27	11
1961...............	6	44	19	5
3 years...........	0	67	26.5	25

as they are in other wolf ranges. Many of the trails reported by Cole (1957) were still used during the present study, but less-used side trails varied from year to year. Side trails seem to originate as routes used by wolves in pursuit of moose. Once established, they may be used several times in winter. However, we observed a few occasions when wolves struck out overland without resorting to old trails. Stenlund (1955) also found this in Minnesota. In British Columbia, Stanwell-Fletcher (1942) tracked a pair of wolves which plowed chest-deep for 22 miles in 6 feet of fluffy snow, without lying down to rest.

We were not able to follow either the pack of two or the pack of three for more than part of a day, so extensive information on their movements was not obtained. The north shore from Washington Harbor to McCargo Cove probably was the route used most, but a trail was sometimes found from McCargo Cove to Blake's Point and around into Rock Harbor and Moskey Basin. An alternate route from McCargo Cove to Moskey Basin followed the chain of lakes from Chickenbone Lake to Lake Richie. The Minong Ridge from McCargo Cove to Todd Harbor was used often, and the Greenstone Ridge Trail, packed by moose tracks, sometimes was followed (figure 39).

In summer, wolf tracks and scats have been found frequently on all Park Service trails within the winter range of these packs, so I assume that these trails constitute major summer routes (figure 3). The Minong Ridge and the extensive system of moose trails also are used in summer.

The most-used winter route of the large pack followed the south shore from Washington Harbor to Halloran Lake and Siskiwit Bay, or to Houghton Point, then across Siskiwit Bay (or around its periphery), and along the shore to Malone Bay. From there one route cut across to Siskiwit Lake, Intermediate Lake, Lake Richie, and Rock Harbor; another followed the shore to Chippewa Harbor and then crossed to Rock Harbor (figure 47).

During 31 days, from February 4 to March 7, 1960, when the entire route of the 16 wolves was known, the animals traveled approximately 277 miles, or 9 miles per day (figures 51–55). However, during 22 of those days the wolves fed on kills, and no extensive movement occurred. Thus, in 9 days of actual traveling, the animals averaged 31 miles per day. During the entire study, the longest distance known to have been traveled in 24 hours was approximately 45 miles. In Alaska, Burkholder (1959) followed a pack that traveled a maximum of 45 miles in a day and averaged 15 miles per day for 15 days' travel, presumably including feeding periods. In Minnesota a pack moved 35 miles overnight (Stenlund, 1955).

The wolves usually travel at a trot, about 5 miles per hour. They rest every few miles, especially on the day after leaving a kill. Generally they leave soon after dawn and begin

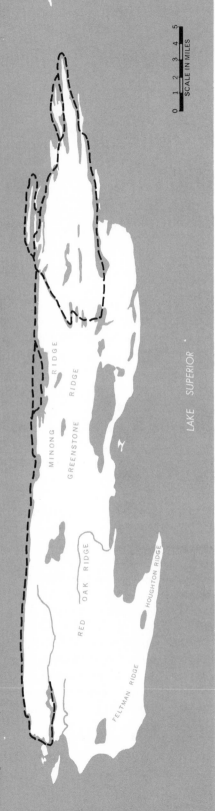

Figure 46—Major winter routes of the small packs.

LAKE SUPERIOR

MINONG RIDGE
GREENSTONE RIDGE
RED OAK RIDGE
FELTMAN RIDGE
HOUGHTON RIDGE

0 1 2 3 4 5
SCALE IN MILES

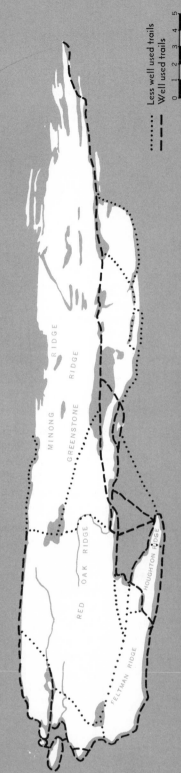

Figure 47—Major winter routes of the large packs.

MINONG RIDGE
GREENSTONE RIDGE
RED OAK RIDGE
FELTMAN RIDGE
HOUGHTON RIDGE

.... Less well used trails
- - - - Well used trails

0 1 2 3 4 5

traveling, but at about 11 a.m. they rest on the ice or on a ridge. About 4 p.m. the animals start traveling steadily. If no moose is killed during the night, they continue throughout the next day, resting often. The calculated rate of movement, 31 miles per day (or 1.3 mph), is an average which includes periods of travel, rest, and hunting. This figure compares favorably with that obtained by another method. For a total of 100 hours in 18 instances throughout the 3 winters, the wolves were timed for various intervals between 10:05 a.m. and 7:05 p.m. They traveled from 3 to 22 miles on each of these occasions and averaged 1.7 miles per hour.

Once the wolves began traveling, their general route usually was predictable. However, the direction the

Figure 48—Two members of the large pack.

animals would take upon leaving a kill could not be predicted. No correlation was found between direction of travel and either wind direction or period since a route was used last. The wolves sometimes doubled right back on their own tracks. Direction of travel seems to be a function of some unexplained whim.

In summer, this pack probably uses the foot trails, ridges, and moose trails which lie within its range, for sign was found on them frequently. However, tracks of a pack of five have been found on beaches along the southeast and southwest shores. A well-defined wolf trail in this area also is visible from the air, so I believe that

Figure 49—Ten of the large pack file through deep snow.

Figure 50—One member of the large pack runs when author steps out of nearby shack.

Figures 51–55—Routes of large pack February 4 through March 7, 1960.

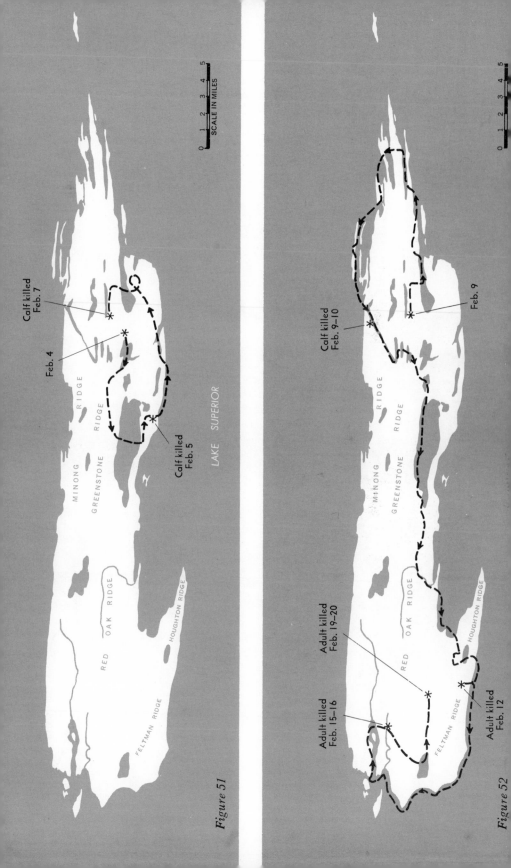

Calf killed
Feb. 7

Feb. 4

Calf killed
Feb. 5

MINONG RIDGE

GREENSTONE RIDGE

RED OAK RIDGE

HOUGHTON RIDGE

FELTMAN RIDGE

LAKE SUPERIOR

SCALE IN MILES
0 1 2 3 4 5

Figure 51

Calf killed
Feb. 9–10

Feb. 9

Adult killed
Feb. 19–20

Adult killed
Feb. 15–16

Adult killed
Feb. 12

MINONG RIDGE

GREENSTONE RIDGE

RED OAK RIDGE

HOUGHTON RIDGE

FELTMAN RIDGE

0 1 2 3 4 5

Figure 52

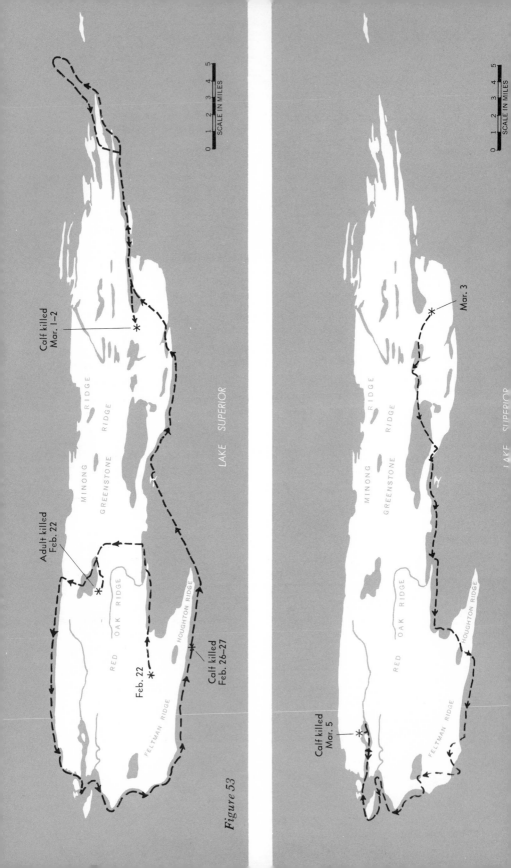

Calf killed
Mar. 1-2

Adult killed
Feb. 22

Feb. 22

Calf killed
Feb. 26-27

MINONG   RIDGE

GREENSTONE   RIDGE

RED   OAK   RIDGE

HOUGHTON RIDGE

FELTMAN RIDGE

LAKE   SUPERIOR

0   1   2   3   4   5
SCALE IN MILES

Figure 53

Mar. 3

Calf killed
Mar. 5

MINONG   RIDGE

GREENSTONE   RIDGE

RED   OAK   RIDGE

HOUGHTON RIDGE

FELTMAN RIDGE

LAKE   SUPERIOR

0   1   2   3   4   5
SCALE IN MILES

SCALE IN MILES
0 1 2 3 4 5

MINONG RIDGE

GREENSTONE RIDGE

RED OAK RIDGE

HOUGHTON RIDGE

FELTMAN RIDGE

LAKE SUPERIOR

Calf killed
Mar. 6–7

Figure 55

in summer the large pack continues to use many of its winter routes.

Most lone wolves were seen along routes used frequently by the packs, but, of course, some of these animals may have been strays from the packs. Banfield (1951) also found single wolves following routes used by packs.

Social Behavior

Although few opportunities existed for studying at close range the actions of the Isle Royale wolves, certain behavior was noticeable from the aircraft. No attempt was made to use foreign urine, dummies, or howling records for analyzing the actions of the wolves, but these techniques are suggested for future workers. The behavioral information presented is based upon distant observation of undisturbed wolves.

ORGANIZATION OF THE PACK

According to Young and Goldman (1944:120):

The pack is generally a pair of wolves and their yearling or two-year-old offspring. At times, however, there will be an intermingling of several wolf families to form a pack; but the duration of such bands is short.

Olson (1938) also asserted that packs are family groups and that larger packs consist of two or more families. Murie (1944), through recognition of individual wolves, ascertained that the "family theory" of the pack held for two groups of wolves in Alaska. He observed members of the East Fork family together at various times from May 15, 1940, to March 17, 1941. In 1941 two females from this pack had young, each in a separate den, but by June 30, one group had moved in with the other. Another pack, seen in August and in December, each time contained the same wolves, three adults and six pups.

Theories conflict regarding the status of the pack in summer. Schenkel (1948) believes that each mated pair leaves the pack toward winter's end, the unpaired, weaker, and younger animals staying in small groups for some time. Cowan (1947) also thinks that in summer the hunting packs are broken up and that the animals hunt in smaller groups. However, Murie observed 15 wolves (including 2 litters of

Figure 56—Part of large pack traveling across ice.

pups) in one group in July. He also saw five adults at a den in June and July. Whether members of a pack dissociate in summer may depend upon the type of terrain, the prey species, the composition of the pack, and several other variables.

On Isle Royale, most spring, summer, and autumn observations have been of single animals, which may have strayed, at least temporarily, from packs (table 9). Tracks, howling, and sightings of three associated wolves in summer and autumn indicate that probably the pack of three functions as an entity most of the year. A larger group also was heard howling several times. This, plus an observation of a group of six adults, and tracks of five adults show that on Isle Royale some wolves associate with others during the summer, at least at times. It may be that bonds among adult wolves are stronger in winter but that members of packs are together frequently in summer.

Murie (1944:45) explained what

TABLE 9.—NUMBER OF WOLVES SEEN OR HEARD FROM MAY TO
OCTOBER

Number[a]	Date	Location	Observer
6	July 1958	Huginnin Cove Trail	Reported
3	Aug. 1958	Head of Tobin Harbor	Reported
1	Aug. 1958	Rainbow Cove	Reported
3	Oct. 1958	S. shore of Amygdaloid Channel.	Reported
1	May 1959	Lake Desor	Author
1	May 1959	Hay Bay	Reported
1	June 1959	Sugar Mountain	Author
1	July 1959	Daisy Farm	Reported
1	July 1959	Lake Desor	Author
3	Oct. 1959	Mt. Ojibway	Author (heard)
Several	May 1960	Daisy Farm	Author (heard)
Several	May 1960	Daisy Farm	Author (heard)
3	May 1960	Daisy Farm	Reported (heard)
1	May 1960	Mt. Ojibway	Reported
Several	June 1960	N. of Siskiwit Lake	Author (heard)
Several	July 1960	Daisy Farm	Author (heard)
Several	July 1960	Daisy Farm	Author (heard)
3	July 1960	Mt. Ojibway	Reported
2 or 3	July 1960	Conglomerate Bay	Reported (heard)
5	Aug. 1960	Attwood Beach	Author (tracks)
3	Aug. 1960	Huginnin Cove Trail	Reported.
3 or 4	Aug. 1960	Chickenbone Lake	Author (from air)
4	Aug. 1960	Chickenbone Lake	Author (heard)
Several	Aug. 1960	Daisy Farm	Author (heard)
5	May 1961	Long Point	Author (tracks)
2 or more	May 1961	Malone Bay	Author (tracks)
3	May 1961	Conglomerate Bay	Author (tracks)

[a] In any of these cases, more animals could have been nearby but unobserved.

might cause a large pack to break up:

The size of the pack may be limited by the law of diminishing returns. Beyond a certain size, advantages may disappear. A pack might be so large that, after the strongest members had finished feeding on a kill, there would be little or nothing left for the rest. In such a situation, hungry ones would go off to hunt again, and the strong ones, already fed, would remain where they were. There thus might result a natural division of a band which was too large to function advantageously for all its members. One would expect that where game is scarce the wolves would operate in smaller units than where food is abundant.

The reason wolves form larger packs in winter seems to be unknown. Possibly, much more food is required during this season, and a larger pack might hunt more efficiently. The latter assumption might not be valid on Isle Royale, for while the large pack chases a moose, usually only five or six animals stay close to it; the others fall far behind. Because of this, it seems that the most efficient pack would contain five or six animals. Two packs of this size, operating independently, could travel twice as far as one, and therefore could locate, on the average, twice the number of vulnerable moose. It may be significant that in 1961, when fewer calves were present, the large group was split into two packs about half the time. Since calves provide much of the winter wolf food (about half during the 1960 study period), a shortage of this age class could cause more difficult hunting, which might force the wolves to operate in smaller groups. Indeed, in the 1961 study

period when the large pack split up several times, the 15 wolves consumed more food than in either of the previous two periods.

At times, a larger pack might be more advantageous. Many a moose stands its ground when cornered by wolves. Such an animal usually is safe, for if the wolves cannot force it to run, they soon leave. Possibly a moose is more inclined to flee when confronted with several wolves than with few. If that is true, a larger pack would be more advantageous, for when a moose runs, it is much more vulnerable.

In the Rocky Mountain national parks of Canada, "the usual winter hunting pack consists of from four to seven individuals, with five or six the most frequent numbers. Packs of 10 or 12 have been reported once or twice in the Jasper area. The largest group recorded was believed to contain 14 individuals" (Cowan, 1947:157). Stenlund (1955) reported that a pack of 15 occurred in Minnesota, and Olson (1938) gave records of packs containing 20 and 30 wolves, also in Minnesota. Murie mentioned a sighting of 22 wolves, tracks of 24, and a report of 50, in Alaska.

According to Schenkel (1948:83) packs are formed in early winter. He provides the following description:

Chorus, howling, joint wanderings and hunting, and fairly early rivalries concerning leadership and sexual partnership denote this period. During this time the pack becomes a close (exclusive) society. Its core comprises the bitch wolf, presumably the only mature one of the pack, and the male "lead wolf." Whether the isolation of the mature female wolves from one another is the result of rivalries, what course these rivalries take in any event, and what effect they have on the formation of a pack is not known. The lead wolf and bitch more and more plainly become a pair—first in the pack group—then at winter's end they separate from the pack and occupy a family area for the summer.

The possible beginning of a breakup in the large pack was noticed in mid-March 1960. The 16 wolves had remained together from February 4 to March 16, but on the 17th and 18th only 13 were seen. On these dates the animals were inland and could have been miscounted, but on March 20 (the last day of the study period) they crossed Siskiwit Bay; only 13 were present. Perhaps this disbanding was only temporary, but it might have been the beginning of a seasonal breakup.

SOCIAL RANKING WITHIN THE LARGE PACK

In the zoological gardens where Schenkel studied wolf behavior, more than one mature male and female were present in a pack, but one of each sex was dominant. These two highest ranking individuals he called "alpha animals." Murie (1944) believed that an unmated male was leader of one of the Mount McKinley packs, for other wolves approached this individual cowering. Apparently, this animal was dominant even to the mated pair within the pack.

Isle Royale's large pack contains at least three mature females, but

only one pair (a male and female closely associated for 2 or 3 weeks) was observed each winter. On February 19 and 22, 1960, the female led the pack, while the male remained beside her, half a body length behind. Copulation was attempted several times. The female appeared inexperienced at leading, for she backtracked twice and was often shortcut by other wolves. Each time after shortcutting the lead pair, the rest of the pack waited "respectfully," and as the leaders passed, each individual assumed the submissive position described by Schenkel (1948: fig. 2). While passing these animals, the leaders held their tails high, in the dominant position (Schenkel, 1948: fig. 30a).

On February 6, 1961, the small female also led the pack, followed closely by a male. Both held their tails in the dominant position when approaching an old kill, whereas the rest of the animals held theirs normally. This pair probably was the "alpha" pair. Apparently, the male usually was leader, but while his mate was in estrus, he took the advantageous position behind her. Fuller and Novakowski (1955) reported that during a wolf-poisoning campaign in Wood Buffalo National Park, Canada, males dominated in taking the bait in two instances in autumn, whereas the only instance during the mating season showed that a female was dominant.

The alpha pair does not always head the string of wolves, but position in line does not necessarily reflect social order. In Alaska, Murie (1944) noticed that the first animal in line was not always the leader. In the present study there were three main activities during which one wolf appeared outstanding: journeying overland, hunting, and arousing the pack from its rest. (I do not know if this wolf is the alpha male as identified above, or even whether it is the same individual each time.) When the pack journeyed through deep snow, the first wolf in line frequently was 25 to 50 yards ahead of the rest, even though it broke trail. When this animal rested, the others did also, and when it began to travel, the others followed.

During hunts in 1959 and 1961, one wolf often seemed more aggressive. Sometimes one animal threatened a moose while the others paid no attention. During several chases, one wolf caught up to the moose before the others did, and in some instances an individual continued chasing for 100 yards farther than the others. In a few cases, although several wolves threatened a moose, only one actually attacked the animal. Once when most of the wolves were lying around waiting for a wounded moose to weaken, one individual, its front legs covered with the blood of the prey, continued to harass the belligerent moose.

A hunt on February 12, 1960, produced some unusual behavior of a different type. After a three-quarter-mile chase during which most of the wolves ran alongside a moose for about 300 yards without at-

tacking it, the lead wolf suddenly stopped, turned around and lunged at those behind, as if to stop them from continuing the chase. It succeeded, for the other wolves turned and ran up their backtrail.

One wolf usually arouses the rest from their slumber. After stretching, this animal goes from wolf to wolf, touching noses and awakening each individual. As each wolf arises, it duplicates the procedure until the entire pack is active. Perhaps it is not necessarily the leader which initiates the arousing; it could be the first animal which awakens. (Murie describes similar arousing behavior begun by an individual other than the leader.) Nevertheless, I frequently saw the leader begin such activity.

Without identifiable individuals in the pack, it was impossible to distinguish the dominance position of the middle-ranking animals. However, status-demonstration was observed often among the wolves in the large pack. Frequent urination, oral, anal, and genital "besnuffling" (figure 57), presentation and withdrawal of anal parts, tail wagging, and mock attack upon weaker members of the pack (an energy displacement) were evident almost every day the pack was observed. Schenkel (1948) describes the above behaviorisms and explains their significance. The large pack performed the most noticeable social behavior in the following situations: (1) upon awakening, (2) when stopping to rest, and (3) while reassembling after a hunt or after splitting up.

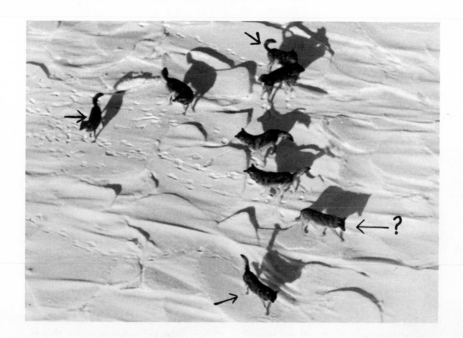

Schenkel (1948:87) explains why this behavior occurs so frequently:

Every mature wolf has an ever ready "expansion power," a tendency to widen, not necessarily his personal territory, but rather, his own social behaviour freedom, and to repress his "Kumpans" of the same sex. Consequently, he maintains a constant watchful interest in all socially important happenings within the pack. In particular, status quarrels are never private affairs between two individuals; the whole society takes a more or less active part in them.

Murie (1944), Young and Goldman (1944), and Crisler (1958) also have observed one or more of the social behaviorisms.

The most repressed individual in the large group of wolves was the most conspicuous. This was the lone wolf which followed the other 15. We first saw the animal on February

Figure 57—Social behavior among members of the large pack. Note oral "besnuffing" in uppermost pair, and varying tail positions. The smaller wolves (arrows) may be females.

23, 1959, about 100 yards behind the pack. It held its head low, ears back, and tail between its legs in the submissive position, and appeared to fear the other wolves. On February 24, while the pack rested on a lake, this animal was able to join the last two wolves in line. These slept for long periods and were not interested in the mating activity in which the rest engaged. The lone wolf wandered around near these two, and suddenly two others bolted toward it. The low-ranking individual ran off, directly past the two friendlier animals, but these remained unconcerned.

After a 100-yard chase, the pursuing wolves cornered the lone wolf near a snowbank and attacked it. They fought the animal for a few seconds and then rejoined the excited pack. The lone wolf followed slowly, and again the two wolves attacked it momentarily. This happened a third time, after which the lone wolf did not attempt to follow the attackers. The details of the fights were not observable, but the lone wolf fought hard and did not appear to be injured. Lorenz (1952) asserts, on the basis of observations in the zoological park, that a wolf submits to its aggressor by presenting its throat, a maneuver which tends to inhibit the aggressive tendency in the attacker. Perhaps this is what caused the hostile animals to end their attacks so suddenly.

The lone wolf continued to follow the pack for the remainder of the 1959 study period and throughout the 1960 winter study period. We did not notice any more attacks on the animal, but it stayed away from most of the wolves and remained submissive. Schenkel reports that "energy displacements" directed at subordinates often occur in packs, and may take the form of ambushes, sneak attacks, and fights. He often saw cases in which several wolves directed their attack against one animal over a long period. This individual ". . . steadily lost the significance of environmental social partnership, was robbed of all social initiative and, in certain

circumstances, with repeated attacks, became mortally wounded" (1948: 88).

Despite the hostilities shown it by certain members, the lone wolf seemed to be accepted by part of the pack. The two friendly wolves mentioned above provide one example. On another occasion, when most of the animals were resting, two wolves backtracked around a point about 25 yards to meet the lone wolf. They sniffed the cowering individual a few seconds and accepted it. The three then moved back around the point a few yards to the rest of the pack. When the lone wolf saw the pack, it ran about 25 yards, lay down, and remained there. A third case of differential behavior toward this individual occurred on March 4, 1959. Ten of the wolves started traveling, while the other five (including the three lighter-colored, lankier animals) rested. The lone wolf joined these five. When they left, it accompanied them and was completely indistinguishable from them; no trouble ensued. A similar situation occurred on March 8. Six wolves, including the lanky individuals, were several miles behind the rest of the pack. The lone wolf joined these and accompanied them, without any apparent fear, to the rest of the animals. When they approached the main pack, the usual sniffing, tail wagging, and other greeting behavior took place; but the lone wolf quickly ran off and remained away from the others.

The reasons for the differential reactions to the lowest-ranking individual are unknown. Possibly, each of the members which accepted it also held low social status. Indeed, there were reasons to conjecture that the three lanky individuals were pups.

Although the lone wolf was suppressed by the large pack, it joined the group in pursuit of a strange wolf. All 16 animals chased the alien for half a mile. According to Schenkel (1948), this type of behavior is not unusual. He observed that despite the sometimes-violent relationships within a pack, the members present a united front toward aliens and become a unit during friendly activity such as chorus howling.

HOWLING

The full significance of wolf howling is unknown. Murie (1944) described situations in which several animals howled before leaving the den area to hunt. From his descriptions, it appears that the howling was merely a manifestation of the wolves' restlessness. This seemed to be the case also during an observation of Isle Royale wolves. On February 9, 1961, four wolves lay on the ice at the head of Washington Harbor from 8:45 to 9:15 a.m., after which they headed into the woods. At 10 a.m. a wolf howled twice from the woods near the shore, and a few minutes later an animal appeared on the ice and howled three more times. Each time, the wolf's muzzle pointed skyward; the howls were low-pitched and drawn out. Five minutes later,

four more wolves appeared, one at a time. They walked about 150 yards onto the ice and lay down.

About 2 p.m. one animal arose, stretched, lay back down, and howled a few times, arousing the nearest wolf. Then it approached this individual, with tail straight up and tip cocked forward, and sniffed its nose. The second animal rolled over and extended its paws toward the first. Meanwhile, the other three wolves arose, and all five walked about 200 yards westward and disappeared up a creek bed. A few minutes later, a single wolf emerged from the woods, sniffed the tracks of the others, cowered, and howled for a few minutes. Then it wandered eastward along the shore for about 50 yards and entered the woods.

Crisler (1958:151) believes that howling is an emotional outlet for wolves. She writes:

Like a community sing, a howl is not mere noise, it is a happy social occasion. Wolves love a howl. When it is started, they instantly seek contact with one another, troop together, fur to fur. Some wolves . . . love a sing more than others do and will run from any distance, panting and bright-eyed, to join in, uttering, as they near, fervent little wows, jaws wide, hardly able to wait to sing.

Seton (1937) and Young and Goldman (1944) believe that wolves vocalize when chasing prey. This supposition seems logical, for vocal expression might help keep members of the pack together as they chase their quarry. However, the only evidence I have found in the literature to support this contention was an observation in 1875 reported to Seton (p. 281) by a logger. During the present study, all hunting was observed from an aircraft, so only indirect information was obtained on the subject.

Two observations indicated that wolves did not vocalize while chasing moose. In one instance, the large pack chased and wounded a moose, while a second animal lay about 100 yards away. The latter moose eventually wandered away but did not seem cognizant of the 16 wolves nearby, as it probably would have if the wolves had been "tonguing." In the second situation, the large pack chased a moose, and a few of the animals caught up with it and held it at bay. Meanwhile, the others were wandering around searching for the moose. They finally found it by following the trail left by those which had cornered it. I believe that if any vocal communication had occurred, these animals would have run directly to the cornered moose.

One function of howling may be to aid in assembling. After long chases, the 15 wolves sometimes were scattered over a large area. On one such occasion, we noticed that a wolf ascended the nearest ridge and appeared to howl. Several others approached the first, and about 150 yards away another animal appeared to howl. Eventually, most of the pack assembled on the ridge. Murie (1944:102) described a similar episode.

On February 4, 1960, when we landed the aircraft within 100 yards of the 16 wolves on Intermediate Lake, the animals eventually scattered into the woods. A few minutes later we heard some howling, which soon increased in volume until the entire pack seemed to be involved. The whining, yelping, and howling (much of which was high-pitched) continued for about 30 seconds and then gradually diminished; a few single howls were emitted after the chorus had subsided. Tracks later showed that the wolves had assembled on a small knoll, where most of the howling probably originated.

Another time the pilot and I frightened the large pack from a freshly killed moose. As the wolves retreated, several barked hoarsely. We remained at the carcass for about 2½ hours, and heard distant howling and barking intermittently throughout the period.

In the last instances some or all of the howling could have resulted from frustration or emotion. This undoubtedly was the case on an occasion in August 1960. From 9 to 11 p.m., I sat 20 feet up in a tree above a freshly killed moose. At 9:30 p.m. at least four wolves began howling about 200 yards away. Howling continued off and on for the next half an hour, but it gradually became more distant. A check the next morning showed that the wolves had not returned to the carcass.

Howling was heard several times near the Daisy Farm campsite (across Rock Harbor from my cabin) in the summer of 1960. The earliest time of day that I heard it was 5:40

p.m., and the latest, 12:30 a.m. It consisted of the usual medley of yips, barks, deep "mournful" howls, and extended calls of ever-changing pitch. Sometimes it occurred for only a few seconds, but once it lasted about 2 minutes. On one occasion when 22 campers were present at the campsite, several wolves howled directly behind the area. The animals sounded to me to be about 100 yards behind the lean-tos, although the campers thought they were closer. The reasons for all the howling in this area are unknown, but perhaps the sound of humans stimulated the wolves. Young and Goldman (1944) wrote that whistles and other human disturbances often stimulate wolves to howl.

Pimlott (1960) found that human

Figure 58—Pilot Don Murray and author examining a fresh kill.

"wolf" howling and recordings of wolf howling would cause wild wolves to perform. After extensive testing of this method he concluded (p. 7):

It appears that the stimulus of wolves to howl is, at least in part, directly proportional to the length of time since they last howled. It is frequently difficult to evoke a response within 15 to 20 minutes, or even longer, after they last howled.

Phonograph records of wolf howling were tried during the present study, and replies were obtained four times. The records were also played after "natural" howls, to determine whether the wolves would vocalize again within a few minutes of their first howl. Although only a few trials were made, results supported Pimlott's conclusion.

MISCELLANEOUS BEHAVIOR

Activity resembling play was noticed on March 6, 1960. The 16 wolves had just left a kill and were traveling along the shore toward Cumberland Point. Several animals chased one another back and forth and in circles, but sometimes a group would chase one individual and then suddenly turn on another. It appeared that the pursued animal carried something, possibly a bone, and that as it dropped the object, another would pick it up and attempt to outrun the rest. The pack cut across Cumberland Point, and in the woods the activity reached its maximum. The entire pack became involved, some in ambushing, others in chasing, until eventually the animals tired. Several other times, I have noticed tracks indicating that the wolves had engaged in similar "sport."

Over-cautious behavior on the part of a single wolf was observed on February 28, 1961. At 6:05 p.m., seven wolves started northward across Hay Bay from Hay Point. Most of the ice was bare, and the wolves were reluctant to walk on it, probably because snow-free ice usually is new and thin. They tried to keep on the chunks of old, snow-covered ice, which were frozen together by new, bare ice. When there were no more snow-covered chunks, the wolves walked on the opaque cracks across the bare ice. However, one wolf would not follow the pack onto the snow-free ice, although it was tempted. Instead, it headed westward into Hay Bay on snow-covered chunks, being careful not to walk on bare ice. When the animal reached the end of these chunks and faced bare ice, it returned the 250 yards to where the pack had crossed. Again the wolf started following the tracks, but once they left snow-covered ice, it would not continue. This time the animal ran about 150 yards southwestward, back into the bay where the snow-covered ice was continuous. It crossed this without hesitation. Meanwhile, the pack had reached shore and was about a mile away. The cautious wolf hurried to them, catching up at 6:35 p.m.

Reproduction

According to Schenkel (1948), pairing begins in early winter, and bonds strengthen as winter progresses. Winter rivalries within the pack occur only among members of the same sex, eventually resulting in an established social order. "In general, the usual conflicts of opinion remain somewhere in the middle between the two possible extremes (status demonstration—battle)" (Schenkel, 1948: 88). However, apparently at times intense battles occur, for Crisler (1958:251) reported an instance in which one female killed another during a fight over a male. Regardless of the form rivalry takes, by mating season pairs are well established.

Young and Goldman (1944) reported that males mature in 3 years and females in 2. These authors (p. 84) provide the following account of wolf reproduction:

Wolves do not breed until between 2 and 3 years of age. They couple much as dogs do but can more readily separate. In captivity oestrum has been noted to continue from three to five days; the female has stood for the male over a period of five days, and then rejected further advances; not until the vulva became noticeably swollen would the female stand. The period of discharge of blood from its start in late December until the swelling of the vulva and the final copulation for five females averaged 45 days.

This places the actual breeding season at mid-February. A captive wolf, which Murie (1944) raised as a pup, first came into heat in early March of her second year, and remained in that condition about 2 weeks. Murie also reported on another captive female, which failed to come into estrus the first year but bred with a dog the second year. "The first 2 weeks that this wolf was in heat she fought off the dog but mated each day during the third week (March 9 to March 15). The male continued to pursue her on the following 3 days but there was no further mating after the fifteenth" (Murie, 1944:17). Four pups were born to this female on May 15, which establishes the gestation period at 60 to 66 days. Pups born in the Philadelphia zoo had a gestation period of 9 weeks (Brown, 1936). According to Bailey (1926) wolves in North Dakota bore young in March, so they must have mated in January.

Murie (1944) reported that Mount McKinley wolves probably breed in early March, since young are born in early May. Fuller and Novakowski (1955), by examining female reproductive tracts, found that estrus probably occurred between March 5 and 21 in northern Alberta. Cowan (1947) believes that British Columbia wolves mate in March and early April.

I first observed mating activity among the Isle Royale wolves on February 21, 1959. This was the first day that the alpha pair was noticed. The male tried unsuccessfully to mount the female several times. One successful copulation was observed but probably not between these two wolves. When the animals coupled, the entire pack (strung out 100 yards ahead) raced back to the pair. After a few seconds of milling around, the pack left the two lying rump to rump. As we flew near the coupled wolves, they stood and snapped at each other but then lay down again. After 15 minutes they parted and hurried to the rest of the pack.

For the next half hour there were several attempted copulations between members of at least three pairs, but in each instance the female thwarted the male by sitting, tail between her legs. Each time mounting occurred, the nearby wolves rushed to the pair, in an apparent free-for-all. Schenkel (1948:93) presents a detailed description of precopulatory behavior in the wolf. I did not ob-

Figure 59—Local snowstorms made flying treacherous.

serve such behavior, but at the time, I was neither aware that it might occur nor close enough to notice it.

On February 24, much mating activity was evident, but only one successful copulation was observed, the animals being coupled back-to-back for at least 6 minutes. The last copulation witnessed in 1959 occurred on February 27, and lasted at least 8 minutes.

In 1960, complete coitus was observed only once, the wolves remaining coupled for at least 5 minutes. The activity of the rest of the pack indicated the presence of at least two other females. Chasing, fighting, and sniffing were noted on February 7, 14, 19, and 20; and on the 22nd, unsuccessful attempts at copu-

lation were seen in one pair. No observations were made on behavior from February 23 to 29, but after the 29th no sign of mating activity was seen.

The only breeding behavior observed in 1961 occurred on February 6. During that day, much chasing and fighting (most evident during the mating season) took place. Flying conditions that year did not allow as much observation as in previous years. Nevertheless, the pack was observed for several hours a day on many days. Probably fear of the aircraft in 1961 caused the wolves to confine their breeding activity to periods when they were undisturbed (see p. 36).

No additional reproductive information was obtained on the Isle Royale wolves. Whether pups were born and raised is unknown. According to data presented by Stenlund

(1955) and Fuller and Novakowski (1955), weight and size are not valid criteria for distinguishing adults from pups in winter. However, since sizes of the Isle Royale wolf packs have remained exactly the same for three winters, I believe that no pups have been added; it would be quite coincidental if exactly the same number of wolves died each year as were raised. As has been discussed, during the first winter, three lighter-colored, lanky individuals were observed in the pack of 15; these rested and played more frequently than the others and possibly were pups. They were not distinguishable in 1960 or 1961.

No active wolf dens were found, although much time was devoted to den hunting. However, on May 21, 1959, a freshly dug den was discovered on an open, south-facing slope about 350 yards north of Siskiwit

Lake, opposite the western tip of Ryan Island. No fresh wolf sign was present, but the size of the entrance and tunnels indicated that probably wolves had dug the den. The entrance measured 28 by 17 inches, and the tunnels were 12 inches in diameter. The mound was 5 feet wide by 10 feet long. These measurements correspond well to those of wolf dens studied by Murie (1944), Cowan (1947), and Banfield (1954). In 1960, this den was partly caved in, but in 1961 it sheltered six fox pups (figure 60).

In 1960, Pimlott's (1960) method of locating wolf dens was tried. Recordings of wolf howling were amplified from 34 locations at various times between 7:55 and 10:15 p.m. (May 17 to August 5), and four re-

Figure 60—Fox pups at a den that once may have been a wolf den.

TABLE 10.—ANALYSIS OF FOOD REMAINS IN 438 WOLF SCATS COLLECTED FROM TRAILS

Food items	1958 Fresh[a]	1958 Old[b]	1958 Total	1959 Fresh[c]	1959 Old	1959 Total	1960 Fresh[a]	1960 Old	1960 Total	Total Fresh	Total Old	Grand total
Number of scats	27	43	70	104	110	214	74	77	154	205	230	438
Number of occurrences	36	54	90	131	124	255	86	85	171	253	263	516
Percent of occurrence												
Moose, unidentified	3		1	12	25	18	9	9	9	9.5	14.8	12.2
Moose, calf	39	48	44	43	2	23	60	14	38	48.2	15.5	31.5
Moose, adult	17	20	19	16	48	32	14	65	39	15.8	47.9	32.1
Moose, total	59	68	64	71	75	73	84	88	86	73.5	78.3	75.9
Beaver	17	17	17	12	10	12	7	7	7	11.1	10.6	10.8
Grass	8	4	6	9	6	8	3	2	3	7.1	4.2	5.8
Snowshoe hare	5	6	6	2	3	3	5		2	3.5	2.6	3.1
Soil	8	6	3	3	tr.	2	1		tr.	3.2	tr.	1.7
Unidentified mammal				2	tr.	1		2	1	.7	1.1	.8
Unidentified	3		1	1	tr.	tr.				.7	tr.	.6
Bird			2		tr.	tr.					1.1	.6
Red fox					tr.	tr.					tr.	tr.
Red squirrel		2	1								tr.	tr.
Deer mouse					tr.	tr.					tr.	tr.

[a] May through August.
[b] Unknown age.
[c] May through August, plus 3 scats from October.

plies were obtained. Three of these originated from the same location on the same evening (although broadcast sites were different), so only in two locations was contact established with wolves. Both areas were searched, but no sign was found. Since in each case no additional replies were obtained on the night following the first contact, it is probable that the replies came from traveling animals.

Food Habits

The timber wolf is a big-game predator. Smaller animals including birds, rodents, and lagomorphs are eaten, but I know of no wolf population which has thrived on small animals alone. Only one record was found which indicated that the majority of wolf scats from an area contained anything other than big game. Tener (1954) reported that on Ellesmere Island 83 percent of 85 wolf scats contained arctic hare (*Lepus arcticus*) remains, whereas 17 percent contained muskoxen (*Ovibos moschatus*).

Murie (1944) found remains of caribou (*Rangifer arcticus*), Dall sheep (*Ovis dalli*), or moose in 935 of 1,174 wolf scats collected in Mount McKinley National Park; and big-game remains composed approximately 70 percent of the 1,350 food items. In eight wolf stomachs and eight scats from Michigan, deer and hare remains were represented equally (Stebler, 1944). Cowan (1947) reported that 80 percent of 420 wolf scats from the Rocky Mountain national parks of Canada contained remains of elk (*Cervus canadensis*), bighorn (*Ovis canadensis*), mountain goat (*Oreamnos americanus*), moose, caribou, or mule deer (*Odocoileus hemionus*). Whitetailed deer remains occurred in 97 percent of 435 scats from Wisconsin (Thompson, 1952), and in 80 percent of 51 wolf stomachs collected in winter from Minnesota (Stenlund, 1955). Fuller and Novakowski (1955) found remains of bison (*Bison bison*) in 32 of 49 wolf stomachs from northern Alberta. Caribou remains composed 58 percent of the items in 62 scats from the Northwest Territories (Banfield, 1954).

On Isle Royale the moose population represents the only potential food supply which could support the present wolf population; beavers (except in winter) and snowshoe hares are available supplements. Of 87 scats collected in May 1952, 56 percent contained moose remains; 24 percent, snowshoe hare; and 20 percent, beaver (Cole, 1952a). In 1954, Cole reported that "sixty-five percent of the scats contained moose hair and 35 percent beaver hair," but the number of scats examined was not given.

A total of 438 wolf scats were analyzed during the present study (table 10). These were collected from 100 miles of foot trails in spring and summer from 1958 to 1960. Since at the time, it was not known whether coyotes were still present, only scats over 1 inch in diameter were considered wolf scats, in accordance with information presented by Thompson (1952). Whenever possible, scats were aged to the nearest month, and those of unknown age were designated "old."

Although grass or sedge made up about 6 percent of the items, these are not considered food. They often are found in canid scats and even have been reported from mountain lion (*Felis concolor*) scats (Robinette *et al.*, 1959). Some vegetation may be eaten inadvertently with the prey. Isle Royale wolves eat bloody snow while waiting for a wounded moose

Figure 61—All that remains of a 2½-month-old calf, killed by wolves.

to weaken; perhaps in summer they eat blood-spattered grass or even bloody soil. Murie (1944) found that some of the wolf scats containing grass also held several roundworms, and suggested that grass may act as a scour.

Moose remains composed 76 percent of the total (516) items. In scats from May through August, they constituted 74 percent of the occurrences, and in "old" scats they formed 78 percent. (Old scats probably were from autumn and winter primarily.) Beaver remains composed approximately 11 percent of the total items, so beavers appear to be the only other important food.

FREQUENCY OF PREDATION

One of the most important figures obtained during this study is the rate of moose kill by the pack of 15 wolves (table 11). (All animals fed upon by wolves are considered "kills," as is discussed on p. 115.) I believe that every kill made by this pack from February 5 to March 4, 1959, and from February 5 to March 20, 1960, was located. In 1961 most of the kills were found, but the wolves' activities were unknown on 11 of the 48 days between February 2 and March

20. During the periods in which the rate of kill was known in 1961, it averaged the same as in 1959 and 1960—one moose per 3 days. However, the wolves once killed two moose in 2 days, and the longest period we found between kills was at least 118 hours, and may have been as much as 137 hours, between March 7 and 12, 1960. The chronological distribution of kills is shown in table 11.

Apparently, the pack of 15 makes fewer kills than do wolves in other areas. Field men in the Rocky Mountain national parks of Canada deter-

TABLE 11.—CHRONOLOGICAL DISTRIBUTION, AND RATE, OF MOOSE
KILL BY THE PACK OF 15

[Underlined dates indicate known dates of kill; others may vary by a day]

1959		1960		1961	
Date	Age and sex	Date	Age and sex	Date	Age and sex
Feb. 5	cow	Feb. 5	calf	Feb. 2	cow
Feb. 8	calf	Feb. 7	calf	Feb. 4	bull
Feb. 11	calf	Feb. 9	calf	Feb. 7–8	calf
Feb. 14	adult	Feb. 12	cow	(Feb. 9–16 unknown)	
Feb. 17	calf	Feb. 16	cow	Feb. 17	bull
Feb. 18	cow	Feb. 20 a	bull	Feb. 18	calf c
Feb. 21	adult	Feb. 22 a	bull	Feb. 23	cow
Feb. 24	cow	Feb. 27	calf	Feb. 25	calf
Mar. 1–4	bull	Mar. 1	calf	Feb. 27	adult
		Mar. 5	calf	Mar. 1–5	fed on old kills d
		Mar. 7	calf	(Mar. 6–11 unknown)	
		Mar 12 a	cow	Mar. 12	adult
		Mar. 15 b	calf	Mar. 14	calf
		Mar. 17	calf	Mar. 16	adult
		Mar. 18–20	calf c	Mar. 18–20	bull
Summation					
28 days: 9 moose		45 days: 15 moose		37 days: 12 moose	

a May have been found dead.   c Human activity interfered with previous kill.
b Found dead, but see p. 137.   d A calf may have been killed during this period.

mined the rate of kill of two packs of five or six wolves (Cowan, 1947). Each pack killed three elk per 2 weeks, "with indications that two small elk might be taken in a week." Conversion of these figures on a basis of pack size for comparison with those from Isle Royale gives a rate of one kill per 1.6 days. Stenlund (1955) estimated that a pack of 3 wolves in Minnesota would kill about one deer per 4 days, so 15 wolves probably would make one kill per .8 day. Through aerial observations of a pack of 10 Alaskan wolves, Burkholder (1959) found 21 kills (14 caribou and 8 moose calves) made in 35 days, an adjusted rate of one kill per 1.2 days. Some of the differences among these figures can be accounted for on the basis of prey size, as will be apparent in the next section. Undoubtedly, variation in availability of prey and in the methods used to derive these figures also contributes to the differences.

Since Isle Royale's smaller wolf packs never were studied closely for several weeks in a row, little is known about their rate of kill. Probably, both small groups (totaling five) did not together kill over a third the number of moose killed by the large pack. During the 1961 study period (48 days), when I became more proficient in locating kills made by the smaller packs, five of these were found. This is a third of the large pack's expected total (16), although all kills of the small packs may not have been found. These groups probably have more difficulty killing

moose than the 15 wolves do, but each carcass should last them longer. Members of the small packs frequently wander far from their kills, so they may hunt new prospects while still able to resort to a previous kill for food. By the time one carcass is eaten, they may have another. In addition, each pack might feed on the other's kill. These speculations are based on limited evidence, but they might indicate direction for future research.

The lone wolf probably kills few moose in winter; it usually feeds on remains left by other wolves. Only once was evidence found that this animal made its own kill. The moose had been wounded and abandoned by the large pack a few days earlier. After finishing it off on March 12, 1961, the lone wolf fed without competition (except from foxes and ravens) at least until March 20.

FOOD CONSUMPTION

No kill was weighed, so all consumption figures are based on moose weights given in the literature. According to information from Kellum (1941), Skuncke (vide Peterson, 1955:77), and Simkin (1962), fully adult cows average about 800 pounds, and bulls, 1,000 pounds (see page 93). Possibly these figures are a bit high for animals killed in winter, but since the amount of possible weight decrease occurring over winter is unknown, these figures will be used. Nine-month-old calves apparently weigh about 300 pounds (modified from Peterson). For ease in assessing kill figures from both the present study and from the literature, I have adapted an arbitrary unit to allow for the varying weights of big game. One "prey unit" is considered to be 100 pounds. Following are the assumed prey units for various ages and species of big game: moose calf, 3; cow, 8; bull, 10; deer, 1; elk, 6; caribou, 3. Adult moose of unknown sex are assumed to be cows, since the sex ratio of kills favored cows strongly.

When the Isle Royale rates of kill are examined in terms of prey units, they do not appear so uniform. The pack of 15 consumed 2.11 p.u. per day in 1959, 1.64 per day in 1960, and 2.21 per day in 1961. Comparable figures calculated from the literature are: Cowan (1947), 3.85 p.u. per day; Stenlund (1955), 1.25; and Burkholder (1959), 2.80. Since Stenlund's figure is an estimate, probably it is not as valid as those from Cowan and Burkholder, which are known rates of kill, or at least minimum rates closely approaching actuality.

Figures of average consumption per wolf-day should include consideration of the weight of uneaten remains. Since remains were not weighed, a standard estimate must suffice. I believe that unconsumed bones, skin, and hair averaged about 50 pounds per adult moose, and 15 pounds per calf. On this basis, the pack of 15 devoured approximately 5,555 pounds of moose in 28 days during 1959, or 13.2 pounds per wolf-day. In 1960, the 16 wolves consumed about 7,000 pounds in 45 days, or 9.7 pounds per wolf per day. The 1961 consumption by 15 wolves was approximately 7,740 pounds in 37 days, or 13.9 pounds per wolf-day.

No average-daily-consumption figures for wolves were found in the literature. However, Wright (1960) reported that African lions (*Panthera leo*) consumed an estimated .11 to .13 pounds per pound of lion per day, and wild dogs (*Lycaon pictus lupinus*) ate .15 pounds per pound of dog per day. On the assumption that the Isle Royale wolf pack contains 5 females at 61 pounds, and 10 males at 78 pounds (weights from Stenlund, 1955), the average wolf weighs 72 pounds. Therefore, the average daily consumption rates per pound of wolf per day would be: (1959) .18; (1960) .13; and (1961) .19. These figures compare favorably with Wright's.

Although average rates are useful figures, they also are misleading, for a wolf's feeding schedule is quite erratic. When food is available, wolves gorge; then they may go several days without eating. Young and Goldman (1944:120) explain it as follows:

Of all the members of the canine family, the wolf, when in its prime, can be most irregular in its feeding habits. Equipped with abundant power to kill, the preference is for large prey in order to sustain its large body. When large prey is not available, long intervals between meals may be endured rather than spend time and energy in quest of small animals. Then when opportunity again occurs the animals fill themselves to repletion.

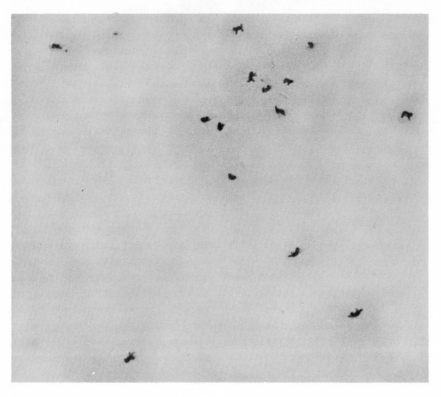

Figure 62—Resting attitudes of engorged wolves.

As would be expected, the capacity of a wolf's stomach is extremely large. Several times, the pack of 15 devoured a calf within 24 hours, a rate of about 20 pounds per individual per day. On one occasion these animals consumed approximately half a cow in less than 2 hours. They killed the moose at 2:40 p.m. on February 12, 1960, and immediately began to feed. By 4:10 p.m. only three wolves were feeding, and the carcass appeared at least half eaten. The cow was mature, but possibly it was smaller than average.

Even if it weighed only 600 pounds, the 15 wolves ate about 20 pounds apiece in 1½ hours.

Other authors have recorded similar feats. Young and Goldman (1944) reported a wolf stomach weighing 18 pounds and another weighing 19 pounds, 3 ounces. According to Cowan (1947), four wolves devoured most of a doe mule deer in 4 hours; and in 5 days, three wolves consumed two mule deer and a calf elk. Cole (1957) found two instances in which a pack of seven or eight Isle Royale wolves ate about three-quarters of an adult moose in 2 days, a consumption rate of about 35 pounds per wolf-day.

Besides being able to consume great amounts of food in short periods, a wolf also can fast several days with no evident hardship. In 1960, the pack of 15 went at least 95 hours (March 8, 3 p.m. to March 12, 2:30 p.m.) apparently without eating anything except possibly hair and bones which they might have gleaned from old kills. In 1961, half of the large pack spent from March 1 to March 5 without any food except a beaver and scraps from old kills. (Possibly the wolves fed on material cached at old kills, but I think this is unlikely. Before leaving a kill, they clean it so completely that there probably is no extra food to cache.) Young and Goldman (1944) reported on a captive wild wolf which fasted a week and then gorged on the eighth day. E. H. McCleery of Kane, Pa., who has raised wolves—as many as 34 at a time—for many years, wrote me that in winter and spring he feeds his animals every 5 days, and in summer, every 5 to 10 days.

FEEDING ROUTINE

Wolves feed for the first few hours after making a kill. Apparently, a cow moose is not quite large enough for the entire 15 animals to feed on at once, for at the one cow we saw killed, two wolves had to wait off at one side; the others, packed solidly around the carcass, were tugging voraciously at it. After gorging on a fresh kill, the wolves usually curl up nearby and sleep. Each probably feeds at least twice during the first half day, for seldom during this period are there no individuals feeding. About mid-morning the whole pack often heads for an open ridge or stretch of ice, sometimes over a mile away, where each animal sprawls in the sun for several hours (figure 62). A few wander back to the kill now and then if it is not far. Around midafternoon the pack returns to feed. On the second day, if the carcass is large, the pack frequently travels leisurely for a few miles to a resting spot. By then little is left of the kill except the intact skeleton. When the wolves return again, they dismember the skeleton and spend hours gnawing bones. Usually 2, and sometimes 3, days are spent at the carcass of an adult, and one or 2 at a calf carcass. Although there is much variability in the above-described routine, it seems to be the basic pattern.

Two calves were examined on the ground soon after being killed, and information was obtained on the parts eaten first. On February 5, 1960, one of a set of twins was killed at 4:40 p.m. By 5:10 p.m. the neck and left side of the chest had been skinned; the heart, part of the lungs, the rump, and the nose were eaten, and there was a hole in the side of the abdomen (figure 63). The second kill, made at 11:45 a.m., March 17, 1960, was investigated within 45 minutes. Most of the meat was missing from one side of the head and throat, and from the upper hind leg and pelvic region; part of one shoulder was eaten. One side of the

Figure 63—Remains of 9-month-old calf 45 minutes after being killed by the large pack.

Figure 64—Remains of the calf in Fig. 63, 24 hours later.

abdomen was wide open, with intestines pulled out and partly eaten, and the liver was gone. Whether these parts are preferred or whether they merely represent the points of attack is unknown.

There is some indication that the pelvic and abdominal regions and the nose are preferred. An adult killed about 7:30 a.m. on August 26, 1960, was examined a few hours later. The wolves had been frightened from the carcass about 8 a.m., and the only meat missing was about 15 pounds from around the pelvis. Undoubtedly, most of the wolves were reluctant to return, for 2 days later just the nose and left side of the abdomen had been eaten. A bull wounded by the large pack and killed by a lone wolf about 6:30 p.m., March 12, 1961, was checked the next day at 11 a.m. The meat and a few pieces of intestine in the pelvic region were all that had been eaten.

Before the wolves abandon a carcass, all the viscera and flesh and about half the skin and hair are consumed. Sometimes the skin is left on the lower legs, but if the carcass is revisited, this is eaten also. Calves killed in winter usually are dismembered completely; all that remain are a chunk of hide, the disarticulated long bones, the mandible and upper tooth rows, and a great patch of hair (figure 64). In summer, the skin and most of the bones of calves apparently are devoured. Cow remains include the skull and anterior half of the backbone in one piece, and the pelvis and posterior

part of the backbone in another. The legs are detached from the skeleton, but most of the bones of each remain together. The ends of the ribs and long bones, and the edges of the scapulae and mandibles are ragged from being chewed (figure 65). Usually, bull skeletons are less pulled apart but are thoroughly cleaned of meat. The completeness with which carcasses are consumed may attest that wolves have difficulty obtaining prey.

Burkholder (1959:9) found the following usage pattern of caribou and calf moose carcasses:

The first parts of the animal eaten are the viscera, except for the stomach contents. The soft parts of the neck and ribs appear to be preferred over the more massive tissue structure. In many cases the entire animal is consumed, including hoofs, long bones, and skull, with only hair and stomach contents remaining.

Parasites and Diseases

Wolves are susceptible to several diseases and physical disorders, and are hosts to many helminth parasites; mange also infests them. Stenlund (1955) has reviewed the literature on the subject. Since his work, Rausch (1958) reported on 43 rabid canids from Alaska, including two wolves. Rausch and Williamson (1959) examined 200 wolf carcasses and listed the helminths found therein.

No wolf carcass was handled during the present study, so little information on parasites and diseases was

Figure 65—Cow moose remains gathered just after the large pack abandoned them.

obtained. However, intermediate stages of two species of helminths, for which the wolf is the definitive host, were found in Isle Royale moose. *Taenia hydatigena* occurred in two of four adults examined, and *Echinococcus granulosus* was found in three of them. Adults of both worms have been reported from wolves in several areas (table 12).

An adult *Taenia* sp. was found by D. L. Allen soon after it had been passed by an animal (presumably a wolf, from the sign). This could have been *T. hydatigena,* or even *T. krabbei,* the larvae of which encyst in the muscles of big game. Moose were not examined for this parasite, so it is not known whether the species occurs on Isle Royale. Rausch and Williamson (1959) found the adults

in 48 of 78 wolves from Alaska, and Erickson (1944) and Stenlund (1955) reported *Taenia* sp., which may have been this species, from Minnesota wolves. Peterson (1955) reported that cysticerci occurred in muscles of an Ontario moose.

The effect of these parasites on the wolf is unknown. Erickson (1944) noted that some wolves harbored so many *Taenia hydatigena* that their intestines appeared blocked. Adults of *Echinococcus granulosus* are only 2 to 8 mm. long (Chandler, 1955), but according to Rausch (1952:159) heavy infections of *Echinococcus granulosus* in the final hosts are usual; "in some cases the cestodes cover nearly the entire mucosal surface of the host intestine." According to Monnig (1938:103), "varying degrees of enteritis may be present [in dogs and cats] from a catarrh to a croupous or haemorrhagic enteritis, especially in heavy infections. . . ."

Choquette (1956) experimentally infected dogs with *Echinococcus granulosus* cysts (as many as seven cysts, from 3 to 10 cm. in diameter, to an individual). He writes (p. 191) that "while it is agreed that dogs can harbor a great number of adult worms without apparent ill effects there are reports of pathogenicity." Haemorrhagic enteritis and rabiform symptoms, diarrhea, asthenia, cachexia, catarrhal inflammation, and death in heavily infected individuals, are listed as effects in dogs. Three of the eight dogs infected by Choquette showed severe diarrhea, weight loss, and asthenia. "Death occurred within a few days of the appearance of symptoms and a month after initial infection. Post-mortem examination showed a severe haemorrhagic enteritis and a very large number of immature worms" (Choquette, 1956:192).

Wolves probably have a greater resistance to these worms than do domestic animals, since the former certainly have evolved with the parasites. Although eight of Choquette's nine experimental dogs became infected, only five passed eggs and segments in their feces, so even all dogs are not equally susceptible. Apparently, the adults of *Echinococcus* are short-lived. One of Choquette's dogs passed eggs for 8 months and then stopped. Autopsy showed it was worm-free. A second dog, still

TABLE 12.—REPORTED INFECTIONS OF WOLVES BY "ECHINOCOCCUS GRANULOSUS" AND "TAENIA HYDATIGENA"

Species	Location	Number examined	Number infected	Percent infected	Source
Echinococcus granulosus:	Minnesota.......	8	5	63	Riley (1939)
	Minnesota.......	18	5	28	Erickson (1944)
	British Columbia.	5	1	20	Cowan (1947)
	N. Ontario......	58	36	62	Sweatman (1952)
	Minnesota......	18	4	22	Stenlund (1955)
	Alaska..........	200	60	30	Rausch & Williamson (1959)
	Ontario.........	520	103	20	Freeman et al. (1961)
Taenia hydatigena:	Minnesota.......	18	8	44	Erickson (1944)
	British Columbia.	5	4	80	Cowan (1947)
	Minnesota.......	18	15	83	Stenlund (1955)
	N. Ontario......	10	10	100	Sweatman & Plummer (1957)
	Alaska..........	78	56	72	Rausch & Williamson (1959)
	Ontario.........	520	39	8	Freeman et al. (1961)

Figure 66—Author checking femur marrow of wolf-killed moose.

Figure 67—Comparison of normal femur marrow (left) with fat-depleted marrow.

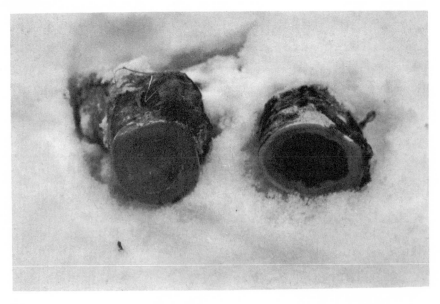

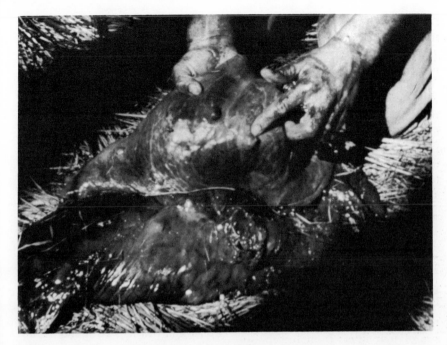

Figure 68—Lung with hydatid cysts from wolf-killed moose.   Photo by D. L. Allen.

Figure 69—Hydatid cysts from wolf-killed moose.   Photo by D. L. Allen.

eliminating eggs, was autopsied 6 months after infection, and senile worms were found. Thus, infections probably do not accumulate for more than 8 months, but in this period, a wolf could become reinfected several times. Wolves probably can support high cestode populations without significant effects, although young, ailing, or old individuals may be affected adversely.

Possible Causes of Population Stability

According to Young and Goldman (1944), the average wolf litter contains seven pups. In Minnesota, Stenlund (1955) found that 8 litters averaged 6.4 young. The mean size of four litters from British Columbia was five (Cowan, 1947). This information alone might lead one to suppose that wolves are prolific and that wolf populations have a high rate of turnover. However, facts do not agree with this supposition.

Cowan found that in the Rocky Mountain national parks in Canada, three packs which had been checked carefully showed no significant increase during two breeding seasons. In northern Alberta, Fuller and Novakowski (1955) poisoned 3 entire packs and found an age ratio of 3 pups to 10 adults. On Isle Royale, two wolf packs have each remained the same size for three winters; indeed, the pack of three apparently has failed to increase since at least early 1957, when Cole reported on

it. The apparent inconsistency between these data and the fact that wolf litters are large probably results from one or more of the following factors: unproductive animals, prenatal losses, mortality factors, and emigration and immigration.

UNPRODUCTIVE ANIMALS

There appear to be at least four categories of unproductive members of wolf packs: (1) surplus males, (2) immature animals, (3) senile individuals, and (4) social subordinates. Murie (1944) found three males and two females, all at least 2 years old, at one den in Mount McKinley National Park; two more adult males joined this pack in late summer. Fuller and Novakowski found one to three extra adults in five out of six packs which they poisoned.

Young and Goldman (1944) quoted a report that the sex ratio was equal in a catch of 68 wolves from New Mexico, and Fuller and Novakowski found an even sex ratio in 58 poisoned wolves in Wood Buffalo National Park, Canada. However, males comprised 15 of 25 wolves shot in British Columbia (Cowan, 1947), and 100 of 156 animals taken in Minnesota (Stenlund, 1955).

An attempt was made to sex Isle Royale wolves on the basis of size and mating behavior. Stenlund found that, in a sample of 114 wolves, males averaged 17 pounds more than females, and Fuller and Novakowski (1955) reported an average difference of 13 pounds, although in each study, weights overlapped between the sexes. On Isle Royale, only one member of the large pack consistently appeared small, but in photographs, three and possibly four smaller animals are evident (figure 57). During all the mating activity observed, I never noticed more than three individuals being pursued amorously at one time. Perhaps other females in estrus were not noticed, or possibly some were not in estrus. Nevertheless, since three or four animals were interested in each of the three "known" females, I believe there is a substantial preponderance of males in this pack. One member of the pack of two, and one of the pack of three, also are smaller and may be females.

Since males mature in 3 years, and females in 2 (Young and Goldman, 1944), most wolf populations will contain a number of unproductive young. In an increasing population, or in one with a high turnover rate, immature animals could compose a high percentage. The only wolves on Isle Royale which were thought to have been immature were the three lanky animals in the large pack.

Wolf populations which are not hunted or trapped heavily probably include a substantial number of old animals. Young and Goldman report that old age for a wolf is 10 to 14 years. Such old wolves, according to these authors, often travel alone and subsist on old kills and carrion; presumably these would be senile. Fuller and Novakowski examined a very old male which had small tes-

ticular volume and no demonstrable spermatogenesis. There is at least one lone wolf on Isle Royale which probably is in this category, and several of the other animals also could be senile.

The most important class of unproductive animals might be the s o c i a l subordinates. Mykytowycz (1960) found that in a captive population of wild European rabbits (*Oryctolagus cuniculus*) the dominant females bred much more effectively than the subordinates. Retzlaff (*vide* Christian, 1958:477) also noticed this phenomenon in a population of laboratory mice (*Mus musculus*). One might gather from Schenkel (1948: fig. 50a) that the same applies to wolves, for he uses the phrase "suppressed, but not entirely 'frigid' females." It would seem advantageous for the alpha individuals in a society to be the most effective reproducers, for probably they are physically the best, or at least the most aggressive. Thus, the non-reproductive members of a group could help supply the food to the reproductive members and their young. Murie (1944) believed that one of the packs he studied was organized in this manner. An extra female even helped care for the young, and stayed with them one night when the mother went hunting.

Laboratory studies of mice by Davis and Christian (1957) have shown a correlation between social status and weight of the adrenal glands, the lowest-ranking individuals (i.e., the most stressed) having the heaviest glands. A similar study by Christian (1956) demonstrated that the animals with heaviest adrenals reproduced least effectively. The same principle might apply to wild wolves, although this would be difficult to prove. It might operate both within a pack, inhibiting the reproductive ability of low-ranking members, and between packs, causing reproductive inhibition in repressed packs. In discussing territoriality, Elton (1950) stated that species having few effective natural enemies tend to be self-regulatory, and Murie (1944) and Stenlund (1955) agreed that territoriality would tend to control wolf numbers. The manner in which this might operate is unknown, but perhaps the above-mentioned relationships are involved.

PRE-NATAL LOSSES

Animals from populations of high densities generally have lower reproductive rates than those in less-dense populations. Hoffman (1958) showed an inverse relationship between density and ovulation rate in *Microtus montanus*. Davis (1949) was able to increase pregnancy rates of brown rats (*Rattus norvegicus*) in Baltimore by reducing the population.

This inverse relationship between density and litter size might be caused by variations in nutrition and/or in social stress. Mason (1939) discussed the effect of nutrition on reproduction. An increase in amount

and variety of nutrients just before the breeding season causes a higher ovulation rate in sheep (Clark, 1934; Stoddard and Smith, 1943; Belschner, 1951). Cheatum and Severinghaus (1950) and Longhurst *et al.* (1952) agree that ovulation rate in deer also is affected by the level of nutrition. According to Frank (1957), the litter size of the vole (*Microtus arvalis*) depends particularly on the quantity and quality of food. Lack (1946) asserted that when avian predators dependent on mice face a food shortage, they fail to breed; when mice and lemmings are excessively common, these birds may raise two broods and have clutches twice the usual size.

Stevenson-Hamilton (1937:257) writes of a similar relationship in African lions:

It was discovered that lions . . . could barely be kept static in numbers. So easy was it for them to catch their prey, that a lioness was accustomed to produce cubs at about twice the normal rate; in place of the usual two or three, she brought forth as many as four or five in a litter; while of these, instead of one or two only, probably all, or nearly all, were able to survive to maturity.

Whereas the effect of nutrition on reproduction has been studied for many years, the role of high-density stress is just beginning to be evaluated. Most of the significant work has been done with laboratory mice. By studying populations of mice given unlimited food and water but varying in number per cage, Christian (1956) discovered that high population density suppressed reproduction in both sexes. One of the manifestations of reproductive suppression was decreased litter size. In a later experiment, Christian and Lemunyan (1958) found that all 10 of their crowded females had bred, but that 7 of these lost all their embryos through both pre- and post-implantation mortality.

Of course, it usually is extremely difficult to separate the roles of nutrition and of social stress in wild populations of high density. However, Kalela (vide Christian, 1958: 491) found that a wild population of the redback vole (Clethrionomys rufocanus) increased in density to a peak and then suddenly collapsed, despite the abundance of available food. Christian et al. (1960), studying a die-off in a herd of sika deer (Cervus nippon), ruled out malnutrition as a cause of mass mortality, and concluded that high-density stress was primarily responsible.

If high-density stress sometimes controls wild populations, conceivably this factor at least contributes to the stability of predator populations, especially in territorial species. In this connection, it may be significant that Isle Royale has one of the highest wolf densities reported (table 6).

MORTALITY FACTORS

Mortality might take one of several forms, but probably it occurs most frequently in the pup class. Cowan (1947) reported on a bitch which apparently had lost an entire litter of young. Fuller and Nova-

kowski (1955) found a ratio of 9 pups to 36 adults in autumn and concluded that this indicated a pup-mortality rate of about 90 percent within the first 6 months. This estimate apparently is based on the questionable assumption that each pair of wolves produces six young each year. Nevertheless, the ratio found by these authors does suggest a high death rate among pups.

There are several possible causes of pup mortality. Conceivably, the bitch might obtain enough food to produce a full litter, and then because of seasonal changes, possible pack break-up, or other adverse circumstances, she might not get sufficient food to nourish all her young. This might apply especially to Isle Royale wolves. Pups should be born there in the third or fourth week of April—about the time the ice goes out. Moose then can take refuge in the water so perhaps are less vulnerable at this time. New calves, which composed much of the wolves' summer diet, are not born until mid-May.

According to Speelman (1939), domestic dog pups require two or three times as much food as adults of the same weight. This should apply to wolf pups as well, so any food shortage could be crucial for them. Stevenson-Hamilton (1937) and Wright (1960) observed behavior in East African lions, which, if duplicated by wolves, would be disastrous to pups. The females and cubs feed on kills only after the males have satiated themselves, and frequently there is little left for the cubs.

Young and Goldman (1944) report that often one or two whelps are more aggressive than the others. Probably if a food shortage existed, these individuals would steal all the food, leading to the eventual death of their littermates. Lee Smits of Detroit, Mich., who has raised wolves, suggested another idea to me. He believes that, during the violent activity which occurs when wolves are fed, one pup might bite another, become excited, and end up devouring it too. In this way, only the most vigorous individuals would survive.

In a special supplement to the Kane (Pennsylvania) *Republican* paying tribute to Dr. E. H. McCleery and the population of captive wolves he has kept for 40 years, McCleery claims that "if a mother lobo has one outstanding pup she may keep that one—eat the others. Also she will eat an injured pup." Although these observations pertain to captive animals, it is possible that under stress, even a wild wolf would act this way.

Social stress during the period that young are being raised could be an important factor. A laboratory experiment with crowded mice produced the following conclusion (Christian and Lemunyan, 1958: 517):

. . . suppressed growth of progeny nurtured by crowded mothers, persisting for at least 2 generations, was due to quantitatively and/or qualitatively deficient lactation resulting from crowding. Such attenuation of the effects of crowding

may explain the long-continued decline in natural populations following peak levels and a precipitous crash in numbers.

Again, interaction of the nutrition and stress factors probably would be more important that the action of either alone.

No information is available on the incidence of pup mortality from injuries by prey, but it might be quite significant, particularly on Isle Royale. Even the large pack of adult wolves must chase many moose before killing one, and the animals obviously are afraid of a threatening moose. MacFarlane (1905) and Stanwell-Fletcher (1942) reported instances in which a wolf was found badly injured by blows from a moose. Naive and inexperienced puppies might not respect moose as adults do, and in the excitement of a chase might be especially vulnerable to the deft kicks of their intended prey. Even experienced adults might perish in this manner, although apparently this has not happened on Isle Royale during the study.

The diseases and parasites discussed previously might be important in controlling wolf numbers in certain locations. It is doubtful that these are directly signficant on Isle Royale, because no evidence of adult mortality was found. If pathogenic organisms were primarily responsible for pup mortality, they probably would cause death to a few adults, too. Indirectly, such parasites as *Taenia hydatigena* and *Echinococcus granulosus* in heavy infections might add to any general stress affecting the wolves, and, therefore, might contribute to whatever reproductive inhibitions there may be.

Old age eventually may be a significant mortality factor on Isle Royale. Seton (1937) writes of a male wolf in the National Zoological Park, which lived over 16 years. If any of the original Isle Royale immigrants remains, it would be at least 14 years old. Wolves over 10 years of age generally are considered old; they usually have worn and broken teeth and find it difficult to obtain food (Young and Goldman, 1944). Such individuals visit old carcasses more often than other wolves. At least one Isle Royale animal, the lone wolf, spent much time at old kills. Since this individual was not fully accepted by the pack, it probably was inferior in some respect, perhaps in age.

EMIGRATION AND IMMIGRATION

Because wolves did immigrate to Isle Royale, the possibility exists that other movements to or from the island have occurred since, or will occur. Significant immigration probably depends upon the following: (1) a high wolf population or a food shortage on the nearby mainland, causing "pressure" for animals to seek new territory; (2) a solid, snow-covered "ice bridge" to the island; (3) the type of reception given the newcomers by the residents; and (4) the ability of the immigrants to kill moose. Since wolves apparently did not populate Isle Royale during

Figure 70—Large pack crossing ice.

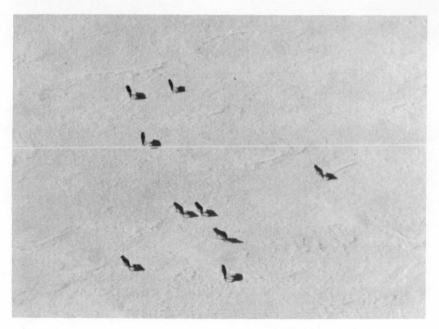

Figure 71—Mature bull moose eating aquatic plants in early June.

this century until about 1949, it seems reasonable to assume that the necessary combination of circumstances does not occur often.

Continuous ice does not connect Isle Royale with the mainland every year, so the ice-bridge factor probably is most critical in determining whether movement in either direction occurs. Cole (1957) collected several reports of years when ice connected the island with the mainland. In two of the three winters during the present study, extensive sheets of thin, drifting ice spanned the lake to Canada several times. Reports, apparently originating from pilots of high-flying aircraft, once claimed that the entire lake was frozen over.

However, after each high wind, the ice piled onto the north shore of Isle Royale, leaving the lake open. Thus, reports of ice bridges to the island should be viewed cautiously. Nevertheless, from February 15 until at least March 21, 1961, the ice withstood several severe winds, and appeared safe for even a vehicle to cross.

Besides depending on suitable ice, movements of wolves *from* Isle Royale also probably would depend on the animals having a strong reason to leave their home range, or at least a great desire to travel (perhaps only temporarily) to new territory. We did witness one apparent attempt by the large pack to leave the island. On March 1, 1960, the 16 wolves were heading northeastward in Rock Harbor at 2:25 p.m., after traveling about 29 miles from their last kill.

They reached Blake's Point, the northeast tip of the island, at 4:40 p.m., and by 4:45 were about a mile due north of the point.

The wolves continued toward Canada another half-mile, gradually curved eastward, and then headed toward Passage Island. The ice was smooth in places, but elsewhere it consisted of older chunks frozen together with new ice. The animals were cautious about crossing from one type of ice to another. Although most of the wolves appeared reluctant to proceed, the leader seemed determined. Several times this animal returned to the hestitant pack and apparently tried to urge the members on. They continued about one-half a mile until encountering ice composed of many small, sharp pieces frozen together. After testing this, the pack returned to Isle Royale (figure 53).

I do not believe the wolves were heading to Passage Island, for they could have taken a more direct route. They might have been able to reach Canada, since there had been little wind the previous week. However, they probably would not have returned, even if they had wanted to, for a few days later the wind had shifted the ice, leaving large cracks.

During the 1961 study period, when a substantial ice bridge existed, the pack certainly could have emigrated, but no sign of an attempt was observed. Nevertheless, it always is conceivable that someday one of the packs might wander off and never

return. Future investigators should attempt to watch the wolves very closely during periods when continuous ice extends to Canada.

Moose Herd

Isle Royale moose probably are intergrades of the eastern subspecies *Alces alces americana* and the northwestern subspecies *A. a. andersoni* (Peterson, 1955:6). The only available weights of wild Isle Royale moose are a few supplied by Murie (1934). However, Kellum (1941: 5) kept six Isle Royale moose and their offspring in corrals on the Michigan mainland from 1936 to 1941, weighed them each month, and obtained the following information:

New born calves weigh from 25 to 35 pounds, and gain from one to two pounds daily for the first month, and from three to five pounds daily the next month. Males weigh more than females at similar ages. A year old male may weigh from 400 to 600 pounds; at two years about 700 pounds; at three years about 900; and from then on his weight will vary with the seasons, from 900 to 1,200 pounds. . . . Females follow similar trends, weighing about 400 pounds when one year old, 600 pounds at two years, and from 600 to 800 pounds during maturity, depending on the condition of the animal and the season.

These weights may be high, for the moose were fed maximally and had little room for exercise.

Skuncke (*vide* Peterson, 1955:77) produced a growth curve for European moose (*Alces alces alces*) based on weights of 637 animals from Sweden. This shows that cows with

Figure 72—Moose feeding in Washington Harbor.

calves achieve maximum weight, about 750 pounds, when 5 years old; cows without calves average about 850. Bulls weigh about 900 pounds when 5 years old and approximately 1,050 pounds in their 11th year. This subspecies supposedly is slightly smaller than most North American subspecies.

From the data of these authors and from Simkin (1962), it seems probable that adult Isle Royale cows average about 800 pounds, and bulls, 1,000.

The food of moose varies with the season; Peterson (1955) discussed the general food habits of the species.

On Isle Royale, moose depend primarily on aspen, white birch, balsam fir, and mountain ash for winter food. Aldous and Krefting (1946), who made an extensive and detailed analysis of the island's winter moose food, listed 28 browse species. Sum-

mer food consists of leaves and twigs of many of these species, plus various forbs and aquatics. Hazelnut, large-leaved aster, thimbleberry, pond-weeds, and water lilies are among the favorite summer foods. The aquatics are sought from early May to late August, especially by bulls. Murie (1934) presented an annotated list of the island's summer moose foods, and Brown (n.d.) discussed the gross changes in vegetation wrought by the high moose population.

Incidental observations made on moose pelage change indicated that the summer coat first became apparent about mid-June and that by mid-July, all animals had new pelage. Calves had winter coats by the end of August.

Great variation was noticed in the degree of antler development among various bulls. Antler formation began several weeks earlier in bulls with large antlers, presumably older individuals. Bulls with large palms were observed about the same time as animals at least 2 years old were noted with nothing but antler pedicels. The following observations provide a general idea of the amount of variation:

May 15 spike horns.
May 15 palmate antlers about 18 inches.
May 16 antler pedicel only.
May 22 antler pedicel only.
June 17 buttons.
June 21 spikes about 4 inches long.
June 22 large palmate antlers fully formed except for small tines.

June 25   spikes about 4 inches long.
June 28   small palm forming.
July 2   spikes about 4 inches long.
July 19   very large palm with outer tines formed but blunt.
Aug. 23   large palm complete and some velvet gone.

Antlers had been shed by most bulls by early February when the winter studies began. However, a few animals were seen with cervina-type antlers during February, and the latest we noticed a bull with antlers was March 12.

NUMBERS AND DISTRIBUTION

The first extensive aerial census of moose on Isle Royale was made by Aldous (Aldous and Krefting, 1946) in February 1945, with a Waco five-seated biplane. Eight parallel strips were flown, and a 30 percent coverage of the island was obtained; 122 moose were seen. Allowing for an arbitrary 20 percent error, the workers estimated the size of the population at 510. Another count in 1947, reported by Krefting (1951), produced an estimate of 600 animals. Cole (1957) made the next aerial census, but he attempted a complete count. A Piper Cub was used to fly narrow strips at 400 to 500 feet altitude until moose or tracks were located. Often only one of a group of animals was spotted, so the pilot spiraled the aircraft downward to about 100 feet, and the running moose were counted. Cole observed 242 animals, and tracks of another 48, and estimated the population at

300. He believed that in favorable weather 90 percent of the island's moose could be counted by this method.

Trotter (1958) in Ontario also was impressed with the results of an intensive-search method of survey. He compared results of three types of censuses made on the same areas: (1) intensive survey by helicopter, (2) transects with a Beaver aircraft, and (3) intensive search with the Beaver. He concluded (p. 6) that ". . . the intensive search method [with Beaver] produced uniformly high counts of moose, whereas the transect method count was low and not consistent enough."

During the present study, Cole's method was used. The island was divided into convenient-sized plots with natural boundaries, a technique suggested by Trotter. With the 90-horsepower Aeronca Champ traveling 70 to 80 m.p.h. at 400 to 500 feet altitude, we flew strips paralleling the

Figure 73—Moose track.

length of the island. Strips varied in width with terrain and cover but approximated one-eighth of a mile, and they overlapped to insure complete coverage. Duplicate counts of the same moose usually were avoided easily because strip length was short (3 to 6 miles) and locations of previously counted animals could be remembered from one strip to the next.

Since I counted moose each day only after observing the wolves, censusing took several days. Each night the possibility existed that moose from a censused area would wander into an uncensused area and vice versa. Because no reason was found for animals to travel consistently only in or out of a censused area, I assumed that these movements would compensate for one another.

Each time we observed a moose, even in an open area, we "buzzed" it at about 100 feet, causing it and any

Figure 74—Aeronca Champ—used throughout the study for following and counting wolves and moose.

nearby unseen individuals to run and be counted. (Lack of fresh snow rendered tracking useless.) This procedure is time-consuming, but results in a much higher count. Banfield *et al.* (1955) also found that frequently moose are not seen from the air until frightened from their beds.

The first census was attempted in 1959, from March 8 to 13. Because of a low gasoline supply, I counted only two-thirds of the island; 176 moose were seen. Eighteen animals had been recorded on the uncensused third incidental to wolf observations, so there was a minimum of 194 moose on the island. This figure undoubtedly was low.

In 1960, many more moose were seen incidental to other work than had been observed the previous year, probably because of better weather. A complete census was taken between February 13 and March 2, involving 45 hours of flying on 10 days, and 529 moose were seen. On the area censused in 1959, 439 moose were found in 1960. The difference (263) between counts during the 2 years obviously cannot be attributed entirely to reproduction. Although other factors may be involved, I believe that the most significant cause of the disparity is variation in weather conditions, especially in wind velocity. Banfiled *et al.* (1955:521) stressed that "unfavorable weather conditions such as strong winds and snowstorms may force big game to take shelter in forests and thus become harder to see from the air." In 1959 strong

winds frequently forced us to discontinue censusing, whereas 1960 was characterized by clear and calm days. Observations in 1960 showed that on windy days significantly fewer moose frequented openings.

The most important effect of wind variation on moose censuses should be emphasized, for, apparently, much greater differences in counts can be caused by this factor than would usually be caused by variations in population. For instance, if Cole's census was hindered by strong winds, his count could have been much too low. Even the 1960 census could be low. However, I do not believe that a much higher count will be achieved unless the population does increase, for apparently optimum conditions prevailed during that census.

Any other factor, such as time of day, which may influence the location

Figure 75—Cow moose with new summer coat.

of moose in reference to conifer cover may affect a count profoundly. Even under the best conditions, many moose undoubtedly are missed. Once when one moose was spotted, circling and diving eventually revealed six other animals were with it; if the one had not been seen, seven would have been missed. Often the pilot sighted moose that I overlooked, but he could not observe much since he had to keep the plane on course. Because many moose are missed during aerial censuses, some authors suggest that a compensatory figure be applied to the results. By comparing aerial and ground censuses on the same area, Edwards (1954) decided that aerial-census figures would be more accurate if increased by 22 percent. Banfield *et al.* (1955) agreed that aerial estimates are about 20 percent low. Peterson (1955) reported that on St. Ignace Island, where conifer cover is dominant, only about a third of the moose present could be counted from the air. During a ground census in Montana, Knowlton (1960) observed 53 moose; in the same area, he counted only 15 from an aircraft 8 days later.

Because of these factors, I believe that a conservative estimate of the number of moose on Isle Royale in March 1960, was 600. The approximate density then is 3 per square mile. Peterson (1955:202) summarized re-

Figure 76—White birch killed by moose many years ago.

ported population data from Minnesota, Nova Scotia, Newfoundland, and Ontario, and concluded the following:

> In summary, it appears that in eastern North America an average density of 1 moose per 5 square miles might be regarded as a "normal" average density for a great portion of the range. One moose per square mile is probably a relatively high density under most conditions, while 2 or more moose per square mile represent an approach to maximum carrying capacity for most large regions. While much higher densities undoubtedly occur in restricted areas, at least temporarily, they have not been observed on large areas (1,000 square miles or more) in eastern North America on a sustained basis.

Moose densities in western North America are not directly comparable to those in the east because, in the former area, summer and winter ranges frequently are miles apart, and reported winter densities are only temporary. In general, western densities are much higher than densities in eastern regions (Peterson, 1955). For instance, Spencer and Chatelain (1953) estimated that the best winter range in south central Alaska (willow, birch, aspen, and cottonwood) can support 5 to 10 moose per square mile "under proper use."

Moose inhabit all of Isle Royale and most of the surrounding islands. Some areas have higher densities than others, however, and local variations are evident between summer and winter distributions. The burns (figure 7) and swamps seem to have the highest concentrations during all seasons, but especially in winter (figure 13). The paucity of animals on the

northeast third of the island in winter probably is caused mostly by a shortage of browse, although lack of extensive swamps also may be a factor. According to Peterson (1955), snow usually does not confine moose to swamps at it does deer, but moose do seem to use swamps for protection from wind. Tracks show that many moose headquarter in swamps and venture from these each day for food.

In spring there is a notable shift of moose to the northeast third of the island. Evidently the attraction there is aquatic plants which thrive in the many beaver floodings in the area. (Terrestial herbs do not appear on Isle Royale until late May, but apparently aquatics begin to grow by early May.) I have seen 8 bulls and yearlings in Ojibway Lake at one time and 12 other moose within half a mile of the lake. It is un-

Figure 77—Moose and tracks in winter, as seen during moose census.

usual to spend a few hours in this location in May or June and not see moose. Use of marshy areas decreases throughout July and August and ends almost completely in September. Peterson (1955) noticed a similar usage pattern of lakes and streams by moose in Ontario.

REPRODUCTION

Accurate knowledge of the sex ratio in any moose population is difficult to obtain, for the sexes differ considerably in behavior, habits, and distribution. Schierbeck (1929) in Nova Scotia found a ratio of 2,232 bulls to 6,175 cows, and Spencer and Chatelain (1953) reported a bull-cow ratio

Figure 78—Mature bull in June.

Figure 79—Cow with 2- to 3-week-old calf.

of 38 to 62 for 5,319 Alaskan moose. However, Pimlott (1953) and Peterson (1955) found even sex ratios in large samples from Newfoundland and Ontario, respectively. Conversely, Pimlott (1959a) stated that kill data from Newfoundland, Sweden, and Norway, and fetal and observational data from Newfoundland show a preponderance of males. Nevertheless, he admitted (p. 447) that ". . . a reasonable doubt exists that the sex ratio of the population actually departs from 50:50."

In Montana, Knowlton (1960) found a summer ratio of 100 cows to 206 bulls (based on 248 identifications), whereas the observed winter ratio for 104 animals was 100 cows to 131 bulls. The sex ratio of hunter-killed moose in the same area was 15 cows to 16 bulls, and of 27 calves in winter was 100 females to 92 males. Knowlton discussed possible reasons for observation of an unbalanced sex ratio when such actually does not exist.

Because of the errors inherent in the method, no attempt was made to determine, on the basis of ground observations, the sex ratio of the Isle Royale moose population. Such information was obtained by a method probably less subject to bias. An aerial survey was made during 11 hours between October 27 and 31, 1959. The same technique was employed as described for the winter moose census, although a 90-horsepower Piper Cub on floats was used, piloted by Jack Burgess of Tower, Minn. D. L. Allen and I alternated as observers. Coverage included the entire area northeast of a northwest tangent to the southwest end of Hatchet Lake (approximately 40 percent of the island), and 150 moose were seen. Of these, 33 were calves, 57 were bulls, and 60 were antlerless. Of the antlerless, 32 definitely were cows, since they were accompanied by calves; the other probably also were females, for according to information by Peterson 1955: 90) and Cringan (1955: 240–246) yearling bulls normally have antlers. However, in Montana, Knowlton (1960) observed animals identified as yearlings, with only 3/4- to 1½-inch buttons as late as September 26, so possibly some apparently antlerless moose on Isle Royale actually had antlers. Nevertheless, because we obtained close aerial views of most animals, and because we did observe spikes and other small antlers on 14 moose, I believe that this type of error was small, and that the census indicated a balanced sex ratio.

According to Murie (1934), the rutting season on Isle Royale extends from mid-September to mid-October, with its height in late September. These dates coincide in general with those furnished by Peterson (1955) for the rutting season in Ontario.

Murie saw the first calf of a season on May 28 and believed that the peak of calving occurred in late May and early June. Information from the present study corroborates this. Co-operators reported the following earliest dates for first calves seen: May 26, 1959; May 20, 1960; May 19, 1961.

The last observation was by W. Leslie Robinette, of the U.S. Bureau of Sport Fisheries and Wildlife, who judged the calf to be a few hours old. Peterson reported that Ontario moose also calve in late May and early June.

The possibility of an unusually early birth on Isle Royale was indicated by the size of twin fetuses removed from a moose found dead on April 24, 1959, and examined on May 8. The male weighed 17¼ pounds and was 29 inches long, and the female weighed 16 pounds and was 28½ inches long. Both had open eyes and were completely covered with hair; their incisors had erupted but were still soft (figure 80). No weights of newborn or fetal twins

Figure 80—One of twin fetuses removed from a moose found dead April 24, 1959.

were found in the literature, but probably a twin would weigh a few pounds less than a single calf. Murie (1934) examined a fetus on May 20 which weighed 22 pounds and was 36 inches long. The smallest of four healthy newborn calves in capitivity in Michigan weighed 24 pounds, although a fifth, which died when 2 days old, weighed only 13 pounds (Kellum, 1941).

An attempt was made to determine the approximate number of calves produced annually by the moose population. Observation forms were distributed to Park Service personnel, commercial fishermen, and other summer residents. These people were asked to record every moose sighting, even if they thought they saw the same animals every day. Since several cooperators seldom left their own sections of the island, many of the

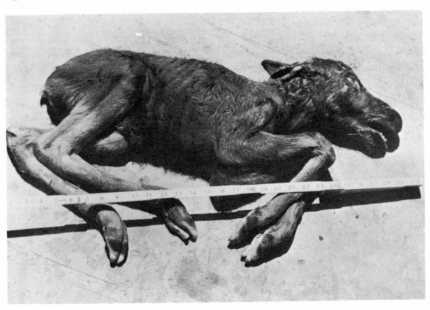

reports probably involved relatively few animals. In 1959, 291 observations were made by 14 cooperators (including the investigator) after May 26, when the first calf was seen, and calves composed 25 percent of them. A critical statistical evaluation of this type of sampling cannot be made, for the number of different animals observed is unknown. If 100 different individuals were observed, the 95 percent confidence limits would be .17 and .33. In 1960, 20 cooperators reported 359 observations, of which calves composed 15 percent. The 95 percent confidence limits would be .10 and .20, if 150 different animals were seen.

All biases in this method would tend to decrease the calf percentage. A higher proportion of yearlings probably is observed than exists in the population, for these recently independ-

Figure 81 — Young bull swimming across Rock Harbor, July 1960.

ent individuals lack the caution of more mature animals and probably also wander more. Secondly, a cow often ventures afield without her calf, especially before the calf is very old (Peterson, 1955). During the remainder of the summer, young moose frequently stray from their parents far enough to be missed by an observer. Another source of bias might be the summer concentrations of bulls, for when an observation is made, several animals may be involved. The latter bias would be important only when relatively few cooperators are reporting, such as during this study.

Other authors (Peterson, 1955; Pimlott, 1959b) also have concluded that surveys of this type indicate lower percentages of calves than actually

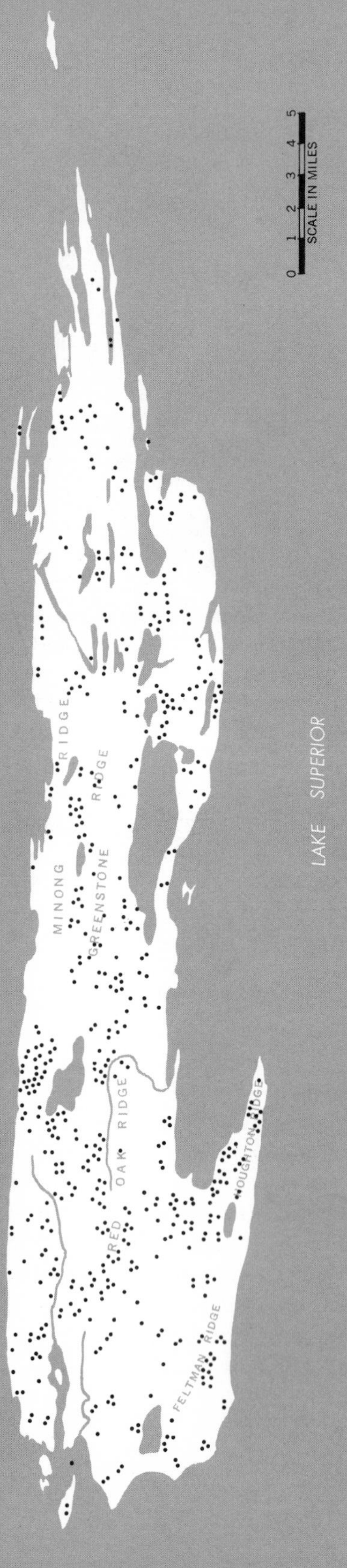

Figure 82—Moose distribution, February 1960.

SCALE IN MILES

LAKE SUPERIOR

MINONG RIDGE

GREENSTONE RIDGE

RED OAK RIDGE

FELTMAN RIDGE

HOUGHTON RIDGE

are present. In Montana, Knowlton (1960) found a ratio of 100 cows to 69 calves (based on 137 observations) in summer, and 100 to 78 (80 observations) in winter, suggesting the unreliability of summer figures. On Isle Royale, Murie (1934) encountered a similar trend. In summer, he found 26 percent of 103 cows followed by calves, whereas in autumn, calves accompanied 40 percent of 42 cows, and in spring, 46 percent of 83 cows. Although there are several possible explanations for these unexpected trends (including small sample sizes), the most likely seems to be a summer bias against calves. In Newfoundland, Pimlott 1959b:399) found that "the percentage of cows observed with calves (35) was approximately half the percentage of pregnant cows (73), the difference being caused by observational biases. . . ." Therefore, calf-total population ratios obtained in summer during the present study must be considered minimum.

The only such ratio obtained in autumn resulted from the aerial survey made in late October 1959. Of the 150 moose seen, 33, or 22 percent, were calves. (The 95 percent confidence limits are .16 and .28.)

Reported twinning rates for North American moose populations vary from 2 percent to 28 percent, on the basis of field observations (Pimlott, 1959b), although some local herds might not include any twins (Knowlton, 1960). Four of the eight rates considered by Pimlott were beween 11 percent and 18 percent. On Isle

Royale, 20 (38 percent) of 53 cows seen with calves in the summer of 1959 were accompanied by twins. If only 25 different cows were seen, the 95 percent confidence limits would be 19 percent and 57 percent. If the lower rate is assumed, the number of calves per cow-with-calf is 1.19. (Also see page 170.)

The most significant moose-population statistic is the yearling-total population ratio. As will be shown later, if an Isle Royale moose survives its first year, chances are excellent that it will live several more. Thus, application of this ratio to the estimate of total population size provides an estimate of annual recruitment. The few yearling-total population ratios which have been obtained for Isle Royale are shown in table 13.

During aerial censuses in late winter, short-yearlings (=calves) sometimes are difficult to distinguish. However, Cole (1957) noted from previous groundwork with Isle Royale moose that when a cow and calf are spooked, they flee together; pairs of adult moose spilt up. Using this information during his aerial survey, he attemped to classify short-yearlings. He believes that possibly 58 (23 percent) of the 252 animals observed were in this category, but his conservative estimate was 15 percent.

During the present study, an attempt was made each winter to sample the yearling-total population ratio. In 1959 a low fuel supply prohibited extensive circling and diving, so not all moose observed were aged. Among the 176 animals seen, there were 52 pairs: 18 cows with calves, 18 pairs of 2 adults, and 16 undetermined pairs. In addition, two cows with twins were seen. If it can be assumed that half of the undetermined pairs were cows with calves, then 17 percent of the sample was composed of calves (95 percent confidence limits are .12 and .22). In

TABLE 13.—YEARLING-TOTAL POPULATION RATIOS REPORTED FOR ISLE ROYALE

Year	Months	Sample size	Percent of yearlings in population [a]	Source
1930	May–June	[b] 128	[c] 21.0	Murie (1934)
1953	Feb.–Mar.	66	20.0	Hakala (1953)
1957	Feb.	252	15–23.0	Cole (1957)
1959	Mar.	176	17.0	Present study
1960	Feb.	529	17.0	Present study
1961	Feb.–Mar.	133	10.5	Present study

[a] Excluding newborn calves.
[b] Cows and yearlings only.
[c] Calculated from Murie's cow-calf ratio, with assumption that sex ratio was equal.

Figure 83—Calf swimming between islands in mid-July. Photo by B. A. Mech.

1960, 89 (17 percent) of 529 moose observed were calves, and since this sample probably was almost a total count, the 95 percent confidence limits are .16 and .18.

Only 133 animals were sampled in 1961, and calves composed 10.5 percent (95 percent confidence limits are .06 and .15). Apparently, this was an exceptionally poor year, for the ratio is the lowest reported from Isle Royale. Since the previous summer's sample indicated that calves composed only 15 percent of the population (compared with 25 percent for 1959), perhaps the calf crop was small.

The average yearling-population ratio probably is about 17 percent,

because this is the mean of all the reported figures and because it constituted three of the seven estimates (table 13).

PARASITES AND DISEASES

Unfortunately, adequate information concerning the general health of Isle Royale moose was not obtained. Since Isle Royale is a National Park, wildlife is protected by law, so no hunter-killed carcasses were available for examination; and no animals could be collected during the present study. In all, only six relatively intact carcasses were examined: two adults which died as a result of accidents, two wolf-killed adults, and two wolf-killed calves. Only the lungs, livers, and hearts of five of these were searched for parasites, but the stomachs and intestines of the six also were inspected. In addition, the bones of 48 other (wolf-killed) moose were examined. Although information from these sources applies primarily to wolf-killed moose, it was established that certain parasites and diseases occur in the Isle Royale herd.

The Winter Tick. The following excellent account of the life history and significance of the winter tick (*Dermacentor albipictus*) is provided by Cowan (1951:42):

> This is a one-host tick. The newly hatched seeds become active with the first autumn frosts, climb the vegetation and, with front legs widespread and waving, wait a passing large mammal. Once on a host they feed three times with appropriate periods of rest and two molts. Except in the [West] Coastal area the tick remains on its host all winter long. Although it is at first so small as to escape detection, by early spring the distended, blood-filled bodies of the adults are conspicuous and frequently reported.
>
> The female lays about 4,000 eggs that hatch in six weeks or so but the young remain sluggish and clumped together until the autumn frosts waken them to a winter of blood sucking. It is one of the most serious parasites of big game mammals. It is frequently present in vast numbers. The writer once estimated 7,200 ticks to be present on a mule deer that was at point of death from tick attack at Devona, Alberta, and has seen moose and elk with many more than that. The ticks congregate on the ears, along the lower throat and chest, and on the shoulders, rump and tail region and flanks but may occur anywhere on the body.
>
> This species is particularly damaging because of the period of its activity when the game animals are having their worst time of the year with food shortages and severe weather. Young animals are most subject to attack and suffer more severely. Individual calf moose that have been watched through the winter appeared to be in excellent condition in the autumn, became weaker, thin, and began to rub the hair from parts of the body by late December, suffered progressive weakness, partial paralysis, and death in February or March. Older animals are not immune and James Hatter has well documented accounts of many moose in the Cariboo region perishing from tick attack. In March and April, when the ticks are dropping off, the wounds left bleed freely and the animal's trail is spotted with blood, when it shakes itself the snow over several feet is pink with blood spatters, and every bed is blood-soaked. The stronger animals recover, the weaker die.

Additional life history details are furnished by Cameron and Fulton (1927).

It has not been proved that ticks are a primary cause of moose mortality, although many weak, emaciated, or dead animals have been found heavily infested (Cameron and Fulton, 1927; Lamson, 1941; Olsen and Fenstermacher, 1942; Peil, 1942; Hatter, 1950a; Peterson, 1955). Olsen and Fenstermacher selected mostly ailing and abnormally acting moose to examine, and these may have been infested secondarily; a third of the 36 moose examined harbored no ticks, whereas others harbored thousands. Hatter (1950b) found that high moose mortality in British Columbia resulted from a tick-malnutrition complex, and Ritcey and Edwards (1958) concluded that ticks alone do not seriously weaken moose. Murie (1951) believes that the many dead elk which he found heavily tick-infested were parasitized secondarily, but he did suspect ticks of killing one young moose. Whether ticks are a primary or secondary factor, they do affect moose populations significantly.

Hickie (1936) reported heavy tick infestations on Isle Royale moose, but found that wild-trapped individuals kept in corrals showed no ill effects from the parasites. However, since most animals which he found dead of malnutrition were heavily parasitized, possibly ticks were partly responsible for their deaths. Although Cole (1956) did not mention finding these parasites on Isle Royale moose, he noticed that several animals had lost considerable hair in February and March, a good indication of tick infestation.

Figure 84—A moose lacking most of its hair in May. This may have resulted from a heavy tick infestation the previous winter.

Only three intact carcasses could be examined for ticks during the present study. A calf killed by wolves in mid-March 1960, had a "moderate" infestation. A 4-year-old bull, which died as a result of an accident in late January 1961, harbored approximately 2 ticks per square inch on about half its body, but a wolf-killed bull (probably at least 13 years old) was infested with approximately 10 ticks per square inch in several places on his rump. The hides of most wolf-kills were torn and scattered, so the degree of infestation could not be determined from these. However, all seven of those that could be checked for ticks in 1961 harbored them. The hide of one very old individual was relatively intact; a high tick population (14 per square inch in places) was present. Lamson (1941) re-

ported a density of 12 ticks per square inch on 116 square inches of a Maine moose.

Because of irritation from these ectoparasites, infested animals rub against trees (Fenstermacher and Jellison, 1933). The hair comes off easily where ticks are numerous (Wallace, 1934), and the neck and flanks usually are denuded first. Naked areas are noticed on many Isle Royale moose by late February. Between mid-May and early June 1960 and 1961, large bare areas were evident on all of 65 animals observed plainly. These denuded areas may have resulted from shedding, which occurs at this time (Peterson, 1955). However, since so many moose in February and March are in this condition, and since most moose show such large naked areas weeks before new hair is apparent, I believe the condition results from tick infestations (figure 84). If that is so, most, if not all, Isle Royale moose are parasitized by ticks to some extent.

Hydatid Cysts. These cysts contain the larvae of the tapeworm *Echinococcus granulosus,* which inhabits the intestine of the wolf and other carnivores. Eggs and mature proglottids pass out with the feces and into water or onto vegetation. The intermediate host, which may be a moose or any of several other big-game species, ingests the eggs while eating or drinking. Schiller (1954) demonstrated that mice could be infected experimentally by blowflies (*Phormia regina*) fed on infected feces, so this method of transmission

also may be important. After an egg hatches in the digestive system of the herbivore, the larva enters the bloodstream, circulates, and eventually encysts in a lung (usually). The cyst grows and, after about 5 months, reaches one centimeter in diameter (Faust, 1949) ; numerous brood capsules containing more larvae begin to form (Monnig, 1938). Cysts frequently reach golfball size in moose, but Chandler (1955) reports one containing 10 to 15 quarts of fluid (host not mentioned). The life cycle is not complete until the cyst is eaten by an appropriate carnivore, in which the larvae become adults.

Apparently, the parasite is widely distributed, for it has been reported from Minnesota (Olsen and Fenstermacher, 1942), Ontario (de Vos and Allin, 1949), Manitoba (Hadwen, 1933), Saskatchewan (Harper et al., 1955), Alberta (Cowan, 1948), British Columbia (Cowan, 1947), Northwest Territories (Banfield, 1954), and Alaska (Rausch, 1959). Peterson (1955) found that *Echinococcus* was the most common parasite encountered in Ontario moose. The reported incidences of infection in moose vary between 30 percent and 68 percent (table 14).

Hydatid cysts may affect animals seriously, for they sometimes occur in large numbers. Although Ritcey and Edwards (1958) found a mean of 7.7 and a mode of 1 cyst in the lungs of 23 infected moose, 1 harbored 32. They provided (p. 143) the following description of the effects of heavy infection:

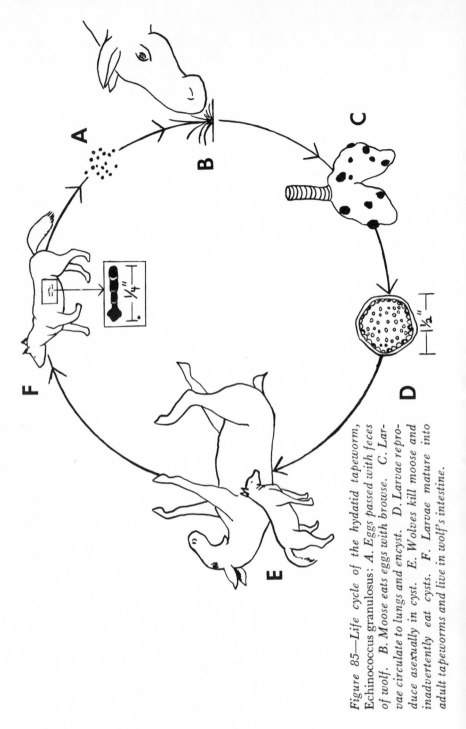

Figure 85—Life cycle of the hydatid tapeworm, Echinococcus granulosus: A. Eggs passed with feces of wolf. B. Moose eats eggs with browse. C. Larvae circulate to lungs and encyst. D. Larvae reproduce asexually in cyst. E. Wolves kill moose and inadvertently eat cysts. F. Larvae mature into adult tapeworms and live in wolf's intestine.

Another cow, on March 6, 1955, was trapped in a large corral for tagging. As men approached the trap she advanced with defiant behavior, stopped, began to tremble violently, then sank slowly to the ground breathing heavily. Breathing became weaker, and the animal was dead in four minutes. Autopsy revealed she was about four years old. She had the heaviest hydatid infection that we have encountered. There were three hydatid cysts in the liver and at least 30 in the lungs, ranging from ¼ to 2 inches in diameter. The cow was pregnant with twin calves, had heavy fat deposits on the omentum, and fat ¾–1 inch thick over the kidneys. The only unusual feature found, aside from cysts, was an excessive amount of fluid in the pericardial sac.

Other sick, abnormally acting, or weak moose with heavy hydatid infections were reported by Law and Kennedy (1933), de Vos and Allin (1949), and Peterson (1955). Cowan (1948) examined an elk lung which was replaced almost completely with cysts, and Fenstermacher (1937) found 50 cysts in the lungs of one moose, and 250, replacing about three-quarters of the lung, in another.

The first record of hydatid cysts from Isle Royale was reported by Sweatman (1952:481); he stated that "five of eight moose were found infected in 1933 on Isle Royale by Dr. D. Coburn." During the present study, three of the four adult moose examined harbored these parasites. The most heavily infected was a cow about 8 years old with 57 cysts (5 to 20 mm. in diameter) in her lungs. Because such a heavy infection was found and because wolves have been devouring moose for several years on Isle Royale (and therefore propagating the worm), it seems probable that the parasite infects a majority of the island moose.

There is more than one possible explanation for the present occurrence of *Echinococcus* on Isle Royale. Coyotes or foxes, which probably spread the parasite before 1933, might have continued to do so. Although probably neither of the smaller canids killed moose, undoubtedly both fed on carcasses. Cowan (1948) suspected coyotes of

TABLE 14.—REPORTED INCIDENCES OF INFECTION OF MOOSE WITH HYDATID CYSTS ("ECHINOCOCCUS GRANULOSUS")

Location	Number of animals	Percent infected	Source
Minnesota	33	36	Olsen & Fenstermacher (1942)
Ontario	29	60	Sweatman (1952)
Alaska	11	36	Spencer & Chatelain (1953)
Saskatchewan	96	30	Harper *et al.* (1955)
British Columbia	34	68	Ritcey & Edwards (1958)
Alaska	[a] 78	31	Rausch (1959)

[a] Adults only.

maintaining hydatid tapeworms in Alberta. According to Riley (1939), foxes are primary hosts of the parasite in Europe, although he knew of no records of fox infection in the United States. Another possibility is that wolves visited Isle Royale occasionally and spread enough eggs to propagate the species. However, the most likely explanation is that the progenitors of the present wolf population harbored adults of *Echinococcus* when they arrived.

Taenia hydatigena. Cysts of this species usually are found in the livers of various big-game animals. After a cyst is eaten by a wolf or other suitable carnivore, the larva develops into a tapeworm which dwells in the intestine of this primary host. If the eggs, which are passed with the carnivore's feces, are eaten by a moose or other ungulate, they hatch in the intestine, and the larvae migrate to the liver where they encyst.

Cowan (1951) reported that in Alberta and British Columbia the incidence of infection with this parasite is high, but that seldom are there over 12 cysts per animal. In Minnesota, the opposite was found. There were 75 cysts in one moose (Fenstermacher, 1937), but only 5.8 percent of 34 moose were infected (Olsen and Fenstermacher, 1942). Sweatman and Plummer (1957) reported that 15 of 17 moose from Ontario harbored *Taenia hydatigena* cysts. Of 32 moose autopsied in British Columbia, 84 percent were infected (Ritcey and Edwards, 1958). The only comment on their effect was that they cause no apparent harm (Cowan, 1951).

No previous record was found of this parasite on Isle Royale, but during the present study, *Taenia hydatigena* cysts were discovered in two of four moose livers examined. One contained 5, the other 10. These specimens were identified by W. W. Becklund of the U.S. Department of Agriculture and were deposited in the U.S. National Museum Helminthological Collection as 57208 and 57210.

Jaw Necrosis. Of 91 moose mandibles and/or upper jaws from Isle Royale, 13 (14 percent) were swollen, porous, and abscessed (figure 86). No attempt was made to isolate a causative organism, but the symtoms are similar to those described for "lumpy jaw," or actinomycosis (Monlux and Davis, 1956). According to these authors, "an anaerobic microorganism, *Actinomyces bovis,* which is more closely related to fungi than to true bacteria, produces these lesions involving the jaws." The disease infects either or both jaws, and since many of the moose remains found had upper or lower jaws missing, the incidence of this disease probably is higher than the figures indicate. In 1929 and 1930, of the 20 remains of Isle Royale moose, 11 (55 percent) showed similar symptoms (Murie, 1934).

The causative organism requires a laceration or abrasion through which to enter the jaw. Most infected specimens collected during the present study were from old moose, and the abscess usually centered around the first molar. This molar is the oldest and, therefore, the first to wear below the gum line. When this occurs, apparently the occluding upper molar wears into the gum, permitting entry of the pathogen. While attemping to age moose by tooth wear, Passmore *et al.* (1955:233) found that "necrotic lesions appeared to have developed very readily when excessive wear had reduced the height of any tooth below that of the normal gum line." Ritcey and Edwards (1958) reported that 5 of 34 autopsied moose had actinomycosis, and that it was most severe in old animals.

Murie (1944:117–120) discussed actinomycosis and related disorders in detail. He believes that the disease is chronic and that heavy infections can be debilitating. Certainly the abscesses and misshapen

jaws and teeth resulting from actinomycosis would impair proper mastication, which might be serious to herbivores.

Lungworm (Dictyocaulus). This nematode infects the bronchial passages of moose and other big game, and its larvae are coughed up and out, or are swallowed and passed with the feces. They eventually climb low vegetation to await ingestion by a new host (Cowan, 1951). Olsen and Fenstermacher (1942) discovered *Dictyocaulus viviparus* in 42 percent of 33 sickly moose from Minnesota, and Lamson (1941) reported *D. hadweni* (considered by some workers as a synonym for *D. viviparus*) from a Maine moose. Heavy infections can be debilitating, as the

Figure 86—Necrotic moose mandibles.

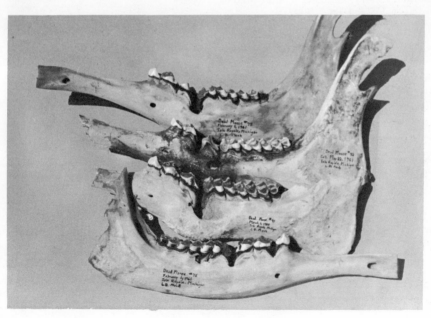

following from Cowan (1951:53) shows:

In addition to the obstructing effect of the adult worms in the lungs, the irritation induced frequently causes a thickening in the walls of the air passages that is characteristic. The inflammation induced and the interference with normal lung function often provides the opportunity for bacterial invasion and a bronchopneumonia results. This causes the animal to have a husky cough and difficulty in breathing; diarrhoea is usual. Even if death does not result directly from the lung-worm attack the animals are so weakened that they are vulnerable to winter conditions or predator harassment. Animals usually die after a prolonged decline and show the same marrow symptoms of fat loss accompanying other debilitating diseases.

During the present study, *Dictyocaulus* sp. was found accidentally in one moose. While counting *Echinococcus* cysts in the excised lungs of an animal examined on August 26, 1960, I noticed a live lungworm. It was identified by M. B. Chitwood of the U.S. Department of Agriculture as *Dictyocaulus* sp. and was placed in the U.S. National Museum Helminthological Collection as 56879. No carcasses were examined for this parasite, and since it has not been reported previously from Isle Royale, no information is available on incidence of infection or significance to the island herd.

Other Parasites and Diseases. In summer, most moose on Isle Royale are pestered by swarms of flies, and there are raw spots near the hocks on at least a few animals. Murie (1934) observed similar lesions on

Isle Royale moose. Peterson (1955) reports the condition from Ontario animals, and believes that it probably results from the collective efforts of the insects. Both authors identified specimens of the pests as moose flies (*Lyperosiops alcis*). Whether the deer-flies (*Chrysops*) and black flies (*Simulium*), abundant on Isle Royale, also parasitize moose is unknown. Undoubtedly, flies are a great nuisance, but the amount of harm they cause has not been determined.

Since complete pathological examinations of moose were not attempted during the present study, there probably are other parasites and/or diseases not yet discovered in the Isle Royale herd. Peterson (1955) summarized the information available on moose parasites and diseases, and discussed approximately 25 species.

MORTALITY

In areas without wolf populations, moose probably succumb to a variety of factors such as malnutrition, old age, diseases, and accidents. Most of these factors cause a gradual decline, so in areas with high wolf populations, dying animals probably are eliminated by predation, and mortality caused directly by any other factors should be low. Such seems to be the case on Isle Royale. Since the 15 to 16 wolves alone eat (and probably kill) an average of 1 moose per 3 days in winter, presumably few moose get a chance to die directly of causes other than predation.

Information on moose mortality was obtained from investigation of as many carcasses and old remains as could be located. These were discovered by two methods. In winter, the aircraft was used to track wolves to carcasses which they fed upon. Some moose were seen killed, and tracks showed that wolves killed several of the other animals which they ate. In many cases, the network of wolf tracks around a "kill" prevented positive determination that the wolves had dispatched the moose. However, except in two cases, no reason was found to indicate that they had not, and chances are good that even the two excepted moose were killed by wolves. Therefore all remains found fed upon in winter will be considered kills; any error resulting from this assumption undoubtedly is small. Fifty-six such kills were found, 51 of which were investigated on the ground. Although most of these were taken by the large pack, several eaten by the smaller packs are included.

The second method used to locate moose remains was ground search in spring and summer. Reports from alerted Park Service personnel and other field men facilitated this work. (W. L. Robinette and L. W. Krefting, of the U.S. Bureau of Sport Fisheries and Wildlife, provided information from 18 remains they examined during a 3-week browse survey in 1961.) A total of 72 remains are included in this "random" sample, and these should represent year-round mortality from most sources and over a period of several years.

Accidents constitute the only moose mortality factor that is relatively unrelated to predation. Only three accidental moose deaths came to my attention during this study. A cow about 5 years old was found on a rocky shore near Rock Harbor Lodge on April 24, 1959, by a construction crew. This animal had heavy kidney, heart, and omental fat and her femur marrow was normal. No wolf wounds were found, but small patches of hair were sheared from her head and legs, and the four right posterior ribs were broken. The cow may have fallen through ice and drowned. Peterson (1955) believes that this type of mortality is especially important in early winter and spring.

The carcass of a month-old calf washed up on Scoville Point sometime before July 25, 1959, when it was reported; no sign of wolf attack was found. Possibly the animal drowned. Peterson (1955:193) reported that "drowning seems to be an important factor in calf losses. . . ." Murie (1934) found remains of two Isle Royale moose which probably had drowned.

The third known moose death for which wolves were not responsible occurred on January 31, 1961. A 4-year-old bull had tangled his antlers and neck in an extension cord near a building at Windigo. He spent several days there, becoming increasingly entangled. Park Service personnel were eventually forced to kill the bull.

Murie (1934) found remains of 6 animals that had been mired or had caught a foot in roots, but no indications of this type of mortality were found during the present study.

Wolf predation undoubtedly is the most significant moose mortality factor on Isle Royale. A possible measure of its importance is afforded by data from randomly discovered moose remains. Such remains frequently can be judged "eaten by wolves," or "not eaten." (Characteristic signs of wolf feeding are: widely scattered bones; separation of the vertebral column into two pieces; and obvious chewing on the edges of the scapulae, the posterior-ventral angles of the mandibular rami, and the ends of long bones. Chewing is evident even after the bones have lain for several years.) Remains of 47 moose were found which could be judged "eaten" or "not eaten." Of these, 34 (72 percent) had been chewed by wolves. Most of those showing no wolf work were well weathered, and some may have dated from the "pre-wolf" period.

Of course, wolf-chewed moose bones do not mean necessarily that wolves killed the moose; Isle Royale wolves do eat carrion. On June 23, 1959, I investigated the putrid carcass of a bull lying a few feet offshore in Chickenbone Lake. Fully formed antlers without velvet indicated that the moose had perished in autumn or early winter. Wolves recently had detached two legs and eaten them on shore. By July 7, the entire carcass had been dragged ashore and eaten.

However, apparently the wolves sometimes wound a moose and leave it. (The bull mentioned above might have been such a victim.) A wounded animal might wander far before dying, and in summer might decompose before the wolves discover it. The bones would not appear chewed, even though wolves were responsible for the animal's death. Data from such remains would tend to compensate for data from remains of an animal that the wolves had eaten but not killed.

Wolf-Moose Relationships

The welfare of a wolf population is related intimately to the availability of prey. In many areas wolves prey on two or more species, and if one becomes relatively unavailable, another provides sustenance. From most reports it appears that an adult moose is one of the most formidable prey animals in North America, so when another species is available, wolves tend to depend heavily on the other species. Peterson (1955:175) reported that in the St. Ignace Island area, "where moose were much more abundant than white-tailed deer," moose remains composed only 36 percent of 76 wolf scats collected, whereas deer remains comprised 57 percent. In Alaska, Burkholder (1959) established that 14 of 22 wolf kills were caribou and 8 were moose. He believes that these species were killed in proportion to their availability. Nevertheless, six of the seven ageable moose were calves, and the other was a yearling, whereas several of the caribou were adults. In Mount Mc-Kinley National Park, Murie (1944: 57) concluded that although caribou, Dall sheep, and moose are available, ". . . moose are not readily taken by wolves." Cowan (1947) found that, in the Rocky Mountain national parks of Canada, where several big-game species are present, moose remains occurred in 9 percent of 420 wolf scats, and most of the remains were those of calves.

MacFarlane (1905) and Stanwell-Fletcher (1942) each reported on a wolf which had been injured badly in an encounter with an adult moose, so it is evident why wolves are cautious in dealing with these animals.

Isle Royale wolves must resort to moose for their primary food, for no other big game is present. Because of this, the resident packs undoubtedly are expert at hunting and killing moose—any inept individuals probably perished long ago. Aerial observations of 66 hunts provide the basis for the following analysis of the wolves' hunting techniques. The number of hunts observed and hours of observation each year are summarized in table 15. Since the wolves hunt as they travel, the figures are based on observations of the wolves traveling, exclusive of rest periods and time spent on large bays or lakes. Moose often occur in groups, so the number of moose involved is given in each case. All observations included in the table were of the large pack or part of it.

When observing wolves hunting, we habitually flew ahead of them and spotted the next moose along their trail. This allowed observation of both wolf and moose behavior before, during, and after attacks. By refueling when the pack rested or passed through areas devoid of moose, we minimized the possibility of having to leave in the middle of a hunt. The fuel cache at Mott Island plus a 5-gallon can of fuel carried in the aircraft were advantageous in this respect. Each hunt witnessed is described in the appendix.

TABLE 15.—OBSERVATIONS OF WOLVES [a] HUNTING

Year	Hours of observation	Number of hunts	Number of moose involved [b]
1959	9	6	15
1960	35	33	66
1961	24	27	51
Total	68	66	132

[a] Pack of 15 or part of it.
[b] Since moose often are in groups, one hunt usually involved more than one animal.

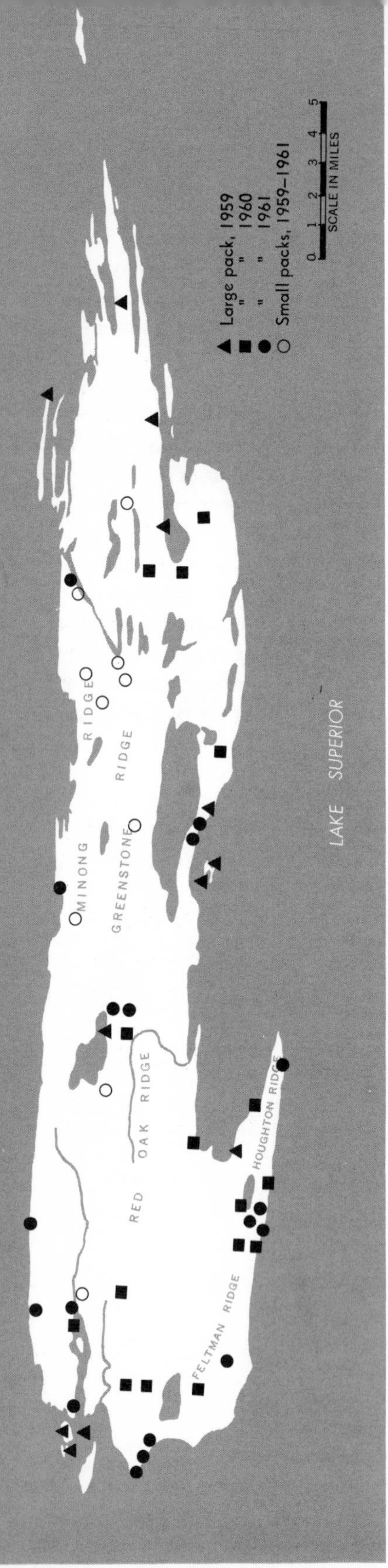

Figure 87—Distribution of kills.

Large pack, 1959 ▲
" " 1960 ■
" " 1961 ●
Small packs, 1959–1961 ○

SCALE IN MILES
0 1 2 3 4 5

LAKE SUPERIOR

MINONG RIDGE
GREENSTONE RIDGE
RED OAK RIDGE
HOUGHTON RIDGE
FELTMAN RIDGE

HUNTING HABITS OF THE WOLVES

After the wolves leave a kill, apparently any moose encountered is subject to attack. Once the animals showed interest in a moose only 35 minutes after leaving a kill. In another case, they killed a moose within 4 to 10 hours after they abandoned their last carcass; and eight times they dispatched a moose within 26 hours after leaving a previous victim. They did almost all of their killing within 48 hours after they left their previous prey. In Alaska, a pack left a moose carcass at noon one day, and by the next morning had dispatched and eaten another moose (Burkholder, 1959). The average distances between kills made on Isle Royale are given in table 8.

The Isle Royale wolves employ a method of hunting moose which differs from methods reportedly used for other species. In Ontario, Dunne (1939) learned that in searching swamps for deer, packs split into twos and threes. Cowan (1947) and Stenlund (1955) found that wolves use a "line abreast" formation upon reaching areas to be hunted. When the predators hunt points and islands for deer in Minnesota, part of the pack drives while a few animals wait on the ice to intercept any prey flushed (Stenlund, 1955). Wolves hunt elk in the Canadian Rockies by traveling single file on ridges and rushing any quarry below them (Cowan, 1947). According to Murie (1944), the Mount McKinley wolves hunt Dall sheep by coursing through the hills hoping to surprise an animal at a disadvantage; when hunting caribou, they merely approach one of the many herds and begin chasing it.

Isle Royale wolves apparently do not have special places to hunt. Everywhere they travel is hunting ground, although more moose are killed in some areas than in others (figure 87). Areas of high moose-kill are characterized by dense moose populations and proximity to well-traveled wolf routes, as is evident by a comparison of figure 87 with figures 82 and 47.

The wolves' most common method of hunting is to travel regular routes single file until they scent a moose (figure 88). Most of the moose detected were within 300 yards upwind of the wolves. However, in one open region, the predators apparently sensed a cow and two calves about 1½ miles away. After getting the weak scent of such distant moose, the pack travels toward them until it locates them more precisely.

In certain cases the wolves detected moose 125 yards downwind or 200 yards crosswind. However, I once saw a moose browse undiscovered for 20 minutes, 100 yards downwind of the resting pack. In several instances wolves seemed to scent moose downwind or crosswind, but apparently could not locate them and eventually left. Commonly, when the wolves sense a moose, all stop and "point." Each stands stiffly with nose upwind and ears alert for 10 to 15 seconds, probably verifying the exact location of the moose. Often

Figure 88—The large pack hunting.

the animals assemble closely, sniff noses, and wag tails before starting toward the prey.

The wolves did not sense all the moose judged to be within range of detection. Of 160 animals in 85 groups which appeared to be within range, 29 (19 groups) went undiscovered. Some of these were within 150 yards, whereas others were as far as half a mile away. Moose were judged within range if circumstances appeared similar to those in which others had been detected during the many observed hunts. Apparently, topography, cover, local wind direction, and previous behavior of the moose all influence its "detectability."

A less-used hunting technique is tracking. When the wolves cross a fresh moose track, they follow it, single file. Sometimes a couple of animals follow downwind of the track parallel to the others but several yards ahead. On one occasion the wolves scented fresh tracks of a moose that had been working up a small valley below them. They did not actually come upon the tracks but were able to follow them from the ridge about 25 yards above. As the tracks got fresher, most of the wolves headed into the valley and began tracking. One paralleled them on the ridge and finally located the moose, which had moved up the side of the valley. Another time the wolves scented moose sign 20 minutes old from about 50 yards upwind, after the moose had left the vicinity.

From the aircraft, I could determine that a moose trail was fresh only when the moose which made it was nearby. Thus, the wolves frequently may have passed up fresh tracks without my knowledge. On February 6, 1961, the pack of 15 crossed tracks 1 minute old, but only 1 wolf followed them. It gave up after 25 yards and returned to the pack. Before and after this occurrence the wolves were chasing moose, so their unconcern apparently did not result from a lack of motivation.

After detecting a moose, the wolves head excitedly toward it single file, but they check their speed until the moose bolts. If the moose makes a stand, the wolves lunge at it from all sides, trying to force it to run. They are readily frightened by its charges, however, and seldom get close (figure 89). When a moose charges, the wolves scurry several yards away, tails between their legs. If they cannot make the moose flee, they leave. They may decide to depart within half a minute, but sometimes they harass a moose intermittently for 5 minutes before leaving. I once saw a pack harry a standing moose for 3 minutes, finally force it to run, and then kill it within about 10 minutes.

If a moose runs at the approach of wolves, the predators suddenly spring forward with great bounds. Their gait appears exhausting, but they can maintain it for at least 20 minutes. After long runs, they rest for at least 10 minutes. During our observations, the wolves ran faster than the moose through snow less than 2 feet deep, and sometimes within 200 or 300 yards they overtook animals which had a 150-yard lead. However, on one occasion the pack took about a one-quarter of a mile to catch up to a moose with a 100-yard head start. Burkholder (1959) reported an incident in which nine wolves covered 300 yards through snow 2 to 3 feet deep while their prey, a yearling moose, ran only 100. In my experience, pursued moose do not always run at top speed; they seem to depend more on endurance.

Young and Goldman (1944) reported that a wolf was clocked at 27 m.p.h. for 200 yards, but Minnesota wardens chased a wolf on a frozen lake for 4 miles, at 35 to 40 m.p.h. (Stenlund, 1955). The latter rate correlates well with the maximum speed reported for moose (35 m.p.h., by Cottam and Williams, 1943). Thick swamps, heavy cover, blowdown, or snowdrifts slowed the wolves but did not hinder moose. Apparently wolves are aware of their limited ability under adverse conditions, for they sometimes fail to chase nearby animals which run through snowdrifts or blowdown. Hatter (1950a) found that in British Columbia "wolves cannot prey successfully on moose in deep soft snow."

The wolves abandoned 20 observed pursuits without catching up to their intended victims. In these cases, either the moose had too great a lead, or adverse running conditions hampered the wolves. Sometimes one or two wolves got within a few yards of a moose and gave up if the rest of the pack was far behind. Usually if a moose maintained a 100-yard lead for 10 or 15 seconds, the wolves discontinued the chase unless they were gaining. Crisler (1958:106), studying wolves and caribou in Alaska, also was impressed with ". . . how quickly the wolves had judged when a chase was useless."

During extended pursuits, most of the wolves follow single file in the trail of the moose until they overtake the animal, undoubtedly making travel easier. Frequently some wolves try shortcutting the moose, but if it turns, these individuals may head in the wrong direction and lose the pack.

After the wolves overtake a moose, most of them remain strung out behind (figure 89), but some stay alongside, apparently awaiting the opportunity for attack. Since pursued moose sometimes travel 2 or 3 miles through several types of cover and over varying terrain without being assailed, probably the physical condition of the moose determines its fate. Although I distinguished no behavioral difference between the three adults seen attacked and the several which fled unharmed, probably the wolves discerned a difference. Two of the moose were killed within 100 yards of where the wolves first encountered them. (The other was wounded within 100 yards but then was abandoned.)

It seems likely that wolves can detect any weakness or inferiority from the behavior of a moose. Certainly if an animal is not strong enough to

Figure 89a—Fifteen wolves approach a moose in burn area.

Figure 89b—The moose stands its ground.

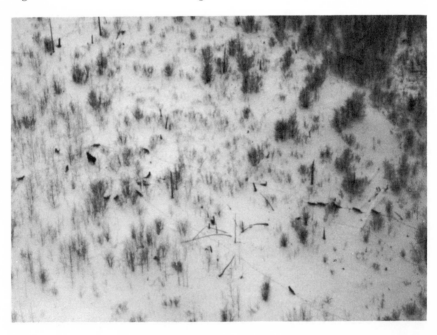

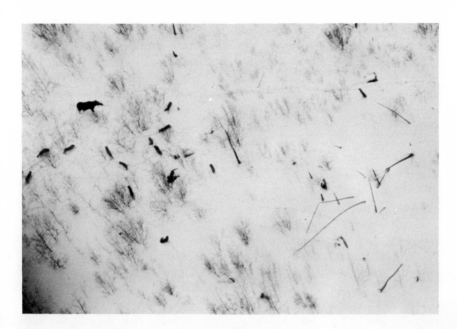

Figure 89c—Wolves harass the moose from a distance.

Figure 89d—The moose holds off wolves; after 5 minutes, wolves leave.

outlast its pursuers, it will be killed, and this presumably is why the wolves chased some individuals so far without attacking them. Perhaps the two animals killed were debilitated enough so that the wolves immediately detected this and did not hesitate to attack. Two reports in the literature are pertinent here. In Wood Buffalo National Park, Fuller (1960) watched at least 10 wolves approach to within 25 feet of 4 bison. The only bison that showed concern was a wounded one; the others continued ruminating. On two other occasions, Fuller saw (from the air) wolves within a herd of bison which paid them no attention. In East Africa, Wright (1960) watched wild dogs pass near several groups of gazelles (*Gazella thomsonii*) without

Figure 90—Wolves pursuing a moose near Malone Bay.

frightening them. Only one individual became panic-stricken and ran— it was chased and killed. In these instances, even humans detected behavioral differences between healthy or "confident" animals and insecure ones.

Extensive observations of wolves hunting caribou in Alaska show that a primary technique is to chase caribou long distances until a weak or inferior individual is located (Murie, 1944; Crisler, 1956). Murie saw tracks of a chase that lasted 3 or 4 miles, and Crisler witnessed a 5-mile chase. Dall sheep may be pursued for one-half mile over rugged terrain (Murie, 1944), and even deer sometimes are chased vainly for long distances (Dunne, 1939). Thus, it appears that the long-chase technique is employed by wolves in many areas and that it probably serves as a test to distinguish vulnerable individuals.

The technique that wolves use when pursuing a cow moose and calf is to attempt to separate them. While some animals harass the cow, others remain beside the calf, and as soon as the cow charges a wolf, those guarding the calf close in. If the cow fails to keep up with the calf, if thick cover causes the two to separate, or if the cow becomes too involved with chasing off wolves, some animals immediately assail the calf. If the others keep the cow occupied for half a minute, the calf probably is doomed, for two wolves can handle a 9-month-old calf easily. It seems amazing that any cow and calf could survive such strategy. However, eight instances were observed in which cows and calves ran from wolves, and only in three of these were calves killed. This further attests to the profound respect the wolves have for the hoofs of a moose.

Since an insufficient number of hunts by smaller packs and lone wolves were observed, generalizations cannot be made regarding the hunting habits of these wolves. The reader is referred to Hunting Account 31 in the appendix, which involves the pack of three, and 42, 43, 70, and 71, concerning a lone wolf. Although no evidence was obtained that a single wolf can kill an adult moose (unless wounded), the fact that an individual was observed seriously attempting this indicates that at least the wolf thought it might succeed. Young and Goldman (1944) stated that one wolf can kill a full-grown moose, and Cowan (1947:159) reported that in the Rocky Mountain national parks of Canada, "several instances of single wolves killing moose and elk were noted."

Figure 91—Wolves pursuing a moose near Grace Creek.

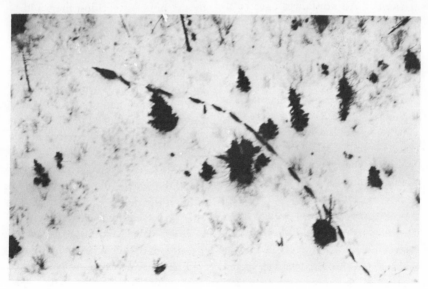

ACCOUNTS OF WOLF ATTACKS

Information on the killing techniques of the wolf was obtained from eight hunts in which moose were killed or wounded. Complete, successful hunts of three calves and one adult were witnessed, plus parts of three hunts in which adults were killed, and one in which an adult was wounded and abandoned. In addition, certain information was obtained from an adult killed in summer. The following accounts (numbered for their chronological position in the hunting accounts included in the appendix) are edited versions of field notes. Because of the distances, speeds, and number of moose and wolves involved in each account, and because of the necessity for constant observation from the rapidly moving aircraft, notes are incomplete in some accounts. All distances are estimated.

2. (February 24, 1959. About three-quarters of a mile northeast of Siskiwit Lake Outlet, and about three-eighths of a mile inland.) At 6 p.m., 10 of the 15 wolves were traveling along the shore of Siskiwit Lake about 1 mile ahead of the others. Suddenly they stopped, and several pointed more or less crosswind for a few seconds toward three adult moose three-eighths of a mile away. Heading inland single file to an old beaver meadow, they traveled downwind a few hundred yards, veered, and continued for 250 yards until directly downwind of the moose. Then they ran straight toward the animals, which were still browsing when the wolves were within 150 yards. Two of the moose sensed the wolves 25 yards away and began running. The wolves gave chase a few yards until they spotted the third moose, which was closer and had not left. They immediately ran the 50 feet to this animal and surrounded it.

A few seconds later the moose bolted and the wolves followed in its trail (figure 90). Soon five or six animals were biting at its hind legs, back, and flanks. The moose continued on, dragging the wolves until it fell. In a few seconds the animal was up, but it fell a second time. Arising again, the moose ran through the open second-growth cover to a small stand of spruce and aspen, while the wolves continued their attacks; one wolf grabbed the quarry by the nose. Reaching the stand of trees, the moose stood, bleeding from the throat, but the wolves would not attack.

Within a few minutes most of the wolves were lying down, including the last five, which had caught up. Two or three continued to harass the moose without actually biting it, and the moose retaliated by kicking with its hind feet. Whenever the animal faced the wolves, they scattered. Although the moose was bleeding from the throat, it appeared strong and "confident." At 6:30 p.m. we left because of darkness.

The next morning at 11:15 a.m. the wolves were gone. The moose lay within 25 feet of where it had made the stand. After we made several low passes, it finally arose and moved on. Although walking stiffly and favoring its left front leg, the moose was not bleeding and seemed in good shape. The wolves were 16 miles away feeding on a new kill.

3. (March 1, 1959. About a quarter-mile south of Lake Desor, and about half a mile southwest of the northeast end of the lake.) From 10:10 a.m. to 5:05 p.m. the 15 wolves lay on Lake Desor, but at 5:05 they began traveling along the shore. Several seemed to point inland, but mating activity obscured this somewhat. After searching the vicinity and finding no moose nearby, we headed for Mott Island to refuel.

When we returned at 6 p.m. the wolves had a bull (as determined later) surrounded in a small stand of hardwoods. He was bleeding steadily from the throat, and had difficultly holding his head up. About 150 square feet of the surrounding snow was covered with blood. The animal's lower left hind leg was bloody, and he leaned against a tree, keeping his right hind leg centered under him. (Chances are good that this animal had been assailed the night before and then temporarily abandoned.)

Most of the wolves were yards away, resting and playing, but a few were licking the bloody snow. One wolf in particular, whose legs were covered with blood, was harassing the moose. It stayed near the bull most of the time, often nipping at the injured leg. However, each time the moose faced it or any nearby wolves, they scrambled away. At 6:30 p.m. we left because of darkness.

Unfavorable weather prevented a check on the situation until March 4. At 10:45 a.m. the bones of the moose were scattered around the spot where we had seen him last. The wolves had just left and were 10 miles away. An examination of the remains showed this to be a bull in wear-class VI (Passmore *et al.,* 1955).

7. (February 5, 1960. About 200 yards south of Siskiwit Lake and 1 mile west of Wood Lake.) At 3:50 p.m. we left the 16 wolves heading across Siskiwit Lake near Ryan Island. After refueling, we tracked them to the southeast shore of the lake, up the first ridge, and along it northeastward. At 4:35 p.m. we saw them running upwind on the open ridge toward a cow and two calves about three-quarters of a mile away. The way the wolves had veered upon reaching the ridge about 1½ miles from the moose suggests they had smelled the animals at that distance.

When still three-quarters of a mile from them, several of the wolves stood on a 100-foot ridge and pointed toward the moose, which now faced them. The first few animals charged off the ridge and ran toward the moose but a little north of them. Two wolves were far ahead, and two others ran south of the trail left by the moose.

The cow and calves eventually headed toward Wood Lake, but upon encountering a steep drop-off, they turned southward. The first two wolves sped after the moose, gained rapidly, and overtook them within a quarter mile. As the moose ran through open second-growth birch, one wolf remained on each side.

The cow was immediately behind the calves, and twice she feinted toward the wolves, which leaped out of the way. Most of the pack began catching up, and as the moose entered a small cedar swamp (the nearest conifer cover), four or five animals tore at the rump and sides of a calf and clung to it. Within 50 feet, the calf went down in a thick clump of cedars. The cow and the other calf continued through the cover with two wolves still following for 20 yards. When these wolves gave up, the moose stopped and returned 50 yards toward the wounded calf. Gradually, however, the moose drifted back toward where they originally had started. Most of the wolves concentrated on the wounded calf, which remained where it had fallen. The cedars obscured our vision, but the calf appeared dead within 5 minutes after it fell.

The snow in the area was only a foot deep, but the wolves were sinking in about 6 inches.

8. (February 7, 1960. A b o u t half a mile southeast of the southwest end of Angleworm Lake.) At 4:10 p.m. the pack of 16 headed north from Moskey Basin for a quarter-mile on an old wolf trail. At 5 o'clock the animals suddenly veered upwind and became alert, often stopping and pointing or scenting the wind. All wolves stayed close together and did not dally. They traveled three-quarters of a mile to within 250 yards of a cow and calf which were browsing directly upwind (5:30 p.m.).

The wolves gave no indication of scenting the moose. Instead, they turned through a thick spruce swamp; but when a third of the way across, they suddenly headed toward the moose. As the pack approached to within 100 yards, the moose started running, the cow behind the calf. The wolves gave chase and soon were racing alongside and behind them.

Throughout the chase, the cow defended the calf, charging the wolves frequently. One animal managed to bite the calf's rump once but did not hinder the animal. The pursuit continued for 200 to 300 yards (through many types of cover and over varying terrain) without an attack, but eventually the wolves separated the moose. Most of the pack pursued the calf, while two animals followed the cow. After a chase of several hundred yards more, a few wolves attacked the rump and flanks of the calf; one grabbed it by the left hind leg. The cow caught up with the group and managed to stamp on one wolf, which arose instantly and appeared unhurt. The others released the calf and continued pursuing it for another hundred yards before attacking again. They finally pulled the animal down and tore at it, but it arose and the cow rushed in. Some of the wolves fled, but others chased the cow. Then the wolves assailed the calf once more. One grabbed it by the nose, and three or four tore at its neck and throat; others ripped at its rump. The calf's hind quarters went down, but the animal continued on, dragging its hind legs and the wolves that were attached to its body. It managed to stand once more, and the cow started to charge again, but one wolf chased her away.

The wolves made a final attack on the calf, and it was unable to arise. Then they lined up side-by-side around the carcass and began feeding. The cow gradually wandered back toward where she had been jumped.

13. (February 12, 1960. About 1½ miles southwest of Halloran Lake and about 200 yards northwest of the Isle Royale shore.) The 16 wolves were traveling along the shore when suddenly they veered inland about 2:30 p.m. toward a lone cow (sex determined later) standing on a ridge 200 yards upwind. The animal ran when the pack was 100 yards away, and the wolves charged up the ridge and continued on her trail. The cow ran slowly and stopped to look back at the approaching pack, which caught up within 100 yards. She stood next to a bushy spruce for protection, and as the wolves lunged, she charged and kicked at them with all four feet. Although she seemed to connect with

her hind feet, apparently no animals were injured.

Meanwhile, the whole pack caught up. The moose defended herself for about 3 minutes while backed against the spruce, but suddenly she bolted and fled toward the end of the ridge. The wolves attacked her rump and flanks but released their holds as she brushed through some thick spruces. They pursued the animal for 25 yards to the end of the ridge, where all plunged down the steep slope.

When the moose landed at the base of the ridge, the wolves were attached to her back and flanks, and one held her by the nose. The downed animal attemped to rise, but the sheer weight of the wolves seemed to anchor her. The wolf grasping her nose held on firmly while she violently shook her head. Most of the animals continued working on her rump and flanks, while two tore at her shoulders.

The moose struggled for more than 5 minutes while the wolves, packed solidly around her, tugged away. Two individuals had to wait at one side, for there was no room around the moose. The "nose-wolf" continued its hold for at least 10 minutes, while the others pulled from all sides. After about 10 minutes, the moose appeared dead. This cow was in wear-class VI.

14. (February 15, 1960. About half a mile downstream of the junction of the Grace Creek Trail and Grace Creek.) At 2:10 p.m. the 16

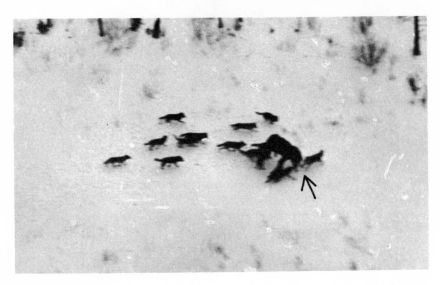

Figure 92—Wolves attacking a moose. Note that one wolf has the moose by the nose (arrow).

wolves were heading down Grace Creek. Suddenly, they pointed toward a cow (as determined later) 200 yards to their left. Then they continued down the creek to where it wound closer to the moose. Heading inland over a knoll, the wolves surprised the cow 25 yards away.

The animal fled, but the wolves caught up almost immediately. One grabbed her right hind leg just above the hoof. However, as the cow trotted through some spruces, she shook the wolf loose. She then ran in a semi-circle toward the creek (figure 91), and several times the wolves overtook her but failed to attack. Once when she ran through a snowdrift, the wolves lost ground, but they quickly caught up again.

As the moose started down a shal-low valley, the wolves attacked her rump. She soon shook them, however, and proceeded to the frozen creek bed, where the wolves attacked again. One animal kept jumping at her nose and finally grabbed it; others fastened onto her rump and flanks. The cow fought hard and dragged the wolves about 100 yards downstream (figure 92). Three or four times, she lifted the "nose-wolf" off the ground and swung it for several seconds before lowering her head. This wolf maintained its grip for over a minute. The moose continued fighting hard and finally shook the wolves and ran back upstream, with the whole pack following.

The cow started into the woods and the wolves lunged again. The moose kicked constantly and trampled two individuals into the snow. One of them crawled away but later seemed unhurt. The moose then stood next to a small balsam along the creek shore and continued to fight off the wolves, which soon gave up temporarily and lay on the ice. At 2:35 p.m. they went 200 yards downstream and assembled. They returned to the animal three times but found her belligerent, although blood from her wounded rump covered several square yards of snow. Nevertheless, there appeared to be no mortal wound.

From 2:50 to 3:25 p.m. the wolves lay on the nearby ice. Meanwhile, at 3:20 the moose walked about 10 yards and lay down. At 3:25, the pack approached and she arose again. Although appearing stiff, she charged the wolves effectively. Many of them were eating the bloody snow where she had stood first (figure 93). At 3:40 the wolves lay down again and at 3:50 so did the moose. About a minute later, a wolf approached the moose and she arose again. At 4:12 this occurred once more. Then the wolves entered some spruces 25 yards south of the moose and curled up. From 4:20 to 4:40 we were refueling,

Figure 93—The large pack waiting for the wounded moose to weaken. See Hunting Account 14. (c) National Geographic Society, courtesy National Geographic Magazine.

but when we returned, the wolves were still there.

At 5 o'clock, they arose, tested the moose, and found her quite pugnacious. Ten minutes later, 14 of the animals left and headed southward while 2 remained curled up within 25 yards of the wounded moose, which was also lying down.

From 5:35 to 6:05, the pack visited an old kill half a mile south of the creek; the animals then traveled back along a ridge until half a mile from the wounded cow. Meanwhile, the two "guards" arose and stood near the moose. The pack headed almost directly toward them, and at 6:40 p.m. when we had to leave, the pack was within a quarter-mile and still heading toward the wounded moose. The next morning at 10:50 a.m. the wolves were feeding on the carcass, which was where we had seen the live animal. Ground observation later showed that this cow was in wear-class VI.

40. (March 17, 1960. About 50 yards southwest of the Island Mine Trail and about half a mile from Siskiwit Bay.) At 11:10 a.m. the large wolf pack was resting along the trail, and at 11:25 the animals slowly headed 150 yards farther up the trail. At 11:35 they suddenly turned upwind and ran about 50 yards into a thick spruce stand. Two moose ran through the stand and split up. Because of thick cover, we could not see the wolves.

Suddenly, however, a calf, pursued closely by two wolves, headed out of the stand, down the trail 100 yards, and into a spruce swamp on the other side of the trail. Within 100 yards, the wolves began nipping at the hind legs of the moose. After another 50 yards, one wolf was clinging to the animal's rump and the other to its throat. The moose stopped and trampled the front wolf, but the wolf would not let go. It clung to the calf's throat for about 2 minutes while the calf continued to pound it and drag it about.

Finally this wolf released its throat-hold, but the other still stuck to the rump. The first wolf then stood on its hind legs, and placing its front paws on the left side of the moose, started chewing the side of its neck for several seconds. The calf soon brushed this animal against a tree, but the wolf then dived under the moose and fastened to its throat. As the running moose straddled the wolf, the wolf ran along with it for about a minute.

Meanwhile, two other wolves caught up. One bit the calf around the head and finally grasped its nose. The other grabbed the right flank and then changed to the rump where it clug for about a minute while the moose continued on. Thus, one wolf had the calf by the nose, one by the throat, and two by the rump. The animal soon stopped and was pulled down under a small clump of trees. In about 3 minutes, it ceased struggling (11:45 a.m.).

When the two wolves first attacked the calf, the cow tried to catch up with it but was too far behind the swamp to find it. Total distance of the chase was about one quarter of a mile. Apparently, the rest of the animals had been chasing the cow; eventually they found their way to the calf also and joined in the feed.

41. (August 26, 1960. West shore of the north arm of Chickenbone Lake about 75 yards south of the outlet.) At 6 p.m. on August 23, four campers noticed a cow moose about 30 feet inland of the above location, with a large open wound on her left hind flank. She seemed reluctant to move. Two days later, Chief Ranger B. J. Zerbey reported that the moose appeared sore and short of breath and would not arise. Two nearby bloody beds indicated that she had arisen a few times but had been hesitant, or unable, to leave the area. At 6 p.m. the same day, two fishery biologists saw her in the mud at the edge of the lake and thought she acted lively. However, the next morning at 8 o'clock, as these men approached the area, they heard wolves barking. Rowing by in their boat, they saw that the moose was dead.

At noon I examined the carcass. There was a surface wound about half an inch wide on the left cheek, and several long gashes on the throat, but none of these had bled much. Horizontally across the upper left hind leg was a wound about 2½ inches deep, 4 inches wide, and 8 inches long. The exposed muscle hung ragged, appearing well chewed; undoubtedly, this was the wound ob-

served by the campers, Zerbey, and the biologists. The only other exposed area was the pelvic region. The flesh there had been eaten through to the coelom, and a few loops of intestine were pulled from the body. Probably most of this damage resulted from feeding, for none of the observers mentioned wounds in this area although they did notice the less conspicuous upper-leg injury.

This cow was in wear-class V and harbored 57 hydatid cysts in her lungs.

During the next 2 days, I saw (from an aircraft) at least three, and possibly four, wolves on a nearby ridge, and heard at least four. These may have represented both small packs or part of the big pack.

71. (March 12, 1961. A b o u t 1½ miles southeast of the northeast end of Lake Desor.) From March 6 to 11, the aircraft underwent its 100-hour check, so no aerial work was done until the 12th. About 10 a.m. the large pack was found at a fresh kill southwest of Halloran Lake. Tracks showed that the last kill had been near Fisherman's Home. While backtracking the wolves from there, we saw a lone wolf also backtracking them along the northwest shore of Siskiwit Bay at 10:30 a.m. We continued following the trail to the above location, where a badly wounded moose lay on an open hillside. Tracks showed that the large pack had wounded this animal, stayed around for at least several

Figure 94—A lone wolf waiting for a wounded moose to weaken.

Figure 95—The wounded moose stands upon approach of the wolf.

hours and then abandoned it. This probably happened about March 8.

At 12:20 p.m. we saw the lone wolf 1½ miles from the moose, still backtracking the pack. From the animal's attitude when approaching I had little doubt that it knew the wounded moose was there. When 250 yards away the wolf ran excitedly up the trail but became cautious when 50 yards away and circled to the west to approach. I learned later that the moose was a bull. He was lying in a blood-soaked patch of snow about 15 feet in diameter which he had not left since the attack. As the wolf came within 30 yards, he arose (12:55 p.m.). The wolf approached to within 10 feet, circled the bull a few minutes, and went off 30 feet and lay down (figure 94). After 5 minutes, the moose lay down; immediately the wolf ran to him, so the moose stood (figure 95). The wolf lay down about 20 feet away, and 10 minutes later the bull lay down. Again the wolf threatened him, tail wagging excitedly, and seemed to try for his nose but failed. The moose just stood without moving quickly or threatening the wolf. A few minutes later the wolf lay down again. The bull continued standing at least from 1:20 until 1:45 p.m. when we left to refuel.

From 2:45 to 3:30 the wolf lay sprawled on its side about 20 feet from the moose, which continued standing.

At 4:45 the bull was alive but lying down, and the wolf was tugging at his rump. Intermittently the moose

watched the wolf but made no threats. He seemed to have no feeling in the rump, or more probably, he was too weak to stop the wolf. At 5:55 the moose was still alive, but by 6:30 p.m. he was dead, lying on his right side.

The next morning at 11 o'clock, I examined the carcass. The only apparent wounded areas were the rump and thighs, but the pelvic region had been fed upon, so it also may have been wounded. The animal was a bull in wear-class VIII and was heavily parasitized with ticks and hydatid cysts, although the femur marrow was normal.

DISCUSSION OF KILLING TECHNIQUES

In all kills witnessed, the first point of attack was the rump. In fact, this region was the only site of severe wounds on the two adults examined from the ground (figure 96). During 1956 and 1957, Cole (1957) observed adult moose on Isle Royale wounded in the thighs. In Alaska, Burkholder (1959:9) chased off a pack of wolves attacking a moose. The animal died that night and was examined from the ground the next day. "The only injuries observed consisted of deep bites and tears on the hams above the hocks. The animal was not hamstrung, the tendons being still intact. No other wounds were noted." Cowan (1947: 159) examined several elk kills and "in each instance the attack had been from the rear and side with the wolf seizing the flank at the point where the leg joins the abdomen." In Minnesota, a moose was reported wounded on the hind flanks by wolves (Stenlund, 1955).

Young and Goldman (1944) reported that wolves hamstring their prey and eat out the hams. However, no evidence of hamstringing was found during the present study; and Burkholder, Cowan, and Stenlund each stated specifically that they observed no instance in which wolves hamstrung their prey. During caribou studies in the Northwest Territories, Banfield (1954:47) found that hamstringing was seldom done. "The method that the wolf generally uses for killing a caribou is to race alongside of it and pull it down by grasping the flank, shoulder, or throat, with the jaws." Stenlund (1955:31) gave the following description of killing techniques used on deer:

No evidence of hamstringing of deer was found on freshly killed carcasses although the possibility does exist. Usually deer are run down from behind, the wolf or wolves biting at the hind flanks and abdomen, or at the hind flanks and head region simultaneously. Often the deer is knocked to the ground two or three times before it is killed. It is possible that some deer might even die from a combination of shock, fright, and exhaustion rather from actual wounds since in some cases it did not appear that animals were wounded badly enough to cause death.

Five of the six times I watched wolves wound moose, several animals slowed down the prey and occupied its attention by pulling at its rump,

Figure 96—Freshly killed moose showing wounded area.

and then one wolf grabbed the nose (figure 92). During the sixth hunt, trees obscured my view after the wolves attacked the animal's rump. Although the nose hold is not mortal, it stops the prey and distracts it from the wolves on the rump. In some hunting accounts furnished by Young and Goldman, mention is made of part of the pack distracting the prey at the front while others inflict significant damage to the rump.

Although the rump region contains no especially vital parts, it seems to be the least dangerous and most advantageous attack point on such a large animal as a moose. After the wolves rip through the 5-inch hair and thick hide, every injury to the upper-leg musculature would hinder the movement of the prey and render the animal more susceptible to intensified attack. Once downed and besieged by several wolves, the moose succumbs quickly. Each of three calves and one adult was killed within 10 minutes.

A p p a r e n t l y many adults are wounded, left to stiffen and weaken from their rump wounds, and then killed (figure 93). Three instances were observed in which this tactic was employed, and Cole (1957) reported two. Probably bulls attacked by the large pack, and any adults tackled by the smaller packs, are likely to be victims of this tactic. This probably is not done purposely; rather it appears to result from the wolves' failure to wound a moose sufficiently to incapacitate it.

Sometimes when the wolves wound a moose, they cannot complete the kill, so they abandon the animal. The moose probably dies within a week, and there are indications that the wolves return and feed on the carcass. The animal involved in Hunting Account 2 was abandoned on February 24, 1959, but on March 13 the pack was feeding on a kill within a quarter-mile of where the animal had been left. Of course, there is no certainty that this moose was the one abandoned. An observation on March 15, 1960, also may be significant. After we followed the large pack all day, the animals began exploring a swamp southwest of Halloran Lake. They did not appear to be hunting but seemed to be searching for something. Eventually they discovered a calf carcass beneath a clump of cedars and began feeding. The femur marrow of the animal was fat-depleted and the stomach was full of cedar. Since this area is heavily hunted by the wolves, it seems unlikely that a moose would get a chance to starve to death. It is more likely that the wolves had wounded and abandoned the animal in this area, and that the only available browse was the small amount of cedar from surrounding trees.

On another occasion, when the wolves had not eaten for 4 days, we followed them all day until they excitedly entered a small clump of trees. Although there was no chase, the animals raced to the clump and gathered there. After about 45 minutes, a few left the clump and lay in the open for the rest of the day.

The next day we found that they had fed on a carcass under the trees. Either they killed the moose while we circled above (doubtful, since their actions did not indicate this), or they found the carcass. The femur marrow was normal, so the animal was not in a state of extreme emaciation. Perhaps it had been wounded and abandoned weeks before.

The moose involved in Hunting Account 72 undoubtedly would have died within a few days if the lone wolf had not finished it off, for it remained for days in a small area, which soon was completely browsed out.

MOOSE DEFENSE

Regarding the senses of moose, Peterson (1955:102) found that ". . . the ears often serve to alert the animal, the eyes to investigate, while the final stimulus, causing immediate reaction, is transmitted by smell." Moose behavior during the present study indicated the same. Since wolves generally traveled upwind to their intended prey, they often approached to within 100 yards before discovery by the moose. Under certain conditions, moose sensed wolves when a quarter of a mile away, but on one occasion the pack came within about 5 feet of two moose in their beds. Differences in wind direction and velocity, cover, terrain, and other factors probably accounted for the varying abilities of moose to sense wolves.

No observations were made on the summer defense of moose against wolves, but two reports indicated that the animals seek refuge in water when threatened. In 1958, campers related to D. L. Allen that they saw a cow and calf enter Tobin Harbor at its head. Then three wolves emerged from the woods, paced the shore about three times, and returned into the brush. A similar occurrence was noticed by Mrs. Alfreda Gale of Tobin Harbor and H. T. Orsborn of Rock Harbor. Mrs. Gale reported that, in July 1959, she and Orsborn spotted a moose "prancing and snorting" about 20 feet from shore in Gutt Bay, Tobin Harbor. Then they spied a wolf on shore near the moose and were convinced that the moose was taking refuge from it. After a few seconds, the wolf ran off, but the moose remained in the water for several minutes.

Sign around remains of a calf killed by wolves about August 5, 1960, indicated that the moose had been killed in the shallow water of an old beaver pond. Apparently, it sought protection in the pond but did not reach deep water. Cowan (1947:160) reported that "on several occasions single deer, elk, and moose have been seen making use of this defensive behavior . . .," and Peterson (1955:-104) agreed that ". . . moose regularly make for the nearest water when seeking protection from predators."

In seven hunts (11 animals) witnessed in winter, moose detected wolves before being discovered, and in each case, the moose immediately left the area. Since it will be shown that a low percentage of moose tested by wolves are killed, it is safe to assume that most of the above-mentioned moose were not highly vulnerable and that, nevertheless, they chose to avoid an encounter with the predators.

During 36 hunts involving 73 moose, the animals fled without being attacked (table 16). They all were pursued, but either obtained adequate headstarts, outdistanced the wolves, or outlasted them. Soon after the wolves discontinued a chase, the pursued animal stopped and watched its backtrail. Several times moose in such situations appeared to be saving their strength until hard pressed. Murie (1944) noticed that caribou frequently stood around w a t c h i n g nearby wolves ". . . when they could have been moving away to a more secure position." Perhaps this was for the

same reason, for caribou also depend upon speed and endurance to escape wolves.

Even when the wolves overtook their quarry, in many cases the moose continued running until their pursuers tired. In seven instances (nine animals) moose ran at least half a mile before the wolves abandoned chase. Three animals, including a cow and calf, traveled about 2½ miles, and another cow and calf ran approximately 3 miles before the wolves gave up. During long pursuits, even after the pack stops, the moose usually continue running for at least a quarter of a mile.

The gait of a moose chased by wolves appears effortless; the animal takes long, deliberate, trotter-like strides. The longest distance I saw moose maintain this gait was an estimated 3¼ miles. This was accomplished by a cow and calf closely pursued by the large pack on March

TABLE 16.—DEFENSIVE BEHAVIOR OF MOOSE ENCOUNTERED BY LARGE PACK OF WOLVES OR PART OF IT [a]

[Parentheses indicate the number of hunts involved]

Year	Number of moose employing each defense		
	Ran [b]	Ran, then stood	Stood [c]
1959	12 (4)	0	2 (1)
1960	27 (12)	8 (7)	11 (7)
1961	34 (20)	4 (4)	11 (9)
Total	73 (36)	12 (11)	24 (17)

[a] Not including hunts in which animals were killed, or in which moose detected wolves first and left the area.
[b] Probably more in this category would have stood, if wolves had been close enough.
[c] More of these animals might have run, if wolves had not been so close.

11, 1960, and it helped them escape. Although healthy moose apparently can outlast wolves, they cannot outrun them. Once wolves catch up to a moose, they usually remain even with the animal unless deep snow or tangled blowdown interferes. However, the maximum speeds of the two species appear to be similar, for if a moose maintains about a 100-yard lead for 15 or 20 seconds, the wolves soon give up. Reported speeds for the moose are: 19 m.p.h. (Peterson, 1955), 22 m.p.h. (Findley, 1951), 27 m.p.h. (Cowan, 1947), and 35 m.p.h. (Cottam and Williams, 1943); a moose maintained the latter speed for a quarter of a mile. Peterson reported that moose gallop occasionally when frightened, but I did not observe this gait used by any moose pursued by wolves.

Running moose were not hindered by blowdown, thick swamps, or 3 feet of snow. Peterson (1955) found that 30 inches of encrusted snow presented little hindrance to moose, but cited findings by Wright et al. that crusted snow lacerates their legs, seriously hampering travel. Murie (1944) also mentioned this hazard. Since strong crusts apparently did not form on Isle Royale until early spring, no observations were made on this subject. However, in late March and early April, crusty snow might be a significant factor in wolf-moose relationships. In British Columbia, changing snow conditions were found to affect predation on moose profoundly. Stanwell-Fletcher (1942) reported that wolves did not hunt

moose "in earnest" until the end of January, when 6 to 8 feet of snow impeded travel by the latter.

Since so many moose escaped by running (even those which the wolves overtook and chased for more than a mile), running appears to be a successful defense. However, each of the five mortal attacks witnessed from the beginning involved running animals. Perhaps this is because a moose does not employ the most effective weapons, its hoofs, so easily when running as when standing still, and because weak or inferior animals, which may be afraid to defy wolves, probably are among those moose that flee. Since any weakness probably affects the ability of a moose both to run and utilize its hoofs effectively, the wolves soon might sense the animal's debility.

Twelve moose, involved in 11 hunts, fled as wolves approached but stopped before, or as soon as, the pack caught up. The moose then stood at bay and held off the wolves. In 17 other instances, 24 moose stood their ground immediately, including 4 cows with calves. In addition, a cow and calf stood at first and then defensively strode off with wolves following for about a quarter of a mile.

None of the 24 moose which stood at bay throughout an attack was killed or wounded. I do not know whether this is because only strong, healthy, "confident" animals defy their attackers or because defiant moose are so formidable. Probably the reasons are of equal importance. It is obvious that moose which stand their ground when confronted by wolves enjoy full command of the situation (figure 1). On February 28, 1961, I saw a moose stride boldly for about 70 yards to meet seven approaching wolves which turned and left when the moose was about 30 yards away.

It is easy to see why wolves fear an enraged moose. With mane erect, ears flattened back, neck extended and head held low, the surrounded animal lashes out at the nearest wolf, and wheels quickly to chase any individual which dares close in behind. Both fore and hind hoofs are used with great facility and exactness. Sometimes a harassed moose backs against a conifer or other protection for its rear. Because my observations were from an aircraft, only the conspicuous manifestations of rage were seen, but Denniston (1956:111) provided a more complete description of the rage pattern:

In this pattern the mane is erected, the ears flattened back against the neck, the lips retracted, the tongue protruded and curled up over the upper lip and nose and repeatedly darted in and out licking the upper lip. The animal usually rears on its hind legs pawing the air with the forefeet, if the stimulus object is at a distance of less than about forty feet.

An informative close-up account of defensive behavior of an Isle Royale moose against a dog is furnished by Hickie (n.d.:28):

The cow . . . charged Togo, ears back, head close to forelegs with outstretched neck and bristling mane, and both fore and hind feet stamping at every jump— and how she came! We barely had time to get around behind a cabin before she charged past. Togo tried to duck to the side, but the heavy snow was too much for him and he floundered. I thought it was all up with him, for she caught him and pounded him with her front feet; but as luck would have it, her aim was poor and he ran toward me. She wheeled and caught him, again rolling him in the snow. This time he managed to roll back under her front legs, scramble out to one side and run down towards the house. After this Togo stayed his distance and as soon she laid back her her ears and moved towards him, he was gone like a flash down the trail.

I once watched a moose beat two wolves into the snow, but these escaped unharmed; apparently the blows were softened by the snow. In another instance a 9-month-old calf pounded a wolf clinging to its throat and finally persuaded the animal to seek a less-hazardous hold; but the wolf was not hurt. In British Columbia, a large male wolf was found barely alive, with broken ribs and legs. "Surrounded by moose tracks, blood patches and moose hair, the wolf had been cripped in a great battle" (Stanwell-Fletcher, 1942:138). In the Canadian Northwest Territories, MacFarlane (1905) found a live adult wolf with a hind leg shattered by a kick from a bull moose.

When a moose stands defiantly at bay, the wolves try to force it to run, but unless it does, they abandon it. Once when a moose stood its ground, the wolves left within 30 seconds, and the longest the pack harrassed an uninjured standing moose was 5 minutes. Cowan (1947) reported instances of a cow elk standing off seven wolves and of a moose discouraging three wolves by standing and striking with its forefeet. Additional evidence that Isle Royale wolves fear moose at bay was afforded by five observed hunts in which the pack chased one of a group of moose until it stopped, and then immediately pursued one of the other fleeing animals. Even when a moose is wounded but throws the wolves and stands its ground, the wolves fail to continue the attack. In each of four instances observed in which a moose was only wounded, the animal finally stood at bay. The wolves then waited for it to weaken considerably before attacking again. In two of the cases they eventually left the wounded moose. This evidence emphasizes that when a moose stands its ground, the wolves are reluctant to attack.

Defense of the calf in winter is quite strong and sterotyped. If wolves are detected soon enough, the cow leads her calf quickly away. If the wolves pursue in such a situation, or if they surprise the moose, the cow immediately rushes to the rear of the calf. In four observations, the two moose stood at bay, and the wolves left within a minute. While standing off a pack of wolves, the cow makes short charges at the animals and instantly returns to the calf's rump. If necessary, the calf employs its front feet for defense, but these probably do not afford adequate protection. In each of the observed cases, the cow provided the effective defense.

In eight hunts the cow and calf ran from the wolves, and in six of these the wolves pursued closely for long distances, once for about 3 miles. During such chases, the moose run slowly and deliberately, with the cow staying close to the calf's rump. If any wolf threatens the calf, the cow charges it but immediately returns to the calf. When the two animals are together they constitute an invulnerable team. The calf charges wolves in front of it, and the cow protects the rear and flanks of the calf and kicks any wolves at her rear. However, while traveling through varying cover and over widely dissimilar terrain, the two cannot always remain together. If a calf gets a few yards from the cow, the wolves close in; if the cow does not rush in promptly, the calf is doomed. Each of the three calves which I saw killed was separated from its parent while running.

Little is known about the summer defense of the calf. Murie (1944) described a cow standing and protecting her newborn calf from two wolf-size huskies. Peterson (1955) discussed the close relationship between cow and calf, and related personal observations of the strong protective instinct of the cow. (For a discussion and analysis of the strong cow-calf bond, see Altmann, 1958.) During the first week or two of a calf's life, the cow would have to stand off wolves instead of leading the calf away, for the calf could not run fast or far enough. On May 22, 1961, I startled a cow and very young calf about 100 feet away. The calf failed to keep up with the cow, so the cow had to wait for it. At times, the calf dropped about 25 feet behind. If the cow were to behave in this manner with a wolf in pursuit, the wolf probably could catch it before the cow could interfere. Undoubtedly, a single bite from a wolf would incapacitate a young calf. Had I been a wolf, however, the cow probably would have stood her ground, or at least remained close to her calf.

An encounter on June 13, 1961, demonstrated the attitude probably assumed by a cow and calves retreating from wolves. While I stood on a moose trail photographing moose in Ojibway Lake, a cow and twin calves ambled down the trail behind me, about 30 feet away. Since there were no nearby trees to climb, I motioned to alert the animals to my presence before they got too close. The cow stopped, grunted, and laid back her ears, and the calves huddled around her hind legs. She acted quite "confident" while I fumbled with my camera. Then she turned and headed slowly and deliberately away, the calves remaining at her heels.

W. Leslie Robinette reported an incident to me which showed what might be in store for wolves which attempt to bother a calf. While studying moose browse in the park, on May 19, 1961, Robinette happened upon a cow and newborn calf (with umbilicus still apparent) south of Siskiwit Lake. After ob-

serving the pair from one tree for 45 minutes, he climbed another for better visibility. Each time he changed position, the cow snorted and her mane bristled. When he descended the second time, the cow charged. Robinette ducked behind the nearest tree just as the animal straddled the tree and pounded the ground on each side of him; her nose was but a few inches from his. Immediately after the initial attack, the cow returned to her calf.

PREDATION EFFICIENCY

Many biologists have suspected that predators have a low rate of hunting success, but quantitative evidence for this belief is not easily obtained. One of the few studies comparing figures on successful and unsuccessful hunts by any predator is Rudebeck's (1950, 1951). By recording observations of all hunts by four species of European raptores for 5 years, Rudebeck found that only 7.6 percent of 688 attempts to secure prey were successful. Success percentages for individual species varied from 4.5 percent to 10.8 percent.

The present study provided the opportunity to obtain figures on the rate of success, or "predation efficiency," of the large pack of wolves (table 17). A total of 160 moose were estimated to be within range of the hunting wolves while under observation, but only 131 were detected. Of these, 77 were tested by the wolves; i.e., the wolves chased them or held them at bay, so those which escaped did so because of their superior condition or ability. Those which were detected but not tested also may have escaped on this basis, but circumstance probably was more important. Therefore, predation efficiency is considered here as the percentage of animals tested that are killed. Since 6 moose were dispatched out of 77 tested, the predation efficiency is 7.8 percent. The almost-exact agreement with Rudebeck's figure undoubtedly is coincidental, but the fact that both percentages are of the same order of magnitude is notable.

Several other authors have reported that wolves make many vain attempts to secure prey (Murie, 1944; Cowan, 1947; Harper, Ruttan, and Benson, 1955; Crisler, 1956), although Burkholder (1959:9) stated that "there was no evidence during this period of my study to indicate that wolves, even singly, had a diffi-

cult time catching adult caribou." After extensive study of wolf-Dall sheep relations, Murie (1944:109) concluded that

Many bands seem to be chased, given a trial, and if no advantage is gained or weak animals discovered, the wolves travel on to chase other bands until an advantage can be seized. The sheep may be vulnerable because of their poor physical condition, due to old age, disease, or winter hardships. Sheep in their first year also seem to be specially susceptible to the rigors of winter. The animals may be vulnerable because of the situation in which they are surprised. . . . My general observations indicate that weak animals are the ones most likely to be found in such situations.

Murie also witnessed several caribou hunts in which wolves appeared to be testing a herd for weak animals. Regarding predation on moose, Murie (1944:186) stated

Wolves perhaps worry many moose which fight them off with such vigor that

TABLE 17.———RESULTS OF HUNTS BY THE LARGE PACK [a]

[Figures in parentheses indicate number of hunts involved]

Year	Total hunts	Number of moose				
		In range	Detected	Tested	Wounded	Killed
1959.........	7	16	15 (6)	7 (5)	2 (2)	1 (1)
1960.........	44	83	66 (33)	48 (26)	5 (5)	5 (5)
1961.........	34	61	50 (27)	22 (15)	....	....
Total......	85	160	131 (66)	77 (46)	7 (7)	6 (6)
Percent in range.....................		81. 9	48. 1	4. 4	3. 7
Percent detected.........................			58. 8	5. 3	4. 4
Percent tested.........................				9. 1	[b] 7. 8

[a] In several of the 1961 hunts, only 7 or 8 wolves were involved, but figures from these hunts are included.
[b] "Predation efficiency."

they are unwilling to expose themselves to the deadly hoofs. However, if any sign of faltering is shown, due to old age, food shortage, or disease, the wolves would no doubt become aware of it, and one would expect them to become more persistent in their attack in hope of wearing down the animal. Moose which are actually known to have been killed by wolves should be closely examined to determine their condition. Unfortunately in many cases the evidence is destroyed.

PATTERNS OF SELECTION IN THE MOOSE KILL

Since such a low percentage of moose tested are killed, wolves probably are selecting certain types of individuals. These could be weak or inferior moose, or merely animals in unfavorable situations. The latter possibility seems unlikely, for observations have been made of unsuccessful hunts occurring on several types of terrain, in various cover, and in diverse situations.

Information on sex, age, and condition of wolf-killed moose was obtained from remains found both from the aircraft in winter and from ground search in summer, as described on page 115.

Sex and Age Distribution. When possible, sex and age data were secured from all moose remains. Sex determination was based on the presence or absence of antlers or antler pedicels. The sex ratio of winter wolf kills was 22 females to 11 males, indicating a strong selection for cows, at least during February and March (assuming an even sex ratio in the population). However, the sexable

remains found by ground search in spring and summer, which should include year-round mortality, showed a ratio of 18 females to 27 males. If there has been an even sex ratio in the population for the last few years, the number of males and females in this category of remains should be even. The preponderance of males might be caused by the probability that the more massive male skulls remained intact longer than female skulls; thus, more females than males would be classified "unknown." Since many of the remains found by ground search consisted only of old, bleached bones, a high proportion of the sample includes animals dead several years. If data from animals which probably died before 1955 are eliminated, the sex ratio is 8 females to 7 males.

Age estimates were based upon mandibles, toothrows, or molariform teeth collected from the remains. Specimens of like molar-wear patterns were segregated, and 10 classes corresponding to those described by Passmore *et al.* (1955) resulted. These authors estimated that classes I to IV correspond to the specimen's actual age but that classes V to IXA contain specimens varying 2, 3, or more years in age; e.g., class VII might contain specimens from 8½ to 10½ years old. However, Sergeant and Pimlott (1959) aged moose on the basis of annuli found in sectioned incisors, apparently a more precise and accurate method. They compared age estimates provided by Passmore *et al.* with their own for the same wear classes, and concluded that both variation in age, and maximum age, were greater in most classes than formerly thought; e.g., class VII included specimens 10 to 17 years old. In the present study, the ages furnished by Sergeant and Pimlott for each wear class were accepted as more representative of actual ages of the specimens.

The similarity in age composition between remains representing year-round mortality and those of winter wolf kills can be seen in table 18. The greatest bias undoubtedly occurs in the calf class of the year-round sample, for calf remains would be hardest to find and would disintegrate sooner. Nevertheless, both samples indicate that calves bear more losses than any other class. This is expected merely because calves form the largest single class. To demonstrate that wolves select calves, one must prove they kill a larger proportion of calves than exists in the population. Since calves composed a 3-year average of 15 percent of the sampled winter population but 36 percent of the 3-year sample of winter kills, a definite selection for calves is indicated, at least in that season.

In Alaska, Burkholder (1959) found that six of seven ageable, winter wolf kills were calves, and one was a yearling.

During summer, calves seem to compose even a higher proportion of the kill, if scat-analysis figures are valid indicators (table 10). In scats from 3 summers, there were 162 occurrences of moose remains identifi-

TABLE 18.—AGE DISTRIBUTION OF DEAD MOOSE

Wear classes [a]	Estimated age [b] (years)	Number of winter wolf kills [c]	Number of remains found by ground search [d]
Calf		18	18
I	1		1
II	2–3		2
III	3–4		1
IV	4–7		4
V	6–10	3	8
VI	8–15	15	8
VII	10–17	3	6
VIII		5	5
IX			4
IXA	[e] 20?	6	
Total		50	57

[a] Passmore et al. (1955).
[b] Sergeant and Pimlott (1959).
[c] Found from aircraft. See page 115 for qualification.
[d] In spring and summer.
[e] Passmore et al. (1955: 238).

able as calf or adult; of these, 75 percent were calf remains. (These statistics might be biased toward calf remains because calves have a higher proportion of hair—the primary identifiable remain in scats—than do adults. Also see page 164.) In addition, three of the four moose found fed upon by wolves in summer were calves. Cowan (1947: 167) reported that, in British Columbia, all remains of moose in the summer wolf scats he examined were calf remains. However, he cautioned that moose calves are more prone to accidents than are the young of other big game, and that "carrion may well make up a fair part of the calf moose item."

Calves probably are especially vulnerable to wolf predation because, like other growing animals, they are smaller, weaker, less experienced, and less independent than adults. In winter, calves may be heavily infested with ticks (see page 107), which probably would predispose them to predation. Fenstermacher (1937) reported that ticks are particularly debilitating, and Peterson (1955:186) believes that ". . . the most serious effects of tick parasitism are manifested in the reduction of the vitality of the moose, making them more vulnerable to other factors, such as diseases, predation, abortion, and malnutrition." In British Columbia, Hatter (1950a) discovered that calves constituted two-thirds of 161 moose found dead from tick-malnutrition complex early in 1947.

Since calves depend so completely on their mothers for protection from wolves, the condition of cows also is all-important to calf survival.

The most significant information in table 18 is that most moose in wear-classes I to IV are invulnerable to wolf predation. This is obvious in the winter wolf-kill sample, but the year-round category also strongly indicates the same. The few specimens in classes I to III of the latter sample could be results of accidents, for animals of any age are susceptible to accidental deaths.

It is surprising that yearlings are so secure from wolf predation. In February and March, short-yearlings are killed despite their mother's protection, but apparently by June, when they become independent, they seldom are taken. Many yearlings in June seem no larger than they do in March, so size probably does not make the difference in early summer. Possibly the primary reason that few yearlings are killed is that wolves change their hunting habits. Just after yearlings are forced away by their parents, a new crop of calves is produced, and wolves undoubtedly prey on these throughout the summer. Meanwhile, the yearlings g r o w quickly and by August probably are large enough to protect themselves. Murie (1944) found that wolves in Mount McKinley National Park preyed heavily upon caribou calves and took only a few adults during the summer.

Moose in wear-class VI, estimated at 8 to 15 years old, seem to be preyed upon most. Of course, individuals older than these would be as vulnerable, or probably more so, but since most kills are in the 8- to 15-year-old class, few older animals remain. Even if a moose population were not hunted by man or wolves, one would expect most adult mortality to occur in the oldest age classes.

No figures are available on the age distribution of moose mortality in other areas for comparison with the Isle Royale statistics. However, Peterson (1955:176), without furnishing figures, stated that "a great majority of the skeletal remains of moose found in the St. Ignace area were of old animals with well-worn teeth." Sources of mortality included wolf predation.

In Mount McKinley National Park, Murie (1944) established that over 50 percent of adult Dall sheep mortality occurs in ages 9 to 14 years. Tener (1954) found that, in the Canadian Northwest Territories, 21 of 24 adult musk-ox remains were from animals at least 6 years old. He believes that many of these had been killed by wolves. During a study of wolves and deer in Minnesota, Stenlund (1955:43) concluded that "there is no indication that wolves tend to take old animals in preference to those in the prime of life." However, his figures seem to indicate that the predators were selecting older animals, for of 29 wolf-killed adults, only 3 were yearlings or 2-year-olds. Burkholder (1959:7) found in his Alaskan studies that four of five ageable wolf-killed caribou adults were over 4 years old, although he states that "all of the wolf kills I could check were in excellent condition and of the 'age of primeness'."

Probably most workers would consider moose 6 to 12 years old in their prime. Indeed, the growth curve for bulls, provided by Skuncke (*vide* Peterson, 1955:77) shows that bulls gain weight until at least 12 years of age. Nevertheless, many of the wolf-killed moose on Isle Royale were in this category. Probably the significant point about wolf predation on any big game is not so much the selection for old animals, but rather *selection against young animals* (other than calves). In the present study, the invulnerability of adults less than 6 years old is striking. In addition, Murie's (1944) sample of remains of 829 Dall sheep shows that a total of only 3.4 percent of the mortality involved animals aged 2, 3, or 4 years. The figures from Tener and Stenlund, and even the limited data from Burkholder, also support the thesis that most big-game animals in their first few years are safe from wolf predation.

Young animals may be relatively invulnerable because they are more alert or they may be faster, stronger, and more agile. Perhaps they should be considered "prime," instead of the more mature individuals usually regarded as such, for security from wolves certainly is a realistic criterion. Of course, young animals could be less susceptible only because they might inhabit areas less frequented by wolves, but, at least in the case of Isle Royale moose, this seems improbable.

Incidence of Debilitating Conditions. One explanation for the vulnerability of apparently prime moose is that they are infected heavily with hydatid cysts (*Echinococcus*). Cowan (1947:17) proposed that the high proportion of elk kills which he found in the "prime"ages might have resulted from the heavy hydatid infections. On Isle Royale, cysts were found in the lungs of one moose each in wear-classes IV, V, and VIII. The youngest animal had only 5, but the others harbored 57 and 35, respectively. Because the parasite is contracted as moose feed, older animals should have heavier infections. Ritcey and Edwards (1958) found this to be true in British Columbia moose. In 6 or 7 years a moose might ingest enough eggs to cause a heavy infection. A very heavy infection in a moose about 4 years old was found in the British Columbia studies.

It has been well demonstrated that a higher proportion of older animals are infected with hydatid cysts than are younger ones. In Saskatchewan, Harper *et al.* (1955) found that only 1 of 12 immature moose examined harbored hydatid cysts whereas 13 of 31 adults were infected. The same trend was noted in deer and caribou. Rausch (1959) showed Alaska harbored cysts, but 15 percent of animals in wear-classes I, II, and III were infected, and 62 percent of those in classes VII, VIII,

and IX. R. O. Skoog found cysts in only 4 of 67 caribou examined, and all 4 were over 7 years old (Rausch and Williamson, 1959).

Undoubtedly, heavily infected animals are more susceptible to predation. Fenstermacher (1937) believes that hydatid cysts are especially debilitating, and Cowan (1951:52) stated: "Infected animals are usually impoverished and of low vitality. They almost certainly have an impaired ability to survive adverse circumstances." However, Rausch (1952) disagrees, for he saw 18 cysts (80 to 90 mm. in diameter) in an Alaskan moose in apparently excellent condition. Nevertheless, it seems that such an animal would have little power to run far, or to fight off wolves. The observation by Ritcey and Edwards (quoted on page 111) is especially significant in this respect.

In Ontario, a fresh wolf-killed moose with diseased lungs was found, and signs showed that it had not fought much (Peterson, 1955). A lung was removed and sent to the Royal Ontario Museum of Zoology. Peterson (1955:176) described it as follows:

When the lung was examined in the museum laboratory it was found to be so completely filled with hydatid cysts of tapeworms that it seemed incredible that it could have functioned sufficiently to keep the animal alive during normal activity, much less allow it to ward off an attack by timber wolves. Well over 50 percent of the volume of the lung was occupied by large cysts up to one inch in diameter.

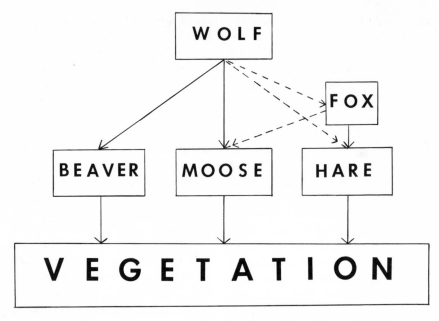

Figure 97—Most important relationships in wolf ecology. (Solid arrows indicate primary relationships.)

Crisler (1956, 1958) described a "tired" caribou running from wolves, faltering, lying down, and being killed. The lungs contained eight cysts, some as big as ping-pong balls. One of the caribou kills examined by Burkholder (1959) also harbored hydatid cysts, but the author did not elaborate.

Philosophically, it seems logical that a heavy hydatid infection should predispose a moose to predation, for the parasite depends for its perpetuation on the moose being eaten by a wolf. The greater the intermediate host's infection, the more beneficial it would be to the parasite to render the host susceptible to predation.

Old moose even without cysts or other debilitating organisms probably would be susceptible to predation because of their general infirmity and lack of agility. However, many old moose undoubtedly are infected with parasites and/or disease, which probably would increase their chances of succumbing to predation. Only two relatively intact carcasses of wolf-killed adults were examined, but each had a heavy hydatid infection. The one checked in winter also was heavily infested with ticks, and had an abnormal liver and badly congested lungs.

All that remained of most kills investigated were bones, but these also showed that many of the moose had been in poor condition. The marrow was fat-depleted or nearly so in the femurs of 5 (14 percent) of 33 adults checked; and 9 (29 percent) of 31 adult skulls or mandibles were necrotic, probably from actinomycosis (figure 86). In the total of 35 adult kills from winter plus 1 from summer, 14 (39 percent) had depleted marrow, jaw necrosis, or hydatid cysts. Some of the animals showed more than one of these conditions and probably also supported heavy tick populations (figure 84). Undoubtedly, a thorough examination of the intact carcasses of these moose would have revealed a much higher percentage of debilitating conditions.

Other studies indicate that adults of big game killed by wolves generally are old or diseased. Murie (1944) discovered that although most Dall sheep mortality occurs in the old-age category, mortality in the prime class includes a much higher percentage of diseased individuals. In the Rocky Mountain national parks of Canada, Cowan (1947) found that 17 (37 percent) of the remains of 46 adult-elk kills were either senile or diseased; and he cautioned that a condition such as hydatid infection is not evident from bones, so many others also may have been diseased. Crisler (1956:346) reported that "at least half of the kills that we observed involved crippled or sick caribou." However, all 5 fresh adult kills (4 caribou and 1 long-yearling moose) examined by Burkholder (1959) were judged to be in excellent condition, although at least one of these was infected with *Echinococcus*.

Species of Lesser Significance

Isle Royale wolves influence species other than moose to a much lesser degree. Some of these are less important prey animals and others are scavengers. Probably none has a great effect on the wolf, but a consideration of wolf ecology must recognize these potential and actual relationships insofar as they are known.

BEAVER

The Isle Royale beaver population apparently reached its peak from 1945 to 1950 (page 19), and in the early 1950's a sharp decline was noticed by park residents. Today beavers are common, but compared to peak numbers, the population appears low. Since wolf sign first was noticed about the time the decrease occurred, a cause and effect relationship was postulated by residents of the island.

Although beavers have not been reported as primary food for any wolf population, they supplement the diets of wolves in many areas. Beaver remains occurred in 7 percent of 420 scats from the Rocky Mountain national parks of Canada (Cowan, 1947) and composed 10.5 percent of the occurrences in 76 wolf scats from Ontario (Peterson, 1955). On Isle Royale, beavers are the second most important wolf food (table 10); beaver remains composed over 10 percent of the occurrences in 438 scats collected during the present study. The data are segregated by year and compared with previous records from Isle Royale, in table 19.

The manner in which wolves hunt beavers is unknown, but possibly they follow shorelines until a beaver is found on land. Such an animal should be easy prey. In autumn and early spring, when beavers are most active on land, they probably are most vulnerable. For much of winter the animals are safe, but under certain conditions a few may be taken as early as March. During thaws, ice sometimes cracks along docks and islands, leaving crevices which beavers could enlarge. In 1961 when thaws occurred in late February and early March, much beaver activity was evident on March 3. Holes in the ice, trails to trees (some 100 feet from the holes) were seen along streams, islands, and docks, and in two of these places, wolves had killed beavers.

The first beaver kill was found near the northeast end of Washington Island. A trail led toward shore from a hole in the ice near a dock, and a few feet out from shore was a large blood-spattered area packed with wolf tracks. There was no sign of moose or moose remains in the vicinity. A nearby wolf was chewing what appeared to be an everted beaver hide. Two wolves were leaving the island, and four others rested about 2 miles away. We could not land and verify our aerial observations, but from the sign and the unusual behavior of the wolves, there was no doubt that they had killed a beaver.

On the same day, we found remains of a beaver killed by the pack of three near a small island in Tobin Harbor. The wolves had investigated two beaver houses situated against the island and had found trails leading from them to some fresh cuttings. A few feet from one trail there was a large bloody area covered with wolf tracks. Beaver fur was scattered about, and a well-chewed skull lay nearby.

TABLE 19.—OCCURRENCE OF BEAVER REMAINS IN WOLF SCATS COLLECTED ON ISLE ROYALE

Year	Number of scats	Percent of occurrence	Source
1952	87	20	Cole, 1952a
1954	?	35	Cole, 1954
1955	8	50	G.A. Petrides [a]
1958	70	17	Present study
1959	214	12	Present study
1960	154	7	Present study
1958–60	438	11	Present study

[a] Analysis by L. D. Mech.

The only literature encountered concerning predation on beaver in winter involved coyotes. Packard (1940) found tracks of a beaver that had emerged from under the ice and traveled half a mile before being killed by three coyotes. On Isle Royale, "Mr. Skadburg related the details of one incident in which coyotes killed a beaver that had been feeding upon a fallen birch from a hole in the ice" (Cole, 1952b). Extensive fieldwork in late March and April probably would produce more observations of predation on beaver.

Ever since wolves arrived on Isle Royale, they undoubtedly have been killing beavers, but whether wolves are directly responsible for the beaver decline is unknown. Before the wolf population was established, many colonies had been abandoned (Krefting, 1963), and supplies of aspen, the preferred food, in the southwest and central sections of the island were judged low (Krefting, 1951). There is a reserve of white birch on most of the island even today, and beavers certainly eat birch, but whether they can thrive on it has not been determined.

The following statements by Cowan (1947:169) indicate that, at least in his study area, wolves were not primarily responsible for a beaver decline:

In 1930 the Athabaska Valley of Jasper Park was superlative beaver range and bore a very heavy population despite the abundance of predatory animals. The re-

Figure 98—Beaver.

moval of trees by these beavers at the time when the elk and moose were eliminating all seedling trees has had the inevitable result of rendering large areas of the park unsuitable for beaver.

There is little doubt that wolves and other predators are effective in reducing a beaver population that has eaten itself out.

I have seen no evidence that predators can prevent a beaver population from increasing until it is so large that safely available food becomes inadequate.

On Isle Royale, beavers that had depleted their aspen supply probably moved to new sites or traveled long distances to obtain aspen, increasingly exposing them to predation. In such a case, predation might be the immediate cause of a beaver decline, but the basic cause would be the shortage of preferred food. Undoubtedly any adverse conditions undergone by a beaver population will result in increased predation; the important distinction to make is whether wolves are primary or secondary causes of the decline. Little work on this aspect was done during the present study, but research is now underway on the ecology of Isle Royale beavers. It should furnish basic information from which a more definite statement can be made about wolf-beaver relations.

SNOWSHOE HARE

The Isle Royale hare population conceivably is a potential food source for the wolves. In British Columbia, Stanwell-Fletcher (1942: 139) found that when the snow crusted ". . . snowshoe rabbits be-

came once more a part of the wolf diet." Murie (1944:58) maintained that "if hares were plentiful they would probably supplement the food supply of wolves considerably." However, it appears that, on Isle Royale, hares are eaten only incidentally and that even a high population hardly would affect the wolf.

Isle Royale hare numbers increased considerably during the present study, as evidenced by increased percentages of hare remains in fox scats, reports from island residents, and observations of hares and tracks (table 20). Even so, the percentage of occurrence of hare remains in 438 wolf scats was only 3.1 percent, and no increase was evident from 1958 to 1960. The low representation of hare is at variance with findings by Cole (1952a) that hare remains composed 24 percent of the winter food of Isle Royale wolves, based on 87 scats. However, since coyotes still were present in 1952, possibly some scats were from coyotes, for Thompson (1952) demonstrated a great overlap in scat sizes of these species. The present figures do agree with statistics by Cowan (1947) and Thompson (1952), who reported that hare remains composed 7 percent of 420 scats from the Rocky Mountain national parks of Canada, and 5 percent of 435 scats from Wisconsin, respectively.

Observations of wolf-hare encounters also indicate that hares are not important to Isle Royale wolves. On February 6, 1961, the pack of

15 accidentally flushed three hares but paid no attention. Even a lone wolf, hunting moose, showed no interest in three hares it flushed, on February 3, 1961. In one of these instances, a hare circled counterclockwise and passed in front of the wolf; 20 seconds later the wolf crossed its trail without investigating.

Figure 99—Snowshoe hare.

To substitute enough hares for the average of 10 to 13 pounds of moose consumed daily, each wolf would have to take two or three a day, which might be an arduous task. Wolves probably have more difficulty catching hares than do foxes (which

TABLE 20.—EVIDENCE OF INCREASE IN HARE NUMBERS

Year	Percent of occurrence of hare remains in fox scats	Weeks of summer fieldwork per hare observation	Hours of flying per hare observation [a]
Summer 1958	17	7.0	
Winter 1959			115
Summer 1959	46	5.0	
Winter 1960			46
Summer 1960	52	.7	
Winter 1961			22

[a] Seen from aircraft during moose census or observations of wolves hunting.

feed regularly on them), because the latter can follow hares into thicker cover and smaller hiding places, and over deep snowdrifts. It probably is more efficient for wolves to concentrate on moose.

RED FOX

Foxes seem to be common on Isle Royale but not abundant. A strong limitation on numbers probably is winter food supply, for mice are relatively unavailable, and at least during the first year of the study, hares were scarce. Information on the diet of the fox was obtained by analysis of 295 scats collected from trails during three summers (table 21). Probably the sample was biased toward winter, for summer scats containing berries disintegrate quickly. Nevertheless, the dependence of foxes

on hares, at least during winter, is evident. Since the hare population is growing, perhaps fox numbers also will increase.

It is interesting that the most foxes observed from the air per day (10, on February 27) were seen in 1961. This is six more than the maximum per day seen during the first two winters. Although complete figures were not kept on number of animals observed per study period, until 1961, the highest number (29) definitely was seen in 1961. However, conclusions on population changes should not be based on observations alone, for biases are many. Most foxes are seen at moose remains on lakes, bays, and shores, where they are most apparent from the air. Variations in amount of time spent over any of these locations could produce widely

Figure 100—Red fox.
Photo by Don Murray.

different totals of animals seen. Since foxes were studied only incidentally, no evidence was obtained that allows absolute, or even relative, estimates of population size.

The most important relationship between the fox and the wolf involves the food gleaned by foxes from remains of wolf-killed moose. Although moose remains composed only 6 percent of the occurrences in the fox scats collected, a higher percentage of the winter diet may consist of moose. Scats on trails (the only places where scats were collected) would be left primarily by traveling animals, but many foxes apparently remain near moose kills for days; most of their scats would not be represented in the collection. During winter, foxes feed on almost every kill soon after the wolves leave, and on one occasion four animals were seen feeding on a carcass.

Although wolves generally benefit foxes, they sometimes kill them. Twice, foxes were seen to flee instantly upon sensing wolves. Another time, on March 15, 1960, I watched a wolf kill a fox. About 5:05 p.m. the large pack was heading through a spruce swamp about a mile southwest of Halloran Lake when suddenly the lead animal sprang toward a running fox 125 yards away. As the wolf passed a moose carcass, from which the animal had run, a second fox scurried off. Within about 15 yards the wolf caught the fox and shook it violently. It then carried the limp

TABLE 21.—ANALYSIS OF FOOD REMAINS IN 295 FOX SCATS COLLECTED FROM TRAILS

	1958	1959	1960	Total
Number of scats..................	20	113	162	295
Number of occurrences............	34	152	191	377
Food items	*Percent of occurrence*			
Snowshoe hare.....................	17	46	52	47
Bird.............................		10	15	12
Muskrat..........................	6	11	8	9
Moose............................	6	6	6	6
Insect...........................	17	7		4
Mouse............................	9	2	3	3
Red squirrel.....................	3	5	2	3
Snake............................	9	5	2	3
Unidentified mammal..............		3	5	3
Strawberry.......................	12	1	1	2
Shadberry........................	9		2	2
Miscellaneous *a*................		3	2	3
Unidentified fruit...............	12			1
Unidentified.....................			2	1

a Fish, soil, grass, fox, *Cornus* fruit, mountain ash fruits, string, paper, and cloth.

carcass under some trees. Half an hour later, I found that the wolf had ripped out the intestines of the fox and abandoned the animal, at least temporarily. The next day the carcass was gone; it may have been eaten or just carried back under the trees.

A contrasting observation was made on the day after the fox was killed. While the wolves fed on the moose carcass, a fox lay curled up about 100 feet away, apparently fast asleep. On another occasion, a fox ventured to within 100 feet of a lone wolf feeding on a moose carcass. Cole (1957) twice saw foxes closely approach wolves near moose carcasses, and found that "they seemed

Figure 101—Ravens about to tease some resting wolves.

to have little fear of the larger animals when abundant supplies of food existed nearby." Murie (1944) also reported instances in which foxes showed no fear of wolves. He concluded, in his Mount McKinley study, that "the relationship between the wolf and the fox seems to be one of mutual gain." Foxes secure food from wolf kills, and wolves enlarge fox dens for their own use.

On Isle Royale six fox pups were produced in 1961 in a den which certainly was large enough for a wolf den (page 71 and figure 60). In the previous 2 years it was vacant, and its original occupants remain unknown. This was the only den found, so nothing is known about this aspect of wolf-fox relationships on Isle Royale.

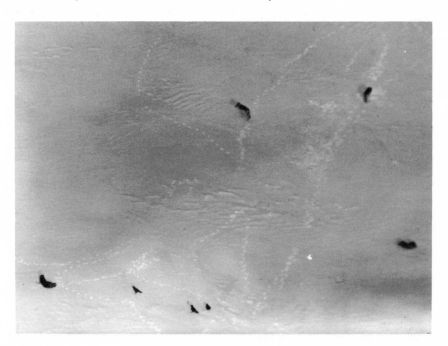

RAVEN

A peculiar relationship exists between the large pack of wolves and a flock of ravens. At every fresh kill, ravens perched in nearby trees, waiting to feed. The instant the wolves finished eating, these scavengers alighted on the carcass. Apparently kill remains provide the primary winter food for Isle Royale ravens.

Probably because these birds are so dependent on the wolves, small flocks regularly accompany the animals during their travels. They fly ahead of the pack, perch in trees until the wolves pass, and then "leapfrog" them again. Frequently, I even saw ravens tracking wolves. A bird so engaged flies directly over a string of tracks. Upon discovering a wolf scat, it thoroughly picks this apart and presumably swallows all edible portions, and then continues along the trail. I cannot remember any raven backtracking, so perhaps the birds deliberately track the wolves to overtake them and only feast on scats incidentally.

Once while the wolves attacked a moose, the ravens swirled around them excitedly. After the wolves wounded the moose, one bird sat in a tree and cawed as they tried to make the moose run. Sometimes the scavengers joined wolves in eating bloody snow.

Wolves and ravens often seem to play together, especially when the wolves rest on the ice, fully gorged (figure 101). The following account of activity noted on March 5, 1961, includes the range of "playful" behavior witnessed between wolves and ravens. As the pack traveled across a harbor, a few wolves lingered to rest, and four or five accompanying ravens began to pester them. The birds would dive at a wolf's head or tail, and the wolf would duck and then leap at them. Sometimes the ravens chased the wolves, flying just above their heads, and once, a raven waddled to a resting wolf, pecked its tail, and jumped aside as the wolf snapped at it. When the wolf retaliated by stalking the raven, the bird allowed it within a foot before arising. Then it landed a few feet beyond the wolf, and repeated the prank.

Crisler (1958) who observed similar activity from the ground, described it as follows:

He [a raven] let the pups trot to within six feet of him, then rose and settled a few feet away to await them again. He played this raven tag for ten minutes at a time. If the wolves ever tired of it, he sat squawking till they came over to him again.

Although Isle Royale wolves almost caught teasing ravens several times, I never saw them succeed; neither were raven remains found in any of the 438 wolf scats analyzed. Therefore, it appears that either the ravens are thoroughly familiar with the wolf's capabilities, or the wolves do not seriously attempt to capture the ravens.

COYOTE

Coyotes were present on Isle Royale from the early 1900's, but by February 1957, very few remained (page 19). Since no coyote or coyote sign was found during the present study, undoubtedly the species has been extirpated from Isle Royale. The cause of this is unknown, but the wolf may be responsible. During a study of British Columbia fauna, Munro (1947) recorded a report from a native who had found remains of a coyote killed and eaten by wolves. The man believed that where wolves invade an area, they drive the coyotes out. Minnesota wardens also discovered a coyote killed by wolves (Stenlund, 1955:46): "The male coyote had run onto the lake from the woods and was immediately killed by the wolves [three] which were running on the ice." Since coyotes and wolves are closely related and since wolves are strongly territorial, it is not unlikely that on a limited range, such as Isle Royale, wolves would chase, and probably kill, every coyote encountered.

Dynamics of Wolf-Moose Coaction

SINCE the approximate size and reproductive rate of the moose herd, and rate of kill by the wolves are known, deductions can be made about the long-range effect of predation on moose numbers. Unrefined calculations suggest that annual production and loss in the moose herd are about equal. If the winter rate of kill for the large pack (one moose per 3 days) applies year around, this pack removes about 122 moose per year. The smaller packs (totaling five or six members) probably kill about a third as many, or 41, giving a total annual mortality of 163 moose. An estimated 564 are present in late May when calves are born. Since calves composed 25 percent of the summer observations, extrapolation suggests that at least 188 calves are produced, indicating that the population would remain stable or increase slightly. However, a precise evaluation obviously is not this simple.

A more thorough appraisal of moose-population dynamics requires consideration of two key figures, annual calf production, and percentage of yearlings in the total population. As used here, the term "short-yearling" is a calf in its first winter or spring, and "long-yearling" is an animal 1 to 1½ years old.

Pregnancy rates are not known for the Isle Royale herd, so data from other studies must be used. In British Columbia, 75 percent of 80 adult uteri were pregnant, including some from before the end of the breeding season (Edwards and Ritcey, 1958). Pimlott (1959b) found that in Newfoundland 81 percent of 239 adults taken after November were gravid, and he believes this is less than the actual percentage. The assumed rate for Isle Royale moose is 80 percent, a conservative estimate, in view of the fact that heavily cropped populations usually are most productive.

Calf-production figures are derived from the pregnancy and twinning rates, and number of adult cows present in calving season. The estimated size of the herd on March 1 is 600 (page 98), including 102 yearlings (17 percent), but by calving season it should decrease to about 564 because of continued predation.

The known kill of the large pack is 19 adults and 17 calves in 110 days (based on data from three winters, table 11). If the small packs take a third as many moose, the kill for the entire population is 25 adults and 23 calves in 110 days. At this rate, the wolves remove 19 adults and 17 calves from March 1 to May 20, when calving season begins, so the herd then should contain about 479 adults and 85 yearlings. Half of the 479, or 239, would be adult cows, assuming an even sex ratio. If 80 percent (191) breed and bear an average of 1.19 calves each (see page 105), the calf crop is 227.

Yearling-total population ratios for Isle Royale are given in table 13, and the average annual ratio for early March is believed to be about 17 percent (page 106), which agrees with statistics from other areas. Figures from de Vos (1956) indicate that long-yearlings composed 10 percent of the population minus calves in the Chapleau Crown Game Preserve, and 13 percent in the general Chapleau District of Ontario. The ratio calculated from Knowlton (1960) for the Gravelly Mountains of Montana was 25 percent, for short-yearlings. Pimlott (1959b) found that reported ratios varied from 9 percent to 23 percent. Such variations might result from differences in methods of obtaining the figures. Some are based on summer observations, others on hunter-kill data and still others on winter aerial observations. Probably the study most comparable to the Isle Royale work is that of Spencer and Chatelain (1953). Pimlott calculated that short-yearlings composed 17 percent of their 9,436 winter aerial observations made in four Alaskan areas over a 3-year period. Most low ratios reported were from summer, whereas the Isle Royale figure applies in March, so it compares favorably with the others. This ratio is significant because it is an excellent

indicator of annual increment to the herd. Mortality statistics demonstrate that very few individuals aged 1 to 5 are lost (table 18). As calculated above, an estimated 85 animals survive their first year.

Having estimated calf production and annual increment, we can compare them with expected annual mortality. Since the calculated kill is 25 adults and 23 calves per 110 days in winter (see above), annual adult mortality approximates 83 animals, assuming the same rate of adult kill year round. The rate of calf kill cannot be projected for the entire year because summer calves are so much smaller than calves in winter. If the rate is constant from November 1 to May 20, 42 calves are consumed in this period. An indication of summer calf loss can be obtained from the percentage of calves present in the autumn population. The only autumn sample taken showed that 22 percent of 150 moose were calves (page 104). Theoretically, 40 adults should have perished between May 20 and late October, when the survey was made, leaving 524. If calves composed 22 percent of the total population, then 148 calves survived; this indicates that approximately 79 died from May 20 to November 1. On this basis, annual mortality would be 83 adults and 121 calves (42 plus 79), or a total of 204. Since approximately 227 animals are believed to be produced each year, the herd would increase annually by about 23, on the basis of the above computations.

However, more substantial figures show that about 85 calves survive to their first year; 227 minus 85 equals 142 calves lost, 21 more than previously calculated. This discrepancy could result from a mistaken assumption that the winter rate of calf kill applies from November to May. Most likely more calves are taken in autumn and early winter, when they are smaller, more numerous and presumably more vulnerable. If this is true, a more realistic figure than 42 for calf mortality from November to May would be 142 minus 79 (summer kill), or 63.

The annual calf kill is a useful figure, but the statistics most indicative of the future trend in moose numbers are annual adult kill and annual increment. The calculated figures are 83 and 85 respectively. If these approximate actual numbers, the Isle Royale herd will remain stable for as long as they apply.

The annual-kill figure can be checked by comparing the approximate weights of animals killed with the total annual consumption (based on figures averaged from all three winter study periods). The large pack consumed a total of approximately 20,295 pounds in 110 days, or 184 pounds per day (page 77), and if the smaller packs ate a third as much, consumption for the entire population would be about 245 pounds per day, or 89,425 per year.

The weight of animals killed is more difficult to determine. Assuming that 85 adults are taken annually and that each provides about 800 pounds of food, then adults contribute 68,000 pounds per year. If 63 calves at 275 pounds are killed between November 1 and May 20, they provide 17,325 pounds. The estimated 79 calves taken between May 20 and November 1 should average about 81 pounds apiece—calculated from weekly calf weights given by Peterson (1955), Denniston (1956), and Dodds (1959)—so these furnish approximately 6,399 pounds. The three estimates total 91,724 pounds, which compares well with the calculated annual consumption. The close agreement is not important, since most of the figures are estimates; the significant point is that both numbers are within the same order of magnitude.

Another figure that compares favorably with production and loss statistics is the summer ratio of calves to total population (25 percent) based on field observations (page 103). The calculated calf production (227) is 33 percent of the estimated herd, but numbers undoubtedly dwindle rapidly during the first few weeks because of predation. Probably the loss rate declines as calves grow and provide more food. Since the summer calf ratio is an average of observations from about May 20 to September 20, it should be less than the percentage present on May 20 and more than the September ratio. Although the latter is unknown, the figure for November, based on 150 moose, is 22 percent. Thus the conservative estimate of the average summer ratio falls into line.

The following non-assessable factors could affect the production-loss calculations, but probably none is influential enough to destroy the worth of the proposed figures: the importance of beavers as summer food, possible waste of adult moose killed by small packs in summer, moose mortality other than predation, and difference in wolves' summer food requirements. Regarding the latter factor, E. H. McCleery, who has maintained a wolf kennel for years, wrote me that he feeds his animals an estimated five-sixths as much in summer as in winter.

The computed proportion of calves in the summer kill does not correlate well with the wolf-scat analysis (table 10). Calf hair composed 48 percent of the occurrences from May to August, and adult hair constituted 16 percent. If 40 adults and 79 calves are killed between May 20 and November 1, calves furnish about 6,399 pounds of food, whereas adults provide about 32,000. There could be several reasons that the scat analysis might not accurately indicate absolute or even relative ratios of calves to adults consumed: (1) Calves are covered with a higher proportion of hair than are adults; (2) all hair is consumed from summer calf kills, whereas large chunks of hide are left at adult kills at least in winter; (3) a wolf could eat much meat from an adult without getting hair, but this would be difficult with a calf; and (4) when an adult is killed in summer, probably the wolves travel little until it is finished, so most scats would be left nearby; however, wolves probably finish a calf quickly and then continue, leaving a higher proportion of scats containing calf remains on trails. These and other possible biases indicate that scat-analysis figures are not a valid check on calculated kill rates.

Postulated seasonal trends in the moose herd are diagramed in figure 102. This model is not a precise estimate of actual numbers; rather

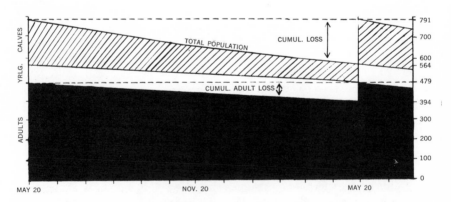

Figure 102—Seasonal trends in the moose herd.

it is an idealized scheme based on limited data. As such, it should be useful for considering the effects of wolves on moose numbers, even though future work may necessitate its modification.

The age-structure curve of the moose herd also can be plotted. Remains of 39 ageable adult moose were discovered at random and segregated into wear classes indicating relative age (table 18); these provide estimates of the percentage of mortality (from wolf predation and all other factors) occurring in each class. Assuming an annual increment of 85 yearlings and a mortality of 85 adults, one can determine the number of individuals in each wear class by subtracting the calculated mortality from the previous class, starting with 85 members in class I. When these are plotted on a graph, a profile of the age structure of the herd (just

before calves are dropped) results (figure 103 and table 22). This total moose in each wear class, 493, compares favorably with the estimated population size just before calving season (564).

The browse-moose-wolf complex can be summarized for the Isle Royale ecosystem in terms of weight, on the basis of data from this study and one figure from the literature. Since no attempt was made to measure browse consumption of moose, figures from other studies will be used. Hickie (1937) determined that a captive moose requires 25 pounds of browse per day, and Kellum (1941) found that captive animals that were supplied "unlimited" food consumed 40 to 50 pounds per day in winter and 50 to 60 in summer. He believes that summer consumption appears higher because of the high water content of summer foods. In addition, Palmer

TABLE 22.—CALCULATED AGE COMPOSITION OF THE MOOSE HERD JUST BEFORE CALVING SEASON

Wear class [a]	Number of moose remains found	Percent of total mortality [b]	Mortality	Population
I.	1	2.56	2.17	[b] 85.00
II.	2	5.12	4.34	82.83
III.	1	2.56	2.17	78.49
IV.	4	10.24	8.68	76.32
V.	8	20.48	17.36	67.64
VI.	8	20.48	17.36	50.28
VII.	6	15.36	13.02	32.92
VIII.	5	12.80	10.85	19.90
IX.	4	10.24	8.68	9.05
IXA.				.37
Total.	39	99.84	84.83	492.80

[a] Passmore et al. (1955).
[b] Calculated annual adult mortality and annual increment is 85.

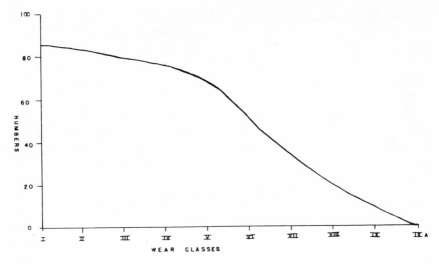

NUMBERS

WEAR CLASSES

Figure 103—Profile of the age distribution of the herd.

(1944) estimated, on the basis of tests with caribou, reindeer, and muskoxen, that a 1,200-pound moose requires about 35 pounds per day. Because wild moose must gather their food, they probably do not consume as much as captive animals, so I will assume that an adult eats 25 pounds daily in winter and 35 pounds in summer.

The Isle Royale wolf population annually devours an estimated 89,425 pounds of moose (page 163), which equals about 112 adults at 800 pounds each. (Since browse consumption figures are based on adults, the wolves' consumption must be converted to adults only.) If the summer rate applies from May 1 to September 1 and the winter rate for the rest of the year, each moose eats about 10,325 pounds per year; the

112 would consume 1,156,400 pounds annually. Since the average Isle Royale wolf is assumed to weigh 72 pounds (page 77), the entire population should weigh about 1,512 pounds. The ratio of moose to browse is 7.7 percent; of wolves to moose, 1.7 percent; and of wolves to browse, .13 percent. Thus, yearly, about 762 pounds of browse are consumed for each 59 pounds of moose, in turn consumed for each 1 pound of wolf.

The above calculations demonstrate the tremendous energy loss that occurs from one trophic level to another. However, since it takes an estimated 564 moose to produce the weight or number consumed, the annual weight of browse consumed is more realistically in the neighborhood of 5,823,300 pounds—or 3,851 pounds of browse per pound of wolf! The true amount of available or total browse, versus the amount consumed by the herd, is unknown.

Control of the Moose Population

Although the wolves are killing many moose and the herd seems stable, is it accurate to say they are controlling the moose population? It might be argued that they are not, for Isle Royale supports one of the highest year-round moose densities reported (page 98), and the yearling-total population ratio compares favorably with figures from wolf-free areas. This agrees with work by Cowan (1947) in the Rocky Mountain national parks of Canada. He found that yearlings composed 22 percent of 178 moose observations in wolf-inhabited areas and 23 percent of 187 observations in wolf-free areas. There also was no apparent difference in survival rates of young elk, deer, or sheep in the two areas. Evidently wolf predation compensates to a greater or lesser degree for other types of calf mortality. The important question is whether wolves merely substitute for other mortality factors or whether they kill more animals than other factors would.

The history of the Isle Royale moose herd affords an answer. Before wolves became established, the herd increased to an estimated 1,000 to 3,000 animals in the 1930's, decreased drastically a few years later, and built up again in the late 1940's (page 22). The limiting factor was food supply. Signs of severe over-browsing are still evident. In fact one species, Canada yew (*Taxus canadensis*), has been suppressed greatly on Isle Royale, whereas it grows luxuriantly on nearby Passage Island, which is uninhabited by moose. Today there appears to be sufficient browse, because much of the second-growth birch, aspen, and willow in the 1936 burn is growing beyond the reach of moose, and new stands of balsam fir and aspen a few feet high have become evident in other areas for the first time in decades. Apparently the wolves are maintaining the moose population below the level at which food would restrict it. If the wolves were exterminated, a significant increase in moose numbers probably would be noticed within a few years; when the population overtook its food supply, another die-off would occur, and the cycle would repeat itself. Malnutrition, disease, and parasitism probably would be the mortality factors, and these tend to cause catastrophic losses instead of the low, steady mortality which characterizes predation.

Apparently the Isle Royale wolf and moose populations have reached a state of dynamic equilibrium. Each is relatively stable, so any substantial fluctuation in one probably would be absorbed by the other until another equilibrium is reached. For example, wolves must travel long distances and test many animals before dispatching one. If some extraordinary factor suddenly reduced the moose population by half, the wolves probably would have such difficulty killing enough animals that inferior individuals might not be allowed to share what prey is taken. Conversely, if the moose population increased significantly, wolves would find easier hunting and might eat only preferred parts of their prey, as the wolves did in Minnesota when deer were more plentiful (Stenlund, 1955). Increased predation then might reduce the herd to a level that again rendered hunting more difficult.

Probably a close predator-prey equilibrium would most likely occur in such a situation as the Isle Royale ecosystem, where populations are discrete and the wolf depends on only one prey species. Undoubtedly the low prey-predator ratio, 30 moose per wolf, also is important. In Mount McKinley National Park, where Murie (1944) concluded that wolves controlled the Dall sheep, there is an estimated 25 to 37 sheep per wolf (calculated from Murie). However, in areas where wolves do not control prey populations, the ratio is much larger. Figures from Cowan (1947) show that there are 300 to 400 head of big game per wolf in the Rocky Mountain national parks of Canada. Cowan concluded (p. 172) the following about predation in the area:

Under the existing circumstances the predators present, coyote, wolf, fox, lynx, wolverine, mountain lion, grizzly, and black bear, together are not taking the annual net increment to the game herds, nor even removing the cull group, a large part of which becomes carrion following death from disease, parasitism, or malnutrition.

In wolf-inhabited areas of Minnesota, there are about 153 deer per wolf (calculated from Stenlund, 1955), and Stenlund estimated that wolves were killing about 16 percent of the herd, much less than the annual turnover.

In British Columbia, Hatter (1950a) found that wolves could not control the irrupting moose population. Arnold (1954) reported that in Michigan, where deer greatly outnumber wolves, the wolves were not controlling the herd. In Alaska, Klein and Olsen (1960), found that deer-inhabited areas free from wolves are characterized by stable or slowly increasing populations exceeding carrying capacity; heavy winter mortality; and severely deteriorated range, whereas in wolf-inhabited areas, range and deer appeared to be in fair to good condition, with light winter mortality from starvation. The authors emphasized that factors other than the wolf may be involved.

Maintenance of a Healthy Herd

An obvious result of intensive predation on Isle Royale moose is the elimination of heavily parasitized, diseased, old, or otherwise inferior individuals. Since 14 of 36 wolf-killed adults (39 percent) showed debilitating conditions even though only bones were examined from most, it seems safe to assume that every adult killed is either inferior or a victim of some circumstance predisposing it to predation. This becomes especially evident when one considers that the 15 to 16 wolves tested an average of 13 moose for

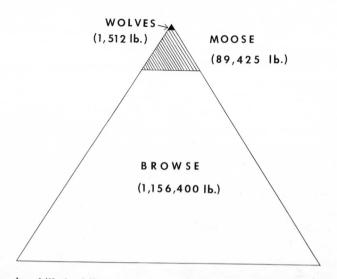

WOLVES→
(1,512 lb.)

MOOSE
(89,425 lb.)

BROWSE
(1,156,400 lb.)

each one they killed while under observation (page 144). If this ratio applies from November 1 to May 20, when a calculated 146 moose should be killed, approximately 1,898 moose would be tested in that period and undoubtedly many others are tested during summer. Since the wolves travel to every part of the island (figures 46, 47, and 3, showing the foot trails used by wolves in summer), they should detect any weak or inferior moose in a short time. Culling benefits any population, but it probably is especially important to Isle Royale's dense herd. It may even be the reason that such a high population has survived. Inferior animals undoubtedly use food less efficiently and reproduce less effectively, so in a herd crowding its environment, these animals would be least desirable.

Research in several other locations has shown that predation on big

Figure 104—Pyramid of biomass— based on biomass consumed only.

game exerts a culling effect. Murie's classic study (1944) of wolves and Dall sheep proved this beyond question in Mount McKinley National Park. Although evidence from other studies is not as conclusive, collectively it strongly supports the hypothesis. H i b b e n (1937) found that all of the 11 puma-killed deer he examined were either ill-proportioned, diseased, parasitized, or otherwise significantly abnormal compared to 74 hunter-killed deer. Cowan (1956) reported that on Vancouver Island, British Columbia, domestic dogs preyed primarily on malnourished and heavily parasitized deer. In the Canadian Northwest Territories, Banfield (1954) studied the hunting techniques of wolves in caribou country and concluded that weak or inferior caribou would be among those most likely to succumb to the wolves' methods. Other results similar to these (Cowan, 1947; Peterson, 1955; Crisler, 1956, 1958) already have been discussed, as has work by Stenlund (1955) and Burkholder (1959), who found no evidence of a culling effect. However, one should remember that seldom are intact carcasses of wolf-killed animals available for examination, and even if they were, the psychological or behavioral factors that might predispose big game to predation still would go undetected.

A heavily cropped herd composed of healthy animals with sufficient food should reproduce vigorously. Probably one of the most sensitive indicators of a moose population's reproductive abilities is the twinning rate. Pimlott (1959b) summarized results of many studies, including his own, and found wide variation (2 to 28 percent) in rates of twinning; he also discussed the effect of nutrition on reproduction and concluded that "variations in adult fecundity may be caused by a number of nutritional factors that differ from one range to another." In Alberta and British Columbia, Cowan (1950) found that elk on overgrazed range had a twinning rate of less than 1 percent, whereas herds in better nutritive condition had a rate of 25 percent.

At present, Isle Royale moose appear to have one of the highest twinning rates reported. Of 53 cows seen with calves in the summer of 1959, 20 were accompanied by twins, a rate of 38 percent (figure 105). (If only 25 different cows were seen, the 95 percent confidence limits would be 19 percent and 57 percent.) In 1960, which appeared to be a year of unusually low production, the twinning rate was 15 percent, on the basis of 47 observations of cows with calves. (The 95 percent confidence limits would be 1 percent and 29 percent if 25 different cows were observed.) In contrast, in 1929 when wolves were not present and moose overpopulated the island, Murie (1934) observed that only 1 of 45 cows with calves was accompanied by twins.

Future of the Wolves and Moose

Apparently the Isle Royale wolf population has increased to its maximum (under present conditions), for if it were going to increase further, it would have done so years ago. Numbers may fluctuate every few years, but probably there will be no significant variation. It seems likely that as long as the large pack remains on the island, the smaller groups will not breed. As individuals from these groups die of old age, the large pack may increase by a few members, although old animals from this pack may drop out and form other small groups; this also may stimulate breeding in the large pack. This is purely conjecture, however, for we know very little about the effects of pack interaction on breeding. Of course, emigration or immigration could complicate the whole situation. The most likely cause of variations in size

Figure 105—Cow and twin calves in early September.

of the wolf population probably would be a significant change in moose numbers.

The moose herd should remain stable for the next several years. Certainly if the wolves were going to deplete the population, they would have done so by now; instead they seem to have kept the herd within its food supply, culled out undesirable individuals, and stimulated reproduction. Indeed, the Isle Royale moose population probably is one of the best "managed" big-game herds in North America.

However, moose are dependent on the vegetation, and they flourish on earlier successional stages. Cowan *et al.* (1950) reported that, in British Columbia, moose numbers declined as the forest approached climax. These authors found that later successional stages supplied only about a third as much browse as

earlier stages, and in regard to quality, they concluded (p. 249) the following:

There is an increase of carotene values and possibly of total mineral content in the vegetation on more advanced forest areas, but . . . in ascorbic acid content, ether extractives, total carbohydrates, and proteins, the vegetation upon the younger forest areas is superior to that on older areas.

One of the primary sources of winter browse on Isle Royale is the 1936 burn (figure 8), but the trees in much of this area are fast growing out of reach of the moose. Since modern fire detection systems make it improbable that many forest fires will escape in the future, it appears that within the next decade the moose population will decrease significantly, with a corresponding decline in wolf numbers. The level that either population will reach is unpredictable, but continued study of both wolf and moose throughout this period should prove highly enlightening.

Acknowledgments

THIS investigation was carried out with the support and cooperation of several institutions and individuals, and it is a pleasure to recognize their contributions. Primary financial support was a National Science Foundation grant to Dr. Durward L. Allen, the responsible investigator, but additional funds were made available by the National Park Service, the Wildlife Management Institute, and the National Wildlife Federation. Purdue University and the Purdue Research Foundation provided my stipends and part of the travel expenses. Personal contributions to the project were made by Lee Smits and Andrew W. Barr of Detroit, Mich.; George W. McCullough of Minneapolis, Minn.; Hugh McMillan, Jr., Sharon, Conn.; and Dr. Robert M. Linn, Houghton, Mich.

Dr. Durward L. Allen of the Department of Forestry and Conservation, Purdue University, conceived the study, enlisted financial support, supervised the research, and assisted with the autumn moose survey and the field work during February 1961. Throughout the investigation, he was available for guidance and useful advice, and his helpful criticisms and suggestions during the preparation of this manuscript were invaluable. For his integral role in this study and for his interest, encouragement, and academic guidance throughout the previous 4 years, I shall remain deeply indebted.

The following faculty members of Purdue University—Dr. Charles M. Kirkpatrick, wildlife physiologist; Dr. Alton A. Lindsey, plant ecologist; Dr. Raymond M. Cable, parasitologist; and Dr. Meyer X. Zarrow, endocrinologist—all served for 4 years on my advisory committee under the chairmanship of Dr. Allen. They read and criticized most of the manuscript for this publication, when it was submitted as a doctoral dissertation. To them I also extend my gratitude.

Indispensable assistance was furnished by the Isle Royale National Park staff in the form of facilities and manpower. The splendid cooperation of successive Superintendents John G. Lewis and George W. Fry, Chief Ranger Benjamin J. Zerbey, and Chief Naturalist Robert M. Linn in this regard is especially appreciated. Zerbey and Linn also spent several lonely weeks keeping camp facilities operating during the winter study periods, as did District Rangers Roy Stamey, Peter L. Parry, and David G. Stimson. Stimson's offer of the use of his summer residence as a camp during the first two winters was particularly generous.

The most significant aspects of this study depended on the fine service of

Northeast Airways, Eveleth, Minn. Arthur C. Tomes, president, took a very personal interest in the study, flew several of the supply trips, and continually strove for the highest standards of safety during winter operations. I also wish to thank Jack Burgess of Tower, Minn., for piloting the research craft during the October moose survey and the first week of the winter study, and for making several of the supply flights.

Especial gratitude is extended to Donald E. Murray of Mountain Iron, Minn., who piloted the research craft for approximately 385 of the 435 hours involved in the investigation. He obtained leaves of absence from his usual occupation and left his family each winter to serve the project. His reliability, experience, and facility with the aircraft under adverse conditions made flying with him a particularly gratifying experience. Almost as important was Don's good humor and companionship and the intense interest he shared with me in pursuit of knowledge about the Isle Royale wolves. It is with sincerity that I extend my thanks to him.

Helpful advice and suggestions on field work were available from the following: Dr. Douglas H. Pimlott and Rodger Stanfield of the Ontario Department of Lands and Forests; Laurits W. Krefting of the U.S. Bureau of Sport Fisheries and Wildlife; Milton H. Stenlund, Minnesota Department of Conservation; Raymond D. Schofield, Michigan Department of Conservation; and C. Gordon Fredine, National Park Service. In addition, unpublished reports by Park Service Biologist James E. Cole, who also spent parts of three winters on Isle Royale, were made available for reference. Dr. Pimlott graciously loaned me a translation of Schenkel's (1948) paper on wolf behavior. He also read this manuscript and offered many helpful criticisms.

Numerous Park Service employees and summer residents of Isle Royale recorded observations for me and extended their friendship and hospitality, which were greatly appreciated. In particular, I am grateful to Mr. and Mrs. Edwin C. Holte for allowing my wife and me to occupy their summer residence in 1959, Mr. and Mrs. Robert A. Janke for special hospitality to my family and me, Philip C. Shelton for assistance with summer field work in 1960, and Mr. and Mrs. Peter Edisen for their general help and neighborliness.

My wife, Betty Ann, did the illustrations and much of the rough-draft typing despite the burden of three young children, but her most appreciated contributions were her ability to live happily under more primitive circumstances than most women are used to, and her enduring patience in managing our family both while I was away on Isle Royale in winter and especially while I prepared this manuscript.

To all the above-mentioned agencies and individuals, and to all others who directly or indirectly contributed to this investigation, I extend my most sincere gratitude.

Following are descriptions of all observed moose hunts by the Isle Royale wolves. The methods of observation are discussed on page 117, and limitations on page 126. Tables 15–17 summarize information from these accounts. Most hunts involved the large pack or part of it, but there are a few observations of hunts by a lone wolf and one by the pack of three. Successful attacks, described in the text, are referred to by page number in this section. All accounts are edited from field notes, and distances are estimated.

1. (February 24, 1959. Southeast shore of Lake Richie.) Ten of the 15 wolves were traveling southwest on Lake Richie at 1 p.m., when suddenly they dispersed and pointed upwind for a few seconds. Then they regrouped, wagged tails, and started inland, single file, directly upwind toward two adult moose feeding one-quarter of a mile away. When the pack was within 200 yards, the moose fled, one heading toward Lake Richie, the other away. The wolves chased the latter animal through deep snow, but soon all but the first wolf gave up. Eventually it got within 25 to 50 feet of the moose but stopped. The remaining wolves were resting 100 yards behind.

The other moose stood 150 yards away, nose upwind, between the wolves and the lake. The lead wolf returned to the others and then headed toward the south arm of the lake, which it reached minutes before the rest. It raced down the ice to a point downwind of the moose, where it sat and waited for the others. When they appeared, the leader ran to meet them; all stood, nose-to-nose, and wagged tails for a few moments. Then they went to the middle of the lake and rested from 1:35 to 3:30 p.m. Soon after the wolves gave up, the first moose lay down and the other began browsing.

2. See page 126.

3. See page 127.

4. (March 4, 1959. Isle Royale shore about 1½ miles southeast of Rainbow Point.) At 6 p.m., 10 of the 15 wolves were traveling along a beach about 2 miles ahead of the others. Suddenly several pointed inland toward five moose, the closest 30 yards away. As the wolves watched with wagging tails, the moose ran into a nearby stand of thick spruces. Two wolves started toward them a few steps as they disappeared. The moose had been feeding in a clearing full of blowdowns and deep snow, which may have been why the wolves did not follow. When the moose entered the spruces, still only

150 yards away, they stopped and looked toward the wolves, which had continued along the shore.

5. (March 7, 1959. Isle Royale shore opposite Malone Island.) While 5 wolves visited a kill on Wright Island, the other 10 traveled into Malone Bay (6:15 p.m.). The leader, 25 yards ahead, started toward Malone Island but suddenly stopped and turned toward shore. A few moments later it was chasing two moose 125 yards inland. The moose separated, and the wolf chased one 125 yards farther, coming within 30 yards of it, but as the moose entered some spruces, the wolf stopped and returned to the pack on shore. All wolves assembled, wagged tails, and ran to Malone Island. See the following account.

6. (March 7, 1959. Malone Island.) At 6:20 p.m. the 10 wolves involved in the previous account filed onto Malone Island and directly toward a cow and calf lying near the opposite side. They had scented the moose about 1/4-mile downwind. As the pack came to within 100 yards, the cow arose and ran to the calf, 25 yards away. The wolves surrounded the moose but did not attack. Slowly the moose moved to thicker cover 25 yards away. The cow stayed close to the calf, protecting its rear, and several times she feinted toward the wolves, making them scurry. The wolves lunged at the moose for 4 minutes but did not attack. Then the wolves headed

onto the ice, where they assembled, wagged tails, and lay down. We left them there at 6:30 p.m.

The next day, tracks showed that they had made another try. They had chased the moose onto the ice, where a large area packed with wolf tracks indicated that the moose had stood off the wolves for some time. No blood was seen anywhere. The moose finally had left the island from the north shore and the wolves from the west end.

7. See page 127.

8. See page 128.

9. (February 9, 1960. A ridge southeast of Duncan Bay.) The large pack (15 plus a lone wolf) was heading upwind toward the bay at 3:35 p.m., when 200 yards ahead a moose ran along the shore. The wolves were on a high ridge and probably could see it; they became excited and ran to where the moose had started but did not follow.

10. (February 11, 1960. Half a mile north of Mud Lake.) The 16 wolves left a swamp and struck out into an open burn; they appeared to be on a fresh moose track. When 250 yards crosswind of three adult moose (two lying, one standing), they stopped and scented the air (5:15 p.m.). The first animals lay on a ridge 200 yards from the moose for a minute, while the rest caught up. Then they continued along the trail, noses to the ground. Two

wolves remained downwind and about 25 feet ahead of the trackers. All three moose then were lying down, but when the first two tracking wolves got within 25 feet, they arose. Meanwhile the rest of the wolves caught up. The moose ran, one though the burn, and the other two into a dense stand of mature aspens, birches, and spruces; the wolves just stood a few minutes.

Meanwhile the single moose, which had run 100 yards into the burn, started back in a westward arc toward cover and thus toward the resting wolves. It came to within 50 yards of them and then strode back through the burn. The wolves started half-heartedly toward the animal, which continued trotting half a mile into the burn and again circled westward toward cover. By this time the wolves were traveling westward across the animal's intended trail, apparently having given up. The moose got within 25 yards of the two lead wolves, and again ran half a mile into the burn. The wolves tracked the moose 50 yards, lay down, and rested for 5 minutes. The moose then circled far behind the wolves and headed for cover while the pack continued on.

11. (February 12, 1960. About 1½ miles northwest of the west corner of Halloran Lake.) As the 16 wolves passed just south of the Feldtmann Trail at 11:35 a.m., they scented three adult moose 200 yards upwind and started toward them. When they came within 150 yards,

the moose ran, two one way and one another. The first two wolves overtook the two moose within 200 yards but did not attack. They continued the chase for half a mile through thick, second-growth birch.

The rest of the pack caught up with the lone moose within 300 yards and pursued it another 300. They ran behind and alongside the animal but did not attack. Suddenly the first wolf stopped and tried to prevent the others from continuing. It actually lunged at the other wolves, which turned and ran. The single moose continued through the dense second growth cover, bypassing an acre of thick spruces. The wolves returned to a nearby trail and assembled. The two that chased the other two moose arrived, and all rested for a few minutes in a nearby swamp. The two moose were slowly moving away. It is not known whether they had outrun or outlasted the wolves or had made a stand.

12. (February 12, 1960. About 200 yards south of the south corner of Halloran Lake.) At 1:40 p.m. the 16 wolves were heading southwest along a ridge 100 yards upwind of a cow (lying) and a calf (standing). The wolves stopped directly upwind and sniffed the wind but could not determine the location of the moose. They stood on the ridge for several minutes until the cow arose; then they immediately ran to it. The cow hurried to the rear of the calf, and the two walked 10 yards through the open burn. The wolves followed,

but the cow made short charges and kicked at them. Half a minute later the wolves assembled 25 feet away while the moose stood and watched. The wolves rested in some cover for a few minutes and then left.

13. See page 129.

14. See page 129.

15. (February 22, 1960. Midway between Mud Lake and Ishpeming Point.) At 3:05 p.m. the 16 wolves were traveling through the burn, toward the Greenstone Ridge, 150 yards crosswind of a standing moose. The wolves stopped, milled around, and ran back and forth for 5 minutes, after which they headed away from the moose for half a mile; then they stopped and began backtracking. When the wolves approached to within one-quarter of a mile, the moose bolted and ran steadily for more than half a mile.

At 3:50 p.m. we left to refuel. The wolves were resting on a ridge 50 yards upwind of where the moose had been. Returning at 4:35, we found that the wolves had found the tracks of the moose and followed them. In one place, they had cut downwind paralleling the trail for 100 yards, and then veered back to it. They followed the fresh moose track for one-half a mile before giving up. We found the animals as they were returning on their back trail.

16. (February 22, 1960. About 1½ miles west-southwest of the above location.) The large pack (16) headed along an open ridge just south of a shallow valley on the south side of which a moose was browsing in sparse cover. At 5:10 p.m. the wolves were ¼-mile crosswind of the animal. They scented its tracks in the valley below and followed them. One wolf, remaining near the top of the ridge downwind of the pack, encountered the moose first. The moose ran a few feet toward the valley when the wolf got within 25 yards; then the rest of the pack surrounded it. The moose stood its ground and charged the wolves repeatedly (figure 1). They deliberated for 5 minutes and then headed toward the Greenstone Ridge at 5:20 p.m.

17. (March 1, 1960, Merritt's Lane.) At 4:15 p.m. the 16 wolves ran through Merritt's Lane and cut inland toward two large moose standing on a ridge 200 yards away. As the wolves started up the steep slope 25 yards from shore, the moose fled for a quarter of a mile. The wolves gave up within a minute, headed back onto the ice, assembled, and continued on.

18. (March 4, 1960. North shore of Siskiwit Bay opposite Francis Point.) The large pack (16) was traveling southwestward along the shore at noon. When 150 yards downwind of two standing moose, they started inland, and the moose ran northward. One headed around the side of a small lake, but the other seemed deliberately to avoid the lake. This moose ran in circles and the wolves soon overtook it. The animal stood at bay and threatened the wolves; they stood around for a minute, assembled, wagged tails, and left.

19. (March 4, 1960. About 200 yards northeast of Halloran Lake.) At 2 p.m., the 16 wolves appeared to be tracking a moose through a row of thick spruces. When they came to within 100 yards of two moose, the moose ran toward Siskiwit Bay; the wolves caught up within a quarter-mile. When the moose split up, the wolves followed the closer animal, which was smaller. It continued over small ridges and depressions in an arc to the right, then veered toward the Siskiwit Bay CCC Camp and ran among the buildings. Four or five wolves remained close behind and beside the running animal, but the rest were far behind. The wolves caught up and stayed with the moose in the open but soon lost ground in thick cover or blowdown.

Wolves nipped at the animal's heels four times but could not hold on. The moose continued through the CCC campground and into Siskiwit Swamp for another half a mile. It stumbled while jumping some down trees and then stopped in a clump of spruces. The wolves (now four) lay near the moose but made no attempt to attack. The moose rested a minute, then left and continued running for at least a mile through second growth cover. The

wolves did not follow; instead they assembled and left the area. Total distance of the chase was at least 2½ miles.

20. (March 4, 1960. Half a mile south of the Siskiwit Bay CCC Camp.) Twelve of the 16 wolves had just assembled after chasing the moose in the previous account and had gone a few hundred yards toward Halloran Lake when suddenly they stopped (2:30 p.m.) and rushed toward a moose standing 300 yards upwind. The animal trotted off immediately, and the wolves gave up without overtaking it.

21. (March 4, 1960. Three-quarters of a mile south of the south corner of Halloran Lake.) At 4:10 p.m. the large pack (16) appeared to be following a fresh moose trail. The first few animals came up to two large standing moose but did not attack. The moose stood for half a minute, and then one ran about 100 yards and stopped momentarily. The wolves followed this individual, while the other ran in a different direction.

The wolves chased the first animal but did not catch up. It went by a third moose lying in an open area, and when the wolves discovered this animal, they surrounded it. The moose stood its ground, and after a few seconds the pack continued after their original quarry. It was several hundred yards ahead, alternately running and standing to look back. The wolves continued about 200 yards farther (about one-half mile in all), gave up, and headed for shore. Meanwhile, two of the wolves bringing up the rear almost ran into the third moose, but they quickly retreated and continued toward the rest of the pack.

22. (March 4, 1960. Isle Royale shore southeast of Feldtmann Tower.) The 16 wolves, continuing along the shore, suddenly stopped and headed directly upwind toward a moose standing 75 yards inland (4:35 p.m.). The animal ran hesitantly when the wolves were 50 yards away, continued for 25 yards, stopped near a small tree, and threatened the wolves. They stood around the moose for half a minute and then headed back to the shore.

23. (March 4, 1960. Isle Royale shore due south of Feldtmann Tower.) Two moose standing 100 yards inland seemed to sense the pack at 4:40 p.m. soon after it left the moose in the previous account; perhaps they heard the wolves chasing that moose. They ran inland and by the time the pack was directly downwind were at last one-quarter of a mile away. The wolves started toward these animals but were distracted by three other large moose standing nearby. All three ran, and the wolves split up and chased them all. After half a minute they concentrated on one, chasing it through fairly open cover and gradually heading it toward the Lake Superior shore, which it was paralleling. (One or two animals usually kept alongside the moose on the inland side.)

After 1½ miles of chase, the moose ran up a small open ridge, and the lead four or five wolves gave up. However, the animals that had fallen behind took a short cut and continued the pursuit. This seemed to give impetus to the resting leaders, and the whole pack took up the chase; but by then the moose was 100 yards ahead, and after a few seconds the wolves gave up (4:47 p.m.).

24. (March 4, 1960. About one-half mile northeast of Rainbow Point.) The 16 wolves were following the shore east of Rainbow Point when at 6:40 p.m. they veered inland directly upwind toward a cow and calf standing 250 yards away. The moose stood their ground as the pack approached, and for a few seconds, both charged the wolves. Then the moose began to run slowly, cow behind the calf. The cow continually threatened the wolves, which would scramble away but immediately return, and the calf also charged at least once more. After following the cow and calf for one-quarter of a mile, the wolves gave up and continued north through a swamp at 6:45 p.m.

25. (March 4, 1960. About one-half mile southeast of the south corner of Feldtmann Lake.) At 6:55 p.m. the large pack (16) headed upwind toward three standing adult moose. The moose fled when the wolves were within 100 yards. Then

one stood, and the wolves chased the other two, which split up. The wolves continued after the closer one, a larger animal, staying within a few yards of it. Most of the wolves had fallen behind, but one finally overtook the moose after chasing it about 1 mile and stopped it. However, as soon as the moose stopped, the wolf scrambled away. Then the moose ran again and all the wolves gave up.

26. (March 6, 1960. About one-half mile northeast of Card Point.) The 16 wolves left their last kill at 4:30 p.m. and started toward the mouth of Washington Harbor. However, at a small bay about three-quarters of a mile northeast of Card Point, they headed inland through a small spruce-cedar swamp directly to a standing moose (5:05 p.m.; there was no wind). The animal stood its ground as the wolves approached. After they deliberated for half a minute, the moose slowly walked off, but the wolves did not follow.

27. (March 9, 1960. Malone Island.) At 2:10 p.m. the 16 wolves were found streaming across Malone Island, while a moose stood nearby in a clump of spruces. One wolf approached and walked on by, but the moose just stood there. The wolves then assembled on the opposite side of the small island, wagged tails, headed back across (only a few feet from the moose), and left. Undoubtedly these wolves had tested the

moose and given up just before we arrived.

28. (March 9, 1960. Shore of Isle Royale between Hat and Schooner Islands.) Heading northeastward along the shore about 2:25 p.m., the 16 wolves suddenly cut inland (crosswind). When 50 yards directly downwind of a cow and calf, they veered toward them. The cow went to the calf's rear, and the two ran when the wolves were 25 yards away. They fled toward Siskiwit Lake and then along a ridge, just south of the lake. Their flight was deliberate and not too fast, and the wolves followed beside and behind them for about 2 miles.

Whenever the wolves came close to the heels of the cow, she kicked, stopping them momentarily; but they returned immediately. The cow also charged wolves near the calf's rear. Part of the pack stayed beside the animals, awaiting opportunity to attack the calf. As the cow threatened wolves behind or beside her, others tried for the calf's rump, but the cow charged and made them scatter.

Once or twice the calf got 10 yards ahead of the cow as she fought the wolves. It appeared that if the cow had failed to keep up with the calf, or if the two had separated, the wolves would quickly have pulled down the calf. They did attack it two or three times but were driven off by the charging cow. The calf, which seemed small, chased the wolves that were ahead of it.

After about 2 miles, the moose stopped temporarily (2:40 p.m.) and so did the wolves. Within a minute the moose were off again, but the wolves remained resting. When 150 yards away, the moose began walking, the cow ahead.

A few minutes later, the pack half-heartedly started toward the animals again, and the cow returned to the rear of her calf. When the pack was within 150 yards of the moose, the wolves gave up and rested (2:45 p.m.). The moose continued running for at least one-half mile, but the wolves remained where they were until 3:05 p.m.

29. (March 9, 1960. About 200 yards northeast of Wood Lake.) At 5:15 p.m., the large pack started northward across Wood Lake. When 300 yards downwind of two large moose (one lying, one standing) in dense second-growth hardwoods, the wolves suddenly cut inland toward them. The moose ran when the pack was 15 yards away, and the wolves pursued one animal. It stopped within 50 yards, and they continued after the other. They followed for 50 yards, when the moose stopped. Whenever the wolves approached, the moose charged and sent them scurrying. Then it slowly ran a few yards and stopped. The wolves deliberated for 2 minutes and left.

30. (March 10, 1960. One-half mile north of the southwest half of Siskiwit Lake.) The 16 wolves were heading downwind along a high ridge, at 3:20 p.m., 150 yards from a moose lying on the side of the ridge.

They found a fresh trail nearby leading to the moose, so all followed it. The moose arose when the pack was 50 yards upwind, and ran 200 yards before the animals found its bed. It continued for one-half mile, then stood and watched its backtrail. The wolves tracked for 100 yards, lay down, and rested until 4:30 p.m., after which they left.

31. (March 10, 1960. Greenstone Ridge Trail opposite Hatchet Lake.) At 4 p.m. the group of three wolves started upwind along the Greenstone Ridge Trail. When about 50 yards downwind of two adult moose lying on the side of the ridge, the wolves scented them, ran to the edge of the ridge, and looked over for several minutes. Then they headed downwind and sat until 4:25 p.m., when they turned back upwind and started toward the moose. The closer moose arose when they were 20 yards away, and they eventually came to within 10 yards. The moose stood for about a minute while the wolves watched it. Both moose soon ran, but the wolves did not follow.

32. (March 11, 1960. One-half mile northwest of Feldtmann Lake.) The 16 wolves were heading crosswind at 2:40 p.m. when suddenly they spread out and excitedly ran around, more-or-less downwind of a cow and small calf 300 yards away. They may have been on a fresh trail, but this could not be determined. When directly downwind of the moose, they veered toward them.

The moose fled, cow ahead, when the wolves were 150 yards away. The pack caught up 150 yards from where the moose started running, and just then the calf darted ahead of the cow, where it stayed throughout the chase. Most of the wolves remained in line behind the cow, but a few kept cutting out and trying to get alongside the animals. The moose passed through spruce swamps, alder swamps, and stands of mature white birch and aspen, but they continued running. The wolves beside the moose never attempted to attack. Twice the moose stopped momentarily, but the wolves did not assail them. After chasing their quarry about 3 miles, the wolves dropped 50 yards behind, stopped, and rested at 3:08 p.m.; the moose continued running at least one-quarter of a mile farther.

Each wolf rested where it stopped, but 10 minutes later the animals assembled, wagged tails, sniffed noses, and lay down together for another 10 minutes. During the chase the snow seemed to hinder the wolves more than usual, perhaps because of the light crust.

33. (March 11, 1960. Midway between Grace Creek and the middle of the Feldtmann Lake shore.) The large pack (16) discovered fresh moose tracks at 4:01 p.m. and followed them for 1 minute, jumping three large moose standing about 100 yards away in a spruce swamp. All three ran, and the pack pursued one for 50 yards until it stopped; then

they started after another. This moose was at least 150 yards ahead in the swamp; the wolves tracked it a few yards, stopped, wagged tails, and gave up.

34. (March 11, 1960. One mile southeast of the mouth of Grace Creek.) About 5 p.m. the 16 wolves were following a wooded ridge toward 2 moose lying downwind. The moose sensed the wolves from 100 yards and ran. The wolves did not detect the moose but eventually discovered their tracks and followed them slowly for 50 yards. One moose ran directly away, but the other went 150 yards, stopped, and watched its backtrail. When the wolves came to within 100 yards, it ran another 200. The wolves rested 10 minutes, and the moose continued on. After resting, the wolves appeared to be trailing the moose, but dense conifers prevented positive determination of this. Eventually they gave up.

35. (March 11, 1960. One mile south-southwest of the mouth of Grace Creek.) At 5:50 p.m. the 16 wolves filed through a stand of spruce and mature white birch. When 300 yards downwind of four standing moose, they suddenly started toward them. The moose ran when the pack was within 100 yards, and the wolves chased one of these for one-half mile. The moose traveled through extensive blowdown (mature trees) quite easily, but this hindered the wolves. Once the animal stopped and charged the wolves, which scattered. It continued running and eventually gained a 100-yard lead; the wolves gave up (6 p.m.), but the moose continued running. The pack rested several minutes and started back toward where they had discovered the moose.

36. (March 11, 1960. Same location as 35.) After the episode described above, the wolves returned to where they had begun the chase. A moose was standing in a nearby clearing 150 yards away, and the pack made an arc until downwind of it (6:45 p.m.). Then they started directly toward the moose and got to within 100 yards before it ran. After they pursued for 25 yards, the moose stood its ground. The wolves stood around for a minute, then left.

37. (March 12, 1960. One-half mile southeast of the Windigo Ranger Station.) At 11 a.m. the 16 wolves were resting 150 yards from a cow and twin calves. Tracks showed that the wolves had either chased or tracked the moose to where we found them, that the moose had stood and the wolves had given up.

38. (March 12, 1960. G r a c e Creek Swamp, southeast of Windigo.) At 11:15 a.m. the pack either scented or was trailing the two moose standing crosswind of it in the spruce swamp. One ran when the wolves got within 125 yards, but the other, a bull with cervina-type antlers, waited until they were 75 yards away. Both headed into some open

hardwoods one-quarter of a mile away, where they stood watching their backtrail. The wolves rested when they came to where the moose had started. They eventually trailed the moose 150 yards but then rested again and gave up. (This was the latest date an antlered bull was seen during this study.)

39. (March 15, 1960. L o n g Point.) The large pack (16) was cutting across Long Point as usual, heading northeastward, when 150 yards upwind of two large moose in an open alder and spruce flat, they stopped and pointed. Then they continued to the moose, which remained in their beds until the wolves were within a few feet. When the moose stood up, the wolves surrounded them, but both moose charged several times, scattering the wolves. From 3:13 to 3:16 p.m. the wolves held the moose at bay and then gave up and continued along the shore.

40. See page 132.

41. See page 133.

42. (February 3, 1961. One mile south of the Greenstone Ridge midway between Lake Desor and Ishpeming Point.) A single wolf, which probably was a member of the pack of two, was heading upwind on some open ridges when at 5 p.m. it detected two adult moose lying one-quarter of a mile upwind. The wolf sneaked to within 25 yards of one moose and then ran straight toward it. Both moose fled immediately with the wolf in pursuit. After three-eighths of a mile, one moose stopped. The wolf continued after the other but soon fell 15 yards behind and gave up; the moose ran on for about 1 mile.

43. (February 3, 1961. One-half mile south of Ishpeming Point.) The wolf involved in the previous account started up a gentle slope through thick second-growth cover and detected a moose 100 yards upwind at 6 p.m. It walked slowly to within 15 yards of the moose, but the moose strode boldly toward it. The wolf cowered, hestitated, then circled, and continued on.

44. (February 6, 1961. One-quarter of a mile northeast of Lake Harvey.) We discovered the 15 wolves at 4:30 p.m. in some thick second-growth hardwoods just as they had started to chase three moose, including a cow and calf. The wolves concentrated on the cow and calf, but these had a 150-yard start. The lead wolf pursued the cow and calf for one-quarter of a mile before giving up. The moose continued on for another quarter of a mile.

45. (February 6, 1961. At the base of the Greenstone Ridge south of Lake Harvey.) The large pack (15) was heading from Lake Harvey toward Greenstone Ridge at 5:43 p.m., when a moose crossed in front of the animals and turned upwind. A minute later the wolves struck its fresh track, but only one animal was

interested. It followed the trail for 35 yards and then returned to the pack; all proceeded on.

46. (February 6, 1961. About 200 yards southeast of the Greenstone Ridge Trail opposite the southwest end of Lake Harvey.) At 5:50 p.m. the 15 wolves were traveling along a ridge through dense second-growth hardwoods when a few sensed a moose browsing 200 yards crosswind of them. The moose detected the wolves 150 yards away and fled. The wolves followed hesitantly for 250 yards while the moose traveled one-quarter of a mile. Then the lead wolf sensed two other moose and abandoned the chase.

47. (February 6, 1961. Same location as previous account.) After giving up the previous chase at 5:53 p.m. the "leader" of the pack of 15 started for two adult moose standing 150 yards more-or-less upwind. Immediately the moose ran and the wolf followed. One moose cut to one side and stopped, while the wolf fell 35 yards behind the other. The wolf then started for the first moose. It fled, but the wolf pursued for 150 yards. After the moose gained a 25-yard lead, the wolf gave up. Apparently the rest of the pack had not discovered these moose.

48. (February 6, 1961. Greenstone Ridge Trail about 2 miles northeast of the Hatchet Lake Trail.) The large pack (15) was heading upwind on the trail at 5:56 p.m.

when the animals scented a cow and calf browsing one-quarter of a mile ahead. They continued to within 250 yards before the moose became aware of them and started off. The moose ran for one-quarter of a mile, but the wolves did not follow.

49. (North shore of Isle Royale west of Lake Desor.) At 11:45 a.m. the 15 wolves scented an adult moose lying 75 yards inland, about one-quarter of a mile upwind. They continued along the shore until opposite the moose. Although the whole pack sensed that the moose was nearby, only one approached the animal. When it was 10 yards away, the moose arose, and the wolf fled. The action of the pack is unexplained, but possibly the animals had tested this moose 2 days earlier when they last used the route. This was the only moose in the vicinity, and the wolves might have had a recent unsuccessful experience with it.

50. (February 10, 1961. South section of Wright Island.) D. L. Allen saw eight of the large pack detect a moose upwind of them at 2:30 p.m. The animal ran through heavy blowdown and mixed woods while the wolves followed for a few yards and gave up.

51. (February 24, 1961. Flat on northwest side of Houghton Ridge about opposite Little Boat Harbor.) Seven members of the large pack were traveling upwind along the shore. At 4:15 p.m. they scented

two adult moose lying 50 yards inland and 250 yards ahead. The moose did not detect the wolves until 4:21, when they were 15 yards away. Both retreated along the narrow strip between shore and a high escarpment, and the wolves pursued 10 yards behind. The moose split up, and we followed the only one we could see. It was running, but no wolves were chasing it. Since the other moose was not seen, it must have stopped in one of the small clumps of conifers in the vicinity. We finally saw the wolves leaving the area. The total distance of the chase was about 300 yards.

52. (February 24, 1961. Top of Houghton Ridge above Little Boat Harbor.) The seven wolves in the above account were crossing Houghton Ridge to the southeast side. When on top of the ridge at 4:39 p.m., they sensed two adult moose lying in a depression 75 yards approximately upwind in sparse conifer cover. Four wolves remained on a knoll while the other three explored the area trying to locate the moose. When they were within 20 yards, the moose bolted, and the wolves floundered through deep snowdrifts in pursuit. The moose quickly gained a 25-yard lead, and the wolves gave up (4:42 p.m.).

53. (February 24, 1961. Southeast of the northeast end of Halloran Lake.) As the seven wolves traveled along the Isle Royale shore, they scented a cow and calf lying 150 yards directly upwind at 5:52 p.m. and veered inland through an area of heavy blowdown. Three minutes later, when the wolves were 10 yards away, the moose arose. The cow charged and then went to the rear of the calf, and both walked off a few yards. The wolves followed cautiously, trying to make the moose run, but after half a minute, they gave up. The moose walked away and the wolves returned to shore.

54. (February 24, 1961. Shore of Isle Royale south of the northeast end of Halloran Lake.) A few minutes after leaving the moose mentioned in the previous account, the seven wolves encountered three adult moose standing a few yards inland among sparse conifers and heavy blowdown. The wolves ran 15 yards to the nearest moose, but this animal stood at bay and threatened the wolves. Immediately they headed for the second moose, which started running. However, they soon abandoned pursuit, for the animal had a head start. Then they turned to the third moose, which had watched them chase the other. This animal ran upon their approach and when during the pursuit it charged the wolves, one got ahead of the moose. The moose charged this wolf and chased it down the trail for 50 yards while the rest of the pack pursued it. Finally the moose stood next to a spruce and defied the wolves. Within half a minute they gave up (6:04 p.m.).

55. (February 24, 1961. Isle Royale shore opposite the center of Halloran Lake.) At 6:22 p.m. the seven wolves scented a moose standing in heavy blowdown 50 yards upwind and headed to it. The moose detected the wolves 20 yards away but stood its ground and charged them. They scattered, stood around for half a minute, and then proceeded along the shore.

56. (February 24, 1961. Isle Royale shore south of the southwest end of Halloran Lake.) Three adult moose were standing in an area of heavy blowdown and moderate conifer cover along the shore, and at 6:35 p.m. the seven wolves came within 20 feet of the nearest. The other two animals stood while the wolves chased the closest. This animal ran for 300 yards, and the nearest the wolves came to it was 10 yards. After the moose gained a 50-yard lead, the pack gave up.

57. (February 28, 1961. Half a mile southwest of Little Boat Harbor.) Eight of the large pack were traveling northeast through an area of heavy blowdown and conifer cover along the shore. Trees obscured our view, but at 3:15 p.m. two running moose (unidentified as to age) were seen with wolves within 100 feet. A third moose was making a stand nearby, and 20 feet away the wolves were just leaving it. Evidently some of the wolves had chased the two moose and had given up, while the others held the third animal at bay.

58. (February 28, 1961. Little Boat Harbor.) As the eight wolves continued along the shore, they scented three adult moose (one standing, two lying) 35 yards upwind at the base of a steep, open hill (3:30 p.m.). The moose detected the wolves at the same time, and two got a substantial start up the hill. The third waited until the wolves were within 30 feet before running. The wolves gave chase but floundered in the deep snowdrifts at the base of the hill. They gave up immediately and continued on.

59. (February 28, 1961. Hay Point, about one-half mile from the tip.) Seven of the eight wolves involved in the previous account crossed Siskiwit Bay to the neck of Hay Point. Here they scented three adult moose 200 years upwind at 5:40 p.m. in a moderately open stand of mixed woods. When the wolves were within 50 yards, the moose sensed them. Two ran but the closest stood. The wolves lunged at the moose and tried to make it run. After 2 minutes, the moose bolted and the wolves closed in. One grabbed a hind leg, but the moose kicked loose. The wolves chased the animal for one-quarter of a mile, dropped behind, and gave up at 5:46. The deep snow obviously hindered them.

60. (February 28, 1961. About one-quarter of a mile from the tip of Hay Point.) One of the moose in the previous account was standing 50 yards inland of the southeast shore of Hay Bay when the wolves came up the bay after the last chase. At 5:50 p.m. the wolves scented this animal 150 yards away. A minute later, when they were on the ice 100 yards away, the moose strode deliberately toward them for 70 yards. When the moose was within 30 yards, the wolves left. This is one of the moose which fled when the wolves first approached (see 59).

61. (February 28, 1961. Southeast side of the tip of Hay Point.) At 5:56 p.m. the seven wolves scented a moose 150 yards crosswind, so they cut across the point toward it. They found the animal's track and followed it for 50 yards, but when they were 25 yards away, the moose ran. The wolves chased it for 10 yards, but the deep snow hindered them, and they gave up.

62. (February 28, 1961. Isle Royale shore south of Mud Lake.) The seven wolves were traveling northeastward along the shore at 6:32 p.m. when they scented a moose standing 75 yards upwind in a thick cedar swamp. The moose detected the wolves about the same time and ran. The pack followed, but only one wolf stayed close to the animal. This wolf chased it for 300 yards, out of the swamp and into sparser cover. Suddenly the moose stopped, and immediately the wolf gave up and returned to the others.

63. (March 4, 1961. The Head—a point west of Long Point.) While the large pack (14 or 15) was following the shore westward, the animals discovered four moose lying 150 yards upwind among heavy blowdown and mixed woods at 2:08 p.m. The wolves got to within 50 yards before the moose detected them. All the moose ran. The wolves followed for 50 yards but did not get close; they soon gave up.

64. (March 4, 1961. Rainbow Point.) The 15 wolves were cutting across Rainbow Point at 3:04 p.m. when they discovered the tracks of two large adult moose (both with much hair missing) standing 150 yards downwind. They followed these for 50 yards before the moose sensed them. One moose moved toward the other and stood for half a minute, then both ran. The wolves tried to keep them in the open along the shore. Although the moose had a 30-yard start, the wolves came to within 10 yards of them at times. After a chase of nearly one-half a mile, the moose curved farther inland, and the wolves abandoned the pursuit. A crust hampered the wolves but did not affect the moose.

65. (March 4, 1961. Shore of Grace Harbor.) The 15 wolves were traveling along the shore, and at 4:21 p.m. they scented a moose standing 50 yards upwind in a stand of mixed woods. After they proceeded toward it 10 yards, the animal ran. The wolves followed for a few yards and gave up.

66. (March 5, 1961. About 1 mile north-northeast of Cumberland Point.) At 4 p.m., 13 wolves were heading overland across Cumberland Point. Suddenly they ran, and about 150 yards crosswind of them a moose was running. Trees obscured our view, but apparently the moose had a substantial start. The wolves followed for 25 yards and then gave up.

67. (March 5, 1961. One-half a mile east of Rainbow Point.) As the 13 wolves traveled along the shore, they scented three adult moose standing 200 yards upwind at 5:44 p.m. in open conifer cover. The moose ran when the wolves were within 150 yards, and the wolves chased two of them, while the third stopped. Part of the pack drove the moose in a semicircle, and the rest intercepted one of them. The other continued running, whereas the cornered moose stood and charged the wolves. They surrounded the animal for a minute and then abandoned it (5:46 p.m.).

68. (March 5, 1961. Two miles west of Long Point.) At 6:20 p.m. the large pack (13) was starting through blowdown and conifer cover toward a moose when the animals scented two others lying 200 yards upwind. They got within 100 yards before the moose detected them. One animal ran, but the closer one stood. The wolves surrounded this moose and apparently tried to make it run, but it stood its ground, kicked, and charged, almost connecting with one wolf. Several wolves gathered around the animal's rump, and one grabbed its nose momentarily. The pack spent 5 minutes harassing the moose, but it would not retreat. Finally the wolves left (6:25 p.m.).

69. (March 5, 1961. About 1½ miles west of Long Point.) As they were traveling along the shore at 6:36 p.m., the 13 wolves involved in the previous account scented a moose standing in open conifers 75 yards upwind. When the wolves were within 50 yards, the moose ran; the wolves pursued it for about 50 yards and gave up.

70. (March 12, 1961. About 1¾ miles south-southeast of the northeast end of Lake Desor.) A lone wolf was backtracking the large pack to a wounded moose when at 12:23 p.m. it sensed a moose standing 35 yards upwind in a small lowland tangle of blowdown, conifers, and second-growth hardwoods. It approached to within 10 yards before the moose detected it. The moose walked threateningly toward the wolf, which ran and circled to get by it. Tracks showed that the large pack a few days earlier had made an unsuccessful attempt to attack this animal.

71. See page 133.

Bibliography

ADAMS, C. C. 1909. *An ecological survey of Isle Royale, Lake Superior.* A report from the University of Michigan Museum, published by the State Biological Survey as a part of the Report of the Board of the Geological Survey for 1908. Wynkoop Hallenbeck Crawford Co., Lansing. 468 pp.

ALDOUS, S. 1945. *Daily notes on trip to Isle Royale National Park for moose browse survey.* U.S. Fish and Wildl. Serv. Isle Royale Nat. Park files. (typewritten).

ALDOUS, S. E., and L. W. KREFTING. 1946. *The present status of moose on Isle Royale.* Trans. N. Am. Wildl. Conf. 11: 296–308.

ALTMANN, MARGARET. 1958. *Social integration of the moose calf.* Animal Behaviour 6: 155–159.

ARNOLD, D. A. 1954. *Predator control in Michigan—when, why, and how.* Trans. N. Am. Wildl. Conf. 19: 141–150.

BAILEY, V. 1926. *A biological survey of North Dakota.* U.S. Dept. of Agric., Biol. Surv. N. Am. Fauna 49. 416 pp.

BANFIELD, A. W. F. 1951. *Populations and movements of the Saskatchewan timber wolf* (Canis lupus knightii) *in Prince Albert National Park, Saskatchewan, 1947 to 1951.* Wildl. Mgmt. Bull. ser. 1, no. 4. 24 pp.

—— 1954. *Preliminary investigation of the barren ground caribou. Part II. Life history, ecology, and utilization.* Can. Wildl. Serv., Wildl. Mgmt. Bull. ser. 1, no. 10B. 112 pp.

BANFIELD, A. W. F., D. R. FLOOK, J. P. KELSALL, and A. F. LOUGHREY. 1955. *An aerial survey technique for northern big game.* Trans. N. Am. Wildl. Conf. 20: 519–532.

BELSCHNER, H. G. 1951. *Sheep management and diseases.* Angus and Robertson, Sydney, Australia. 723 pp.

BROWN, C. A.   Undated (1935).   *Ferns and flowering plants of Isle Royale, Michigan.*   U.S. Dept. Int. Emergency Conservation Work, Field Survey.   Univ. Mich. Herbarium.   90 pp.

BROWN, C. E.   1936.   *Rearing wild animals in captivity, and gestation periods.*   J. Mammal. 17: 10–13.

BURKHOLDER, B. L.   1959.   *Movements and behavior of a wolf pack in Alaska.*   J. Wildl. Mgmt. 23: 1–11.

BURT, W. H.   1957.   *Mammals of the Great Lakes Region.*   Univ. Mich. Press, Ann Arbor.   246 pp.

CAMERON, A. E. and J. S. FULTON.   1927.   *A local outbreak of the moose-tick,* D. albipictus Packard (Ixodoidea), *in Saskatchewan.*   Bull. Ent. Res. 17: 249–257.

CHANDLER, A. C.   1955.   *Introduction to parasitology.*   John Wiley and Sons, Inc., New York.   799 pp.

CHEATUM, E. L., and C. W. SEVERINGHAUS.   1950.   *Variations in fertility of the white-tailed deer related to range conditions.*   Trans. N. Am. Wildl. Conf. 15: 170–189.

CHOQUETTE, L. P. E.   1956.   *Observations on experimental infection of dogs with Echinococcus.*   Can. J. Zool. 34: 190–192.

CHRISTIAN, J. J.   1956.   *Adrenal and reproductive responses to population size in mice from freely growing populations.*   Ecology 37: 258–273.

———— 1958.   *The roles of endocrine and behavioral factors in the growth of mammalian populations.*   Naval Med. Res. Inst. Lecture and Rev. ser. no. 58–1: 473–496.

CHRISTIAN, J. J., V. FLYGER, and D. E. DAVIS.   1960.   *Factors in the mass mortality of a herd of sika deer,* Cervus nippon.   Chesapeake Sci. 1: 79–95.

CHRISTIAN, J. J., and C. D. LEMUNYAN.   1958.   *Adverse effects of crowding on lactation and reproduction of mice and two generations of their progeny.*   Endocrinology 63: 517–529.

CLARK, R. T.   1934.   *Studies on the physiology of reproduction in sheep.*   Anat. Rec. 60: 125–159.

Cole, J. E. 1952a. *Presence of timber wolves in Isle Royale National Park.* U.S. Nat.. Park. Serv. Isle Royale Nat. Park files. (typewritten).

——— 1952b. *Report on field trip to Isle Royale, spring, 1952.* U.S. Nat. Park Serv. Isle Royale Nat. Park files. (typewritten).

——— 1953. *Winter moose study—1953.* U.S. Nat. Park Serv. Isle Royale Nat. Park files. (typewritten).

——— 1954. *Report on investigation of Isle Royale National Park.* U.S. Nat. Park Serv. Isle Royale Nat. Park files. (typewritten).

——— 1956. *1956 Winter wildlife study, Isle Royale National Park.* U.S. Nat. Park Serv. Isle Royale Nat. Park files. 56 pp. (typewritten).

——— 1957. *Isle Royale wildlife investigations, winter of 1956–57.* U.S. Nat. Park Serv. Isle Royale Nat. Park files. 42 pp. (typewritten).

Cottam, C., and C. S. Williams. 1943. *Speed of some wild mammals.* J. Mammal. 24: 262–263.

Cowan, I. M. 1947. *The timber wolf in the Rocky Mountain national parks of Canada.* Can. J. Res. 25: 139–174.

——— 1948. *The occurrence of the granular tapeworm* Echinococcus granulosus *in wild game in North America.* J. Wildl. Mgmt. 12: 105–106.

——— 1950. *Some vital statistics of big game on overstocked mountain range.* Trans. N. Am. Wildl. Conf. 15: 581–588.

——— 1951. *The diseases and parasites of big game mammals of Western Canada.* Rept. Proc. Game Conv., Vancouver, B.C., Game Dept. 5: 37–64.

——— 1956. *Life and times of the coast blacktailed deer. In* W. P. Taylor, The deer of North America, Stackpole Co., Harrisburg, Pa., and Wildl. Mgmt. Inst., Wash., D.C.

Cowan, I. M., W. S. Hoar, and J. Hatter. 1950. *The effect of forest succession upon the quantity and upon the nutritive values of woody plants used as food by moose.* Can. J. Res., sec. D., 28: 249–271.

CRINGAN, A. T. 1955. *Studies of moose antler development in relation to age.* App. B, pp. 239–246. *In* R. L. Peterson, North American moose, Univ. of Toronto Press, Toronto.

CRISLER, LOIS. 1956. *Observations of wolves hunting caribou.* J. Mammal. 37: 337–346.

———— 1958. *Arctic wild.* Harper and Bros., New York. 301 pp.

DAVIS, D. E. 1949. *The role of intraspecific competition in game management.* Trans. N. Am. Wildl. Conf. 14: 225–230.

DAVIS, D. E., and J. J. CHRISTIAN. 1957. *Relation of adrenal weight to social rank of mice.* Proc. of Soc. Exptl. Biol. and Med. 94: 728–731.

DENNISTON, R. H. 1956. *Ecology, behavior, and population dynamics of the Wyoming or Rocky Mountain moose, Alces alces shirasi.* Zool. 41: 105–118.

DE VOS, A. 1950. *Timber wolf movements on Sibley Peninsula, Ontario.* J. Mammal. 31: 169–175.

———— 1956. *Summer studies of moose in Ontario.* Trans. N. Amer. Wildl. Conf. 21: 510–525.

DE VOS, A., and A. E. ALLIN. 1949. *Some notes on moose parasites.* J. Mammal. 30: 430–431.

DE VOS, A., and R. L. PETERSON. 1951. *A review of the status of woodland caribou* (Rangifer caribou) *in Ontario.* J. Mammal 32: 329–337.

DICE, LEE R. 1943. *The biotic provinces of North America.* Univ. Mich. Press, Ann Arbor. 78 pp.

DODDS, D. G. 1959. *Feeding and growth of a captive moose calf.* J. Wildl. Mgmt. 23: 231–232.

DUMAS, ALEXANDRE. 1960. *Wolf hunt in czarist Russia* (translation by J. David Townsend). Sports Afield July 1960: 19.

DUNNE, A. L. 1939. *Report on wolves followed during February and March 1939.* Can. Field Nat. 53: 117–118.

EDWARDS, R. Y. 1954. *Comparison of an aerial and ground census of moose.* J. Wildl. Mgmt. 18: 403–404.

EDWARDS, R. Y. and R. W. RITCEY. 1958. *Reproduction in a moose population.* J. Wildl. Mgmt. 22: 261–268.

ELTON, C. 1950. *The ecology of animals.* Methuen and Co. Ltd., London. 97 pp.

ERICKSON, A. B. 1944. *Helminths of Minnesota Canidae in relation to food habits, and a host list and key to the species reported from North America.* Am. Midl. Nat. 32: 358–372.

FAUST, E. C. 1949. *Human helminthology.* Lea and Febiger, Philadelphia. 744 pp.

FENSTERMACHER, R. 1937. *Further studies of diseases affecting moose.* II. Cornell Vet. 27: 25–37.

FENSTERMACHER, R. and W. L. JELLISON. 1933. *Diseases affecting moose.* Univ. Minn. Ag. Exp. Sta. Bull. 294, 20 pp.

FINDLEY, J. S. 1951. *A record of moose speed.* J. Mammal. 32: 116.

FRANK, F. 1957. *The causality of microtine cycles in Germany.* J. Wildl. Mgmt. 21: 113–121.

FREEMAN, R. S., A. ADORJAN, and D. H. PIMLOTT. 1961. *Cestodes of wolves, coyotes, and coyote-dog hybrids in Ontario.* Can. J. Zool. 39: 527–532.

FULLER, W. A. 1960. *Behaviour and social organization of the wild bison of Wood Buffalo National Park, Canada.* Arctic 13: 2–19.

FULLER, W. A. and N. S. NOVAKOWSKI. 1955. *Wolf control operations, Wood Buffalo National Park, 1951–1952.* Can. Wildl. Serv. Wildl. Mgmt. Bull. ser. 11, no. 1. 23 pp.

GENSCH, R. H. 1946a. *Observations on the beaver of Isle Royale National Park, Michigan from May 9 to June 4, 1946.* U.S. Fish and Wildl. Serv. Isle Royale Nat. Park files. (typewritten).

———— 1946 b. *Daily notes on Isle Royale trip, May 7–June 5, 1946.* U.S. Fish and Wildl. Serv. Isle Royale Nat. Park files. (typewritten).

GILBERT, K. T. 1946. *General statement giving coverage to the beaver on Isle Royale.* Memo to Supt., Feb. 15. Isle Royale Nat. Park files. (typewritten).

HADWEN, S. 1933. (Untitled note). Proc. Helminthol. Soc., Wash. J. Parasitol. 19: 83.

HAKALA, D. R. 1953. *Moose browse and wildlife study at Isle Royale, February 17 to March 16, 1953.* U.S. Nat. Park Serv. Isle Royale Nat. Park files. (typewritten).

———— 1954. *Wolf on Isle Royale!* Nat. Mag., 47: 35–37.

HARPER, T. A., R. A. RUTTAN, and W. A. BENSON. 1955. *Hydatid disease* (Echinococcus granulosus) *in Saskatchewan big game.* Trans. N. Am. Wildl. Conf. 20: 198–208.

HATTER, J. 1950a. *The moose of Central British Columbia.* M.S. Thesis. Washington State Col. 356 pp.

———— 1950b. *Past and present aspects of the moose problem in Central British Columbia.* Proc. 13th Ann. Conf. West. Assoc. State Game and Fish Commissioners: 150–154.

HIBBEN, FRANK C. 1937. *A preliminary study of the mountain lion* (Felis oregonensis *sp.*). Univ. of N. Mex. Bull. 318. Biol. ser. 5(3) : 3–59.

HICKIE, P. F. 1936. *Isle Royale moose studies.* Proc. N. Am. Wildl. Conf. 1 : 396–398.

———— 1937. *A preliminary report on the past and present status of the moose* Alces americana (*Clinton*), *in Michigan.* Papers Mich. Acad. Sci., Arts and Letters 22: 627–639.

———— Undated (1943). *Michigan Moose.* Mich. Dept. Cons., Game Div. 57 pp.

HOFFMAN, R. S. 1958. *The role of reproduction and mortality in popuplation fluctuations of voles* (Microtus). Ecol. Monographs 28: 79–109.

INGLES, L. G. 1963. *Status of the wolf in California.* J. Mammal. 44: 109.

JOHNSON, C. E. 1922. *Notes on the mammals of northern Lake County, Minnesota.* J. Mammal. 3: 33–39.

JOHNSSON, R. G., and P. C. SHELTON. 1960. *The vertebrates of Isle Royale National Park.* Wolf's Eye 4(3): 24 pp. (Publ. of the Isle Royale Nat. Hist. Assoc.).

KELLUM, F. 1941. *Cusino's captive moose.* Mich. Cons. 10: 4–5.

KELSALL, J. P. 1957. *Continued barren-ground caribou studies.* Can. Wildl. Serv. Wildl. Mgmt. Bull. ser. 1, no. 12. 148 pp.

KLEIN, D. R., and S. T. OLSON. 1960. *Natural mortality patterns of deer in southeast Alaska.* J. Wildl. Mgmt. 24: 80–88.

KNOWLTON, F. F. 1960. *Food habits, movements, and populations of moose in the Gravelly Mountains, Montana.* J. Wildl. Mgmt. 24: 162–170.

KREFTING, L. W. 1949a. *Observations on the moose of Isle Royale National Park, May 16–June 5, 1949.* U.S. Fish and Wildl. Serv. Isle Royale Nat. Park files. (typewritten).

———— 1949b. *Observtions on the moose of Isle Royale National Park, September 17–25, 1949.* U.S. Fish and Wildl. Serv. Isle Royale Nat. Park files. (typewritten).

———— 1951. *What is the future of the Isle Royale moose herd?* Trans. N. Am. Wildl. Conf. 16: 461–470.

———— 1963. *The beaver of Isle Royale, Lake Superior.* Minn. Naturalist 14(2).

KREFTING, L. W., and F. B. LEE. 1948a. *Moose browse investigation of Isle Royale National Park, May 1948.* U.S. Fish and Wildl. Serv. Isle Royale Nat. Park files. (typewritten).

———— 1948b. *Beaver food investigation of Isle Royale National Park.* U.S. Fish and Wildl. Serv. Isle Royale Nat. Park files. (typewritten).

LACK, D. 1946. *Competition for food by birds of prey.* J. Animal Ecol. 15: 123–130.

LAMSON, A. L. 1941. *Maine moose disease studies.* M.S. Thesis. Univ. of Maine. 61 pp.

LAW, R. G., and A. H. KENNEDY. 1933. Echinococcus granulosus *in moose.* N. Am. Vet. 14: 33–34.

LINN, R. M. 1957. *The spruce-fir, maple-birch transition in Isle Royale National Park, Lake Superior.* Ph. D. Thesis. Duke Univ. 101 pp.

LONGHURST, W. M., A. S. LEOPOLD, and R. F. DASMANN. 1952. *A survey of California deer herds, their ranges and management problems.* Calif. Dept. Game and Fish, Game Bull. no. 6, 136 pp.

LORENZ, K. Z. 1952. *King Solomon's ring.* Methuen and Co. Ltd., London. 202 pp.

MACFARLANE, R. R. 1905. *Notes on mammals collected and observed in the northern Mackenzie River district, North-west Territories of Canada.* Proc. U.S. Natl. Mus. 28: 673–764.

MASON, K. E. 1939. *Relation of the vitamins to the sex glands.* Chap. XXII, pp. 1149–1212. *In* E. Allen, C. H. Danforth, and E. A. Doisy. Sex and internal secretions, 2nd. ed., Williams and Wilkins Co., Baltimore.

MONLUX, A. W., and C. L. DAVIS. 1956. *Actinomycosis and actinobacillosis.* 265–268. *In* Animal diseases, The Yearbook of Agriculture 1956. U.S. Dept. Agr., Wash., D.C.

MONNIG, H. O. 1938. *Veterinary helminthology and entomology.* 2nd. ed. Williams and Wilkins Co., Baltimore. 409 pp.

MUNRO, J. A. 1947. *Observations of birds and mammals in Central British Columbia.* Occasional Papers Brit. Col. Prov. Mus. 6, 165 pp.

MURIE, A. 1934. *The moose of Isle Royale.* Univ. Mich. Mus. Zool. Misc. Publ. 25, 44 pp.

——— 1944. *The wolves of Mount McKinley.* U.S. Nat. Park Serv., Fauna ser. 5, 238 pp.

MURIE, O. J. 1951. *The elk of North America.* Stackpole, Harrisburg, Pa., and Wildl. Mgmt. Inst., Wash., D.C. 376 pp.

——— 1954. *A field guide to animal tracks.* Houghton Mifflin Co., Boston. 374 pp.

MYKYTOWYCZ, R. 1960. *Social behavior of an experimental colony of wild rabbits,* Oryctolagus cuniculus (*L.*). III Second breeding season. C.S.I.R.O. Wildl. Res. 5: 1–20.

NEFF, E. D. 1951. *Can we save the gray wolf?* Nat. His. 40: 392–396, 432.

OLSEN, O. W., and R. FENSTERMACHER. 1942. *Parasites of moose in northern Minnesota.* Am. J. Vet. Res. 3: 403–408.

OLSON, S. F. 1938. *Organization and range of the pack.* Ecology 19: 168–170.

PACKARD, F. M. 1940. *Beaver killed by coyotes.* J. Mammal. 21: 359.

PALMER, L. J. 1944. *Food requirements of some Alaska game mammals.* J. Mammal. 25: 49–54.

PASSMORE, R. C., R. L. PETERSON, and A. T. CRINGAN. 1955. *A study of mandibular tooth wear as an index to age of moose.* App. A., 223–246. *In* R. L. Peterson, *North American moose*, Univ. of Toronto Press, Toronto.

PEIL, J. E. 1942. *Moose and ticks.* Conserv. Volunteer 5: 19.

PETERSON, R. L. 1955. *North American moose.* Univ. of Toronto Press, Toronto. 280 pp.

PIMLOTT, D. H. 1953. *Newfoundland moose.* Trans. N. Am. Wildl. Conf. 18: 563–579.

———— 1959a. *Moose harvest in Newfoundland and Fennoscandian countries.* Trans. N. Am. Wildl. Conf. 24: 422–448.

———— 1959b. *Reproduction and productivity of Newfoundland moose.* J. Wildl. Mgmt. 23: 381–401.

———— 1960. *The use of tape-recorded wolf howls to locate timber wolves.* 22nd. Midwest Wildl. Conf. 15 pp. (mimeo.).

RAUSCH, R. 1952. *Hydatid disease in boreal regions.* Arctic 5: 157–174.

———— 1958. *Some observations on rabies in Alaska, with special reference to wild Canidae.* J. Wildl. Mgmt. 22: 246–260.

RAUSCH, R. A. 1959. *Notes on the prevalence of hydatid disease in Alaskan moose.* J. Wildl. Mgmt. 23: 122–123.

RAUSCH, R., and F. S. L. WILLIAMSON. 1959. *Studies on the helminth fauna of Alaska.* XXXIV. *The parasites of wolves,* Canis lupus *L.* J. Parasitol. 45: 395–403.

RILEY, W. A. 1939. *The need for data relative to the occurrence of hydatids and of* Echinococcus granulosus *in wildlife.* J. Wildl. Mgmt. 3: 255–257.

RITCEY, R. W., and R. Y. EDWARDS. 1958. *Parasites and diseases of the Wells Gray moose herd.* J. Mammal. 39: 139–145.

ROBINETTE, W. L., J. S. GASHWILER, and OWEN W. MORRIS. 1959. *Food habits of the cougar in Utah and Nevada.* J. Wildl. Mgmt. 23: 261–273.

ROWAN, W. 1950. *Winter habits and numbers of timber wolves.* J. Mammal. 31: 167–169.

RUDEBECK, G. 1950. *The choice of prey and modes of hunting of predatory birds with special reference to their selective effect.* Oikos 2: 65–88.

—— 1951. *The choice of prey and modes of hunting of predatory birds with special reference to their selective effect (cont.).* Oikos 3: 200–231.

SCHENKEL, R. 1948. *Ausdruchs-studien an wolfen.* Behaviour 1: 81–129. (Unpubl. Translation from German by Agnes Klasson.)

SCHIERBECK, O. 1929. *Is it right to protect the female of the species at the cost of the male?* Can. Field Nat. 43: 6–9.

SCHILLER, E. L. 1954. *Studies on the helminth fauna of Alaska.* XIX. An experimental study of blowfly (*Phormia regina*) transmission of hydatid disease. Exptl. Parasitol. 3: 161–166.

SERGEANT, D. E., and D. H. PIMLOTT. 1959. *Age determination in moose from sectioned incisor teeth.* J. Wildl. Mgmt. 23: 315–321.

SETON, E. T. 1937. *Lives of game animals.* vol. I. Literary Guild of America, New York. 640 pp.

SHEVLIN, C. E. 1951. *Introduction of wolves at Isle Royale.* U.S. Nat. Park Serv. Memo to Dir., Region II. Isle Royale Nat. Park files. (typewritten).

SIMKIN, D. W. 1962. *Weights of Ontario moose.* Ont. Fish & Wildl. Rev. 1(6) : 10–12.

SMITS, L. 1963. *King of the wild.* Mich. Conservation 32(1) : 45–50.

SPEELMAN, S. R. 1939. *Nutritional requirements of dogs.* Food and life, Yearbook of Agriculture, 1939, U.S. Dept. Agr., Wash., D.C.

SPENCER, D. L., and E. F. CHATELAIN. 1953. *Progress in the management of the moose of south central Alaska.* Trans. N. Am. Wildl. Conf. 18: 539–552.

STANWELL-FLETCHER, J. F. and T. C. 1942. *Three years in the wolves' wilderness.* Nat. Hist. 49: 136–147.

STEBLER, A. M. 1944. *The status of the wolf in Michigan.* J. Mammal. 25: 37–43.

STENLUND, M. H. 1955. *A field study of the timber wolf* (Canis lupus) *on the Superior National Forest, Minnesota.* Minn. Dept. Cons. Tech. Bull. 4, 55 pp.

STEVENSON-HAMILTON, J. 1937. *South African eden.* Cassell and Company Ltd., London. 311 pp.

STODDARD, L. A., and A. D. SMITH. 1943. *Range management.* McGraw-Hill Book Co., New York. 547 pp.

SWANSON, G., T. SURBER, and T. S. ROBERTS. 1945. *The mammals of Minnesota.* Minn. Dept. Cons. Tech. Bull. 2. 108 pp.

SWEATMAN, G. K. 1952. *Distribution and incidence of* Echinococcus granulosus *in man and other animals with special reference to Canada.* Can. J. Publ. Health 43: 480–486.

SWEATMAN, G. K., and P. J. G. PLUMMER. 1957. *The biology and pathology of the tapeworm* Taenia hydatigena *in domestic and wild hosts.* Can. J. Zool. 35: 93–109.

TENER, J. S. 1954. *A preliminary study of the musk-oxen of Fosheim Peninsula, Ellesmere Island, N.W.T.* Can. Wildl. Serv., Wildl. Mgmt. Bull., ser. 1, no. 9. 34 pp.

THOMPSON, D. Q. 1952. *Travel, range, and food habits of timber wolves in Wisconsin.* J. Mammal. 33: 429–442.

TROTTER, R. H. 1958. *Aerial census of moose in Ontario.* N.E. Wildl. Conf. 15 pp. (mimeo.).

U.S. Dept. of Commerce. Weather Bureau. 1956a. *Climatic summary of the United States—supplement for 1931 through 1952.* Climatography of the United States no. 11–16 (Michigan).

———— 1956b. *Climatic summary of the United States—supplement for 1931 through 1952.* Climatography of the United States no. 11–17 (Minnesota).

U.S. Dept. of the Interior. National Park Service. 1937. *Vegetation type map of Isle Royale.* Isle Royale Nat. Park files.

Wallace, F. G. 1934. *Parasites collected from moose,* Alces americanus *in Northern Minnesota.* J. Am. Vet. Med. Assoc. 84: 770.

Wright, B. S. 1960. *Predation on big game in East Africa.* J. Wildl. Mgmt. 24: 1–15.

Young, P., and E. A. Goldman. 1944. *The wolves of North America.* Am. Wildl. Inst., Wash., D.C. 636 pp.

Young, S. P. 1946. *The wolf in North American history.* Caxton Printers Ltd., Caldwell, Idaho, 149 pp.

Zerbey, J. 1960. *Fish and wildlife of Isle Royale National Park.* U.S. Nat. Park Serv. Isle Royale Nat. Park files. 6 pp. (typewritten).

Index

Accidents, moose—106, 108, 114–116, 147.
Accounts of wolf attacks—126–135, 174–189.
Acknowledgment—172–173.
Actinomycosis—112–113.
Adams, C. C.—5–6, 16, 18–20.
Adrenal glands—87–89.
African lions—77, 88–89.
Ageing techniques, moose—145–146.
Age ratio. (*See* individual species.)
Aggressive behavior in wolf. (*see* Wolf: aggression.)
Aircraft—29–33, 95–98, 101, 104–105, 115, 117, 120, 145.
Aircraft hunting of wolves—35.
Aircraft, wolves' reaction to—35–37, 66, 70.
Aldous, S.—19.
Aldous, S. E. and L. W. Krefting—13, 22–23, 25, 94–95.
Allen, D. L.—24, 82, 85, 101, 138, 172.
"Alpha" wolves—61–62, 69, 87.
Altmann, Margaret—142.
Anal "besnuffling," wolf—62.
Anderson, J.—16.
Anderson, V.—16.
Annual increment, moose—105, 161–165.
Antler development—94–95.
Arctic hare as wolf food—73.
Arnold, D. A.—168.
Arousal of pack from sleep—62.
Assembling of wolves—66.

Bailey, V.—69.
Banfield, A. W. F.—47, 71, 73, 109, 136, 169.
Banfield, A. W. F. *et al.*—96, 98.
Barking—66.
Barr, A. W.—172.
Bats—17.
Baudino, P. M.—21.
Beaver: coyote predation—153; decline in numbers—153–154; food supply—20, 153–154; history—17, 19–20, 151, 153; methods of study—31; wolf

food—72, 74, 151–154; wolf predation—151–154.
Becklund, W. W.—112.
Belschner, H. G.—88.
Bighorn as wolf food—73.
"Big Jim"—26, 27, 42.
Biomass ratios—166, 169.
Bison as wolf food—73, 124.
Black flies—114.
Bones, wolf-chewed—116.
Bounties—2–3.
Breakup of pack—42, 58–61.
Breeding season. (*See* individual species.)
Brown, C. A.—13, 15, 94.
Brown, C. E.—69.
Browse—22–23, 94, 99, 171.
Brush wolf. (*See* Coyote.)
Bulls, concentrations of—103.
Burgess, J.—101, 173.
Burkholder, B. L.—36, 42, 47, 50–51, 76–77, 81, 116, 118, 121, 135–136, 144, 146, 148, 150–151, 170.
Burns—13, 18, 23, 98, 167, 171.
Burt, W. H.—17.

Cable, R. M.—172.
Cahalane, V.—25.
Calf. (*See* Moose: calf.)
Cameron, A. E.—107.
Cannibalism—90.
Caribou: escape behavior—139, 150; history—16–18; hydatid tapeworm—149–151; wolf food—73, 76–77, 81, 116–117, 119; wolf predation—124, 136, 144, 147–148, 150–151, 169–170.
Carrion eating—116.
Carrying capacity, moose—98.
Caution, wolf—68.
Census. (*See* individual species.)
Chandler, A. C.—82, 109.
Cheatum, E. L.—88.
Chitwood, M. B.—114.
Choquette, L. P. E.—83.
Christian, J. J.—87–89.
Christian, J. J. and C. D. Lemunyan—89–90.

Christian, J. J. *et al.*—89.
Chrysops—114.
Clark, R. T.—88.
Climate—7.
Coburn, D. R.—22, 111.
Cole, J. E.—3, 18–20, 22–25, 27, 35, 40–42, 49, 51, 73, 78, 86, 92, 95, 97, 105, 108, 135, 137, 152–154, 158, 173.
Color, wolf—35, 42, 71.
Condition of moose a factor in predation—121–125, 140, 145–151, 167–170.
Control of moose population—167–168.
Cooperators in study—31.
Copulation, wolf—61, 69–70.
Cottam, C.—121, 140.
Cover types—10–15.
Cowan, I. M.—43, 47, 49, 58, 60, 69, 71, 73, 76–78, 83, 86, 89, 107, 109, 111–114, 117–118, 125, 135–136, 138, 140–141, 144, 147, 149, 151, 153–154, 167–170.
Cowan, I. M. *et al.*—171.
Cow-calf bond—142–143, 147.
Coyote: history—16–17, 19, 24–25, 154, 159–160; hydatid tapeworm—111–112; wolf relations with—160.
Cringan, A. T.—101.
Crisler, Lois—63, 65, 68, 121, 124, 144, 150–151, 159, 170.
Cross, J.—16, 18, 24.
Culling effect of wolves—168–170.

Dall sheep as wolf food—117–119, 144, 148, 151, 168–169.
Dall sheep mortality—151.
Dassler, C. F. W.—19.
Dassler, J. C.—19.
Davis, D. E.—88.
Davis, D. E. and J. J. Christian—87.
Debilitating conditions, moose—149–151.
Deer: defense—138; hydatid tapeworm—149; Isle Royale—17; wolf food—73, 76–78, 116; wolf predation—76, 118, 124, 136, 148, 168.
Deer flies—114.
Deer mouse—17–18.
Defense. (*See* individual species.)
Denniston, R. H.—141, 163.
Dens—31, 58–59, 65, 71, 158.
Density. (*See* individual species.)
Dermacentor albipictus. (*See* Winter tick.)
Description, wolf—35.
Detection of wolves by moose—138.
Detectability of moose by wolves—120.

De Vos, A.—24, 50, 162.
De Vos, A., and A. E. Allin—109, 111.
De Voss, A., and R. L. Peterson—18, 20.
Diarrhea, moose—114.
Dice, L. R.—10.
Dictyocaulus sp. (*See* Lungworm.)
Diet. (*See* individual species.)
Displacement activity, wolf—64.
Distance between kills—50.
Distribution of moose on Isle Royale—95–99.
Distribution of wolves in U.S.—1–2.
Dodds, D. G.—163.
Dominance. (*See* Wolf: dominance.)
Drowning, moose—115.
Dumas, A.—2.
Dunne, A. L.—118, 124.
Duration of study—29, 31.
Dynamic equilibrium of wolf-moose population—167–168.
Dynamics of wolf-moose coaction—161–171.

Echinococcus granulosus. (*See* hydatid tapeworm.)
Edisen, Pete and Laura—18–20, 24–26, 173.
Edwards, R. Y.—97.
Edwards, R. Y. and R. W. Ritcey—161.
Elk: defense—138, 141–142; hydatid tapeworm—111, 149, 151; winter tick—107; wolf food—73, 76–78, 118; wolf predation—125, 135–136, 151.
Elton, C.—88.
Emigration, wolf—91–93, 170.
Energy loss between wolf-moose trophic levels—166, 169.
Equipment used in study—29–33.
Erickson, A. B.—82–83.
Escape behavior, moose—139–144.
Estrus, wolf—61, 69–70, 87.
European rabbits—87.
"Expansion power," wolf—63.

Family groups, wolf—57–58.
Fasting, wolf—79, 137.
Faust, E. C.—109.
Feeding behavior and routine, wolf—36–37, 48, 50–51, 60, 76–81, 116, 132–133, 137–138.
Fenstermacher, R.—111–112, 147, 149.
Fenstermacher, R., and W. L. Jellison—109.
Fetuses, moose—102.
Findley, J. S.—140.

Lone wolf—37–39, 42, 48, 57, 59, 63, 65, 158; feeding habits—76, 91; frequency of predation—76; predation on moose—76, 125, 133–135, 183–184, 189; snowshoe hare, relations with—155; senility—87, 91.

Longhurst, W. M.—88.

Lorenz, K. Z.—64.

Lumpy jaw—112–113, 151.

Lungworm (*Dictyocaulus* sp.)—113–114.

Lynx—16–17.

Lyperosiops alcis—114.

MacFarlane, R. R.—90, 117, 141.

Maintenance of healthy moose herd—168–170.

Malnutrition, moose—22, 107–108, 114, 147, 167.

Mammals—16–27.

Man, wolf relations with—2, 25–26, 36–37.

Mandibles, moose—112–113, 145–146, 151.

Mange, wolf—81.

Marrow condition, moose—114–115, 135, 137–138, 150–151.

Marten—16–17.

Mating behavior, wolf—42–43, 61, 63, 68–70, 86, 127.

Maturity, wolf—69, 87.

Mason, K. E.—88.

McCleery, E. H.—79, 90, 164.

McCullough, G. W.—172.

McMillan, H., Jr.—172.

Measurements, wolf—1, 35, 71, 86–87, 166.

Mech, B. A.—173.

Merritt, G.—16, 19.

Methods (*see also* individual species)—29–33.

Mice, laboratory—87–89.

Microclimate—9.

Mink—17.

"Mock attack," wolf—62.

Monlux, A. W.—112.

Monnig, H. O.—82, 109.

Moose: accidents—106, 108, 114, 115–116, 147; actinomycosis—112–113; age ratio—31, 102–106, 165; ageing techniques—145–146; annual increment—105, 161–165; antler development—94–95; bare areas on hide—107–109; bones, wolf-chewed—116; browse—22–23, 94, 99, 171; bulls, concentrations of—103; calf-adult ratios—103–106, 161–165; calf, defense of—125, 127–129, 132–133, 147, 175–176, 179–185; calf mortality—161–165, 167; calf numbers as factor in wolf pack size—60; calf production—102–106, 147, 161–165; calf twins (*see* Moose: twins); calf weight—93–94, 102; calves, wolf consumption of—161–163; calves, winter ticks on—107–108; calving period—101–103; carrying capacity—98; census—95–98, 101; condition as factor in predation—121–125, 140, 145–151, 167–170; cow-calf bond—142–143, 147; debilitating conditions—149–151; defense of calf—142–143; defensive behavior (*see also* Accounts of wolf attacks)—60, 90, 120–121, 125, 138–143; defensive posture—141, 143; density—98–99, 119, 167, 169; detection of wolves—138; detectability by wolves—120; diarrhoea—114; diseases—106–114, 167–168; distribution—95–99; drowning—115; escape behavior—139–144, fetuses—102; food (*see also* browse)—94, 98–99; food consumption rate—165–166; gait—129, 140; herd—93–116; history—17, 20–23, 167; immigration—21; Isle Royale subspecies—93–94; jaw necrosis—112–113, 151, kill, rate of—76–79, 114, 161–166; kills (*see* wolf-killed moose); limiting factor—167; lumpy jaw—112–113, 151; lungworm—113–114; malnutrition—22, 107–108, 114, 147, 167; mandibles—112–113, 145–146, 151; marrow condition—114–115, 135, 137–138, 150–151; methods of study—29–33, 95–97, 101–102, 115–117; 145; moose fly—114; mortality, sex ratio of—145; numbers—22–23, 31, 45, 95–99, 161–165, 167; numbers, past—22–23, 95, 167; numbers, stability of—167, 171; old age—114; overbrowsing—22, 167; parasites—106–114, 167–168, past numbers—22–23, 95, 167; pelage—94, 109; pneumonia—114; population, seasonal trends in—31, 45, 161–165; population size—22–23, 31, 45, 95–99, 161–165, 167; population stability—167–168; predation—114–151, 156; pregnancy rate—161; productivity—161–165, 170; range—45, 98–99; rate of kill by wolves—76–79, 114, 161–166; remains—31, 115–116, 145, 148, 150–151; reproduction—

Predation on moose—114–151, 156.
Pregnancy rate, moose—161.
Prejudice against wolf—2.
Pre-natal losses of wolves—88–89.
Presentation of anal parts, wolf—62.
Preulx, C.—16.
Prey availability—116.
Prey-predator ratios—168.
Prey units—77.
Productivity. (*See* individual species.)
Protection of wolves—2, 5.
Pups, fox—158.
Pups, wolf—42, 57–59, 65, 69–71, 87, 89–90.

Rabies—81.
Range, moose—45, 98–99.
Rate, moose kill—76–79, 114, 161–166.
Rate of travel—51, 53, 121.
Rausch, R.—81–82, 109, 111, 149.
Rausch, R., and F. S. L. Williamson—81–83, 149.
Ravens, wolf relations with—76, 159.
Red-backed vole—17.
Red squirrel—17.
Remains, moose—31, 115–116, 145, 148, 150–151.
Repressed individuals (wolves)—63–65.
Reproduction. (*See* individual species.)
Reproductive inhibition, wolf—88.
Reproductive rate of wolf affected by food—88–89.
Response of moose to weather—96–99.
Resting habits, wolf—41–42, 48, 51, 53, 62–63, 71, 79, 117, 120.

Retzlaff—87.
Riley, W. A.—83, 112.
Ritcey, R. W.—107, 109, 111–113, 149.
Robinette, W. L.—102, 115, 143.
Robinette, W. L. *et al.*—74.
Rowan, W.—47.
Rude, S.—18–19, 20, 24.
Rudebeck, G.—143–144.
Running ability. (*See* individual species.)
Rutting season—101.

Scat analysis, wolf—73–74, 116–117, 146–147, 151, 164.
Scavenging, wolf—87, 91, 116.
Scenting ability, wolf—119–120.
Scent posts—45.
Schenkel, R.—45, 48, 58, 60–65, 68–69, 87, 173.

Schierbeck, O.—99.
Schiller, E. L.—109.
Schofield, R. D.—173.
Selection in moose kill—145–151.
Senility, wolf—87.
Senses. (*See* individual species.)
Sergeant, D. E.—145–146.
Seton, E. T.—65–66, 91.
Sex ratio. (*See* individual species.)
Shedding, moose—109.
Shelton, P. C.—173.
Shevlin, E.—24.
Shoreline travel, wolf—38, 50–51, 53.
Similium—114.
Simkin, D. W.—76, 94.
Size, wolf—1, 35, 71, 86–87, 166.
Skadburg, J.—153.
Skoog, R. O.—149.
Skuncke—76, 93, 148.
Smits, L.—2, 26, 90, 172.
Snow conditions—9.
Snowshoe hare: fox food—154–156; history—17–18, 154–156; methods of study—31, 154; numbers—17–18, 154; wolf food—73, 154–156; wolf predation—154–156.
Social behavior, wolf—36–37, 40–49, 57–73.
Social ranking—61–65.
Social status related to wolf productivity—87–88.
Species of lesser significance—151–160.
Speed. (*See* individual species.)
Speelman, S. R.—89.
Spencer, D. L.—98–99, 111, 162.
Stamey, R.—172.
Stanfield, R.—173.
Stanwell-Fletcher, J. F.—51, 90, 117, 140–141, 154.
Starvation, moose—22, 107–108, 114, 147, 167.
Stebler, A. M.—47, 73.
Stenlund, M. H.—2, 27, 35, 43, 47, 49–51, 60, 70–71, 73, 76–77, 81–83, 86, 88, 118, 121, 136, 148, 160, 168, 170, 173.
Stevenson-Hamilton, J.—88–89.
Stimson, D. G.—172.
Stoddard, L. A.—88.
Stomach capacity, wolf—78.
Stress, high density—87–90.
Study area. (*See* Isle Royale.)
Submissive attitude, wolf—48, 61, 63.
Subspecies. (*See* individual species.)
Summer observations of wolves—59.
Summer routes, wolf—53, 57.

Surplus males, wolf—86–87.
Survival, moose—105.
Swanson, G.—18, 20.
Sweatman, G. K.—83, 111.
Sweatman, G. H., and P. J. G. Plummer—83, 112.
Swimming, moose—21.

Taenia hydatigena—82–83, 90, 112.
Taenia Krabbei—82.
Taenia sp., wolf—82.
Tail positions, wolf—61–63.
Tail wagging, wolf—62, 120, 174–175, 178.
Techniques. (*See* Methods.)
Tener, J. S.—73, 148.
Territory, wolf—40, 43, 47–49, 88.
Testing prey—124–125, 139, 143–145, 167–169.
Thompson, D. Q.—47, 73–74, 154.
Thirty-one days' travel of large pack—51.
Tick. (*See* Winter tick.)
Tomes, A. C.—173.
Tracks and trails. (*See* individual species.)
Travel. (*See* Wolf: travel.)
Trophic levels—166, 169.
Trotter, R. H.—95.
Twinning rate, moose—161–162, 170.

Unproductive individuals, wolf—86–88.
Urination, wolf—62.
U.S. Department of Commerce, Weather Bureau—8.

Vegetation—10–15.
Vocal communication, wolf. (*See* Wolf: howling.)

Wallace, F. G.—109.
Warth, W.—47.
Weasel—17.
Weights. (*See* individual species.)
Wild dogs—77, 124.
Winter tick: elk—107; moose—107–109, 135, 147, 150–151.
"Withdrawal of anal parts," wolf—62.
Wolf: age ratio—89; aggression toward moose—62, 126–138; aggression toward other wolves—64–65, 68, 87, 90; aircraft, hunting by—35; aircraft, reaction to—35–37, 66, 70; "Alpha" individuals—61–62, 69, 87; anal "besnuffling"—62; arousal from sleep—62; assembling—66; barking—66; bea-

ver, relations with—72, 74, 151–154; breakup of pack—42; breeding season—69–70; cannibalism—90; carrion eating—116; caution—68; census—37–39; color—35, 42, 71; control of moose population—167–168; copulation—61, 69–70; coyote, relations with—160; crossing ice—24–27, 68, 91–93; dens—31, 58–59, 65, 71, 158; density—45–47; density as population control—88–90; description—35; diet—73–81, 116–117; diseases—81–86, 90; displacement activity—64; distance between kills—50; distribution—1–2; dominance between packs—40, 42–43, 48–49, 65, 88; dominance as related to productivity—87–88; dominance within packs—42–43, 61–65; dominant posture—61; emigration—91–93, 170; estrus—61, 69–70, 87; "expansion power"—63; family groups—57–58; fasting—79, 137; feeding behavior—36–37, 48, 50–51, 60, 76–81, 116, 132–133, 137–138; feeding routine—79–81; fighting (*see also* Wolf): dominance—64–65, 68, 70, 87, 90; food as factor in population control—88–90; food consumption—60, 76–79, 114, 155, 163–164, 166; food habits—73–81, 116–117; food requirements—60, 77–78, 89; fox, relations with—76, 157–158; frequency of predation—75–76; frigidity—87; future—170–171; genital "besnuffling"—62, 70; gestation—69; gorging—77–79; habitat destruction—1; history—24–27; home range—43–47; howling—31, 36, 45, 57, 59, 72–73; howling in relation to pack formation—60; howling, recordings of—67–68, 71–73; howling, significance—65–68; howling while hunting—65–66; hunting accounts—126–135, 174–189; hunting behavior—29, 40, 42, 49–51, 53, 58, 60, 62, 65–66, 87, 116–151; hunting techniques—118–135, 147; hydatid tapeworm—82–86, 109–112; ice, crossing—24–27, 68, 91–93; immigration—24–27, 91–93; injuries by prey—90, 117, 141; intraspecific strife (*see* Wolf: dominance, aggression); introduction on Isle Royale—24–27, 42; Isle Royale subspecies—35; killing techniques—126–138; litter size—86, 89; leader (*see also* "Alpha" wolves)—60–62, 93; lone wolf (*see* Lone wolf); mange—81; man's rela-